W9-BJH-573

Instructor's Manual and Test Bank

for

Eshleman

The Family

✦ Ninth Edition ✦

Prepared by

Marilyn Daniels
Wayne State University
J. Ross Eshleman
Wayne State University

Allyn and Bacon
Boston   London   Toronto   Sydney   Tokyo   Singapore

Copyright © 2000 by Allyn & Bacon
A Pearson Education Company
160 Gould Street
Needham Heights, Massachusetts 02494

Internet: www.abacon.com

All rights reserved. The contents, or parts thereof, may be reproduced for use
with *The Family*, Ninth Edition, by J. Ross Eshleman, provided such
reproductions bear copyright notice, but may not be reproduced in any form for
any other purpose without written permission from the copyright owner.

ISBN 0-205-30761-2

Printed in the United States of America

10 9 8 7 6 5 4 3 2 1   03 02 01 00 99

New to this Edition

This manual conforms to Professor Eshleman's greatly reformatted Ninth Edition. Repeat users of the text and manual will soon see that virtually all the chapters have been reconstituted.

This edition of the instructor's manual offers something new. Some of the lecture and discussion questions are very detailed and very exhaustive of pertinent arguments. It is hoped that these especially thorough lecture items will save you time and effort in class preparation, since most of us face the daunting task of preparing several in-depth analyses for each class session. Further, these very detailed lecture and discussion items anticipate student's questions. They generally provide arguments on "both sides" of the most thorny family issues.

TABLE OF CONTENTS

TABLE OF CONTENTS

Test Bank

PREFACE TO THE INSTRUCTOR'S MANUAL

This instructor's manual is to be used with the textbook **The Family: An Introduction** by J. Ross Eshleman, Ninth Edition. The following elements are included for each text chapter: an outline of chapter **contents**, an **overview** of chapter contents, **lecture and discussion questions with answer guidelines, classroom activities and projects**, and **film and video resources**.

In place of the rather "sketchy" ideas typically offered by instructor's manuals, I'm offering comprehensive **lecture and discussion questions** intended to build upon Eshleman's text with theoretically substantive questions and focused "answer guidelines." You may incorporate these questions into your presentations, or pose them directly to students. I hope the questions will be thought provoking and helpful to you as you prepare your lectures. The **classroom activities and projects** are straightforward suggestions for interacting with students in the classroom.

This edition of the manual features many new **video and film resources**. All titles listed are available in video formats, and most may be obtained in film formats, as well. I have not included dates of release, since most are undated, and filmmakers tend to regularly update older productions. For specific ordering information, consult the film catalogs of your local library, or a comprehensive listing such as **Bowker's Complete Video Directory**, which provides manufacturers' prices and ordering details.

The pages of this manual may be torn out, if you choose, for classroom use. For your convenience, the test bank--prepared completely by J. Ross Eshleman--is separate from the instructor's guide section, and is located in the second half of the manual.

I sincerely hope this instructor's manual will meet your needs.

Marilyn Boyd Daniels

THE **TEST BANK** BEGINS ON PAGE 137

PREFACE

This test bank is designed for use with the ninth edition of <u>The Family: An Introduction</u> by J. Ross Eshleman. All test questions were prepared by the author of the text.

The test bank includes close to 1300 questions. Each of the seventeen chapters include between twenty-five and thirty-five true-false questions, twenty-five to thirty multiple-choice questions, ten to twelve fill-in questions, and ten to twelve short answer/essay questions. Most questions come from the basic textual material but some were created from information provided in the inserts, tables, and figures.

The answer to each objective-type question and the page reference from the text appears to the left of each question. In the instances where the question covers more than one page in the text, the number given refers to the page that has the correct answer.

I hope you will find this test bank helpful. Any corrections, comments or constructive suggestions you have in regard to the test bank questions, the instructor's manual, or the text itself would be much appreciated.

It is my hope that you will find the excitement that I find in teaching and interacting with students. I encourage you to challenge their thinking and force them to question many ideas they hold about families and intimate primary group relationships.

J. Ross Eshleman

CHAPTER 1

MARRIAGE AND THE FAMILY: DISCIPLINARY AND THEORETICAL APPROACHES

CASE EXAMPLE
> Questions to Consider
> Introduction to the chapter

DISCIPLINES INVOLVED IN FAMILY STUDIES

SOCIAL SCIENCE APPROACH TO THE FAMILY
> Sociology of the family
> Uses of family sociology

NATURE OF RESEARCH AND THEORETICAL FRAMES OF REFERENCE
> Concepts and variables
> Conceptual frameworks
> Propositions and hypotheses
> Theory

THEORIES AND FRAMES OF REFERENCE
> Structural-functional frame of reference
> Social conflict frame of reference
> Symbolic interaction frame of reference
> Social exchange frame of reference
> Developmental frame of reference
> Feminist frame of reference

APPRAISAL AND EXPANSION OF CONTEMPORARY FAMILY THEORY

SUMMARY

OBJECTIVES

Based upon their reading and careful consideration of Chapter 1, students should:

1.   Be familiar with the disciplines involved in family study and be able to identify the specific focus of each;

2.   understand the differences in approach of the separate social sciences that study the family;

3. be able to distinguish micro-level analysis in family sociology from macro-level analysis;

4. be able to distinguish between sociological, psychological, and social-psychological approaches to the family;

5. understand *very clearly* the difference between "do gooders" in the realm of the family, and problem solving through social science research;

6. understand the nature of theories, and be familiar with the research terms "concepts," "variables," "conceptual frameworks," "propositions," and "hypotheses;"

7. know the importance of theory in the field of family sociology, and have some idea how theory and research are linked;

8. be conversant with the six frames of reference as discussed by Eshleman: structural-functionalism, social conflict, symbolic interactionism, social exchange, developmentalism, and feminism;

9. be aware of how phenomenological analyses are useful for showing how people construct their own reality, and how phenomenological approaches may be used to examine little-known areas of social life; and,

10. be aware of important shifts in the area of family sociology, including efforts to integrate theoretical perspectives and develop more flexible "vocabularies" of concepts.

OVERVIEW

What does the "**family**" consist of? Sociologically, the family is a group, a social system, and a social institution. It is the site of a number of intimate behaviors. However, some scholars have questioned whether "the family" is a meaningful concept, since the traditional, idealized image of the family is inconsistent with many current realities. Today's family relationships reflect the realities of today, and new patterns are emerging such as remarriages, dual career/dual income households, childless couples, one-parent households, and same-sex unions. It may be necessary to begin to think different about the family—not as "the family," but as a **system of families**.

It is difficult to find terms that differentiate family from nonfamily relationships. It might be better to think about families less in terms of structure, stability, and standards, and more in terms of process, change, and close relationships. It has been suggested that any dyad (or set of dyads) might be considered a "family." This book recognizes a wide range of patterns, structural arrangements, and behaviors as being family or family-like. This book also recognizes that the social institution of the family varies around the world in its range of patterns, structural arrangements, and behaviors.

A wide range of disciplines are concerned with families and family-related topics, including anthropology, psychology, and sociology. No discipline or profession dominates the topic of marriage and family. Each discipline involves a specific orientation, and disciplinary isolation has been a problem. Although interdisciplinary approaches may close some of the gaps that now separate disciplines, each discipline will continue to emphasize specific directions.

All the social science disciplines approach the family-related behavior of human beings with similar aims and methods. The aim is generally to establish relationships based on patterns of regularities and uniformities. It is assumed that all phenomena have regularities operating independently of the researcher, which may be discovered through objective observation.

The sociology of the family seeks to explain both the social order and disorder of the family, with primary focus upon social structure rather than individuals. Family sociology becomes useful in understanding what *is*, in presenting new ways of viewing life, and in acquiring knowledge about relationships and families around the world.

Family theories are neither right nor wrong, but are ways of looking at--and rationally explaining--phenomena related to the family. **Concepts** and **variables**, **conceptual frameworks**, **propositions**, and **hypotheses** are all basic to the development of **theory**. A good theory should be abstract, be testable, have wide application, be cumulative, and provide grounds for prediction. Theory gives meaning to research findings and enables the development of systematic consensual explanations.

The use and application of theory depends upon theoretical **frames of reference**. Six frames of reference are covered in this chapter.

The **structural-functional** frame of reference is identified with the study of the interrelationships between the structures of any system. The concepts **structure** and **function** can be discussed separately, although they are interrelated, and one implies the other. Social structures are units of society that carry out or result in one or more basic functions, and functions are results (or consequences) of given social structures. The social structure of a family refers to the way in which the social units are arranged, to the interrelationship of the parts, and to the patterns of organization. Families perform both manifest and latent functions for persons and society as well.

The type of policy (or the level of analysis) ranges from **macroanalysis** to **microanalysis**. Macrofunctionalsits are concerned with the analysis of large-scale systems and institutions, while microfunctionalists are concerned with the analysis of individual families and small-scale systems (often designated as "group dynamics").

Today, a major thrust of the structural-functional approach centers on explaining the parts or components (structure) of a society and the manner in which these parts interrelate with each other.

It is important to consider how variations in family structure lead to differing consequences for children. Increases in divorce rates, female headship rates, and nonmarital fertility have fueled the growing proportion of children in poverty. These facts have important implications for social policy: If consequences vary by social structure, conditions can be improved by supporting structural arrangements, rather than by focusing on the individuals who suffer the consequences.

The **social conflict** frame of reference assumes that conflict is natural and inevitable in all human interactions. The classical case for conflict theory comes from Karl Marx, who assumed that economic organization, especially the ownership of property, generates revolutionary class conflict. From this point of view, the family serves to support the capitalistic system, exploiting working-class workers and women. According to the social conflict model, the family is not the "haven" posited by an order model such as functionalism.

The **symbolic interaction** frame of reference addresses two major questions, both of which are of central concern to the family: socialization and personality. The interactionist approach makes the assumptions that marriages and families must be studied at their own level; that marriage and family can only be understood within the context of the social setting and society in which they exist; that the human infant at birth is asocial and learns in interaction with others what is acceptable and unacceptable behavior; and that a social human being is an actor as well as a reactor.

The **social exchange** frame of reference rests on the belief that human beings attempt to make choices they expect will maximize their rewards and or minimize their costs. Social exchange theory seeks to explain why certain behavioral outcomes (such as marriage, sex, employment) occur, given a set of structural conditions (such as age, race, gender, class) and interactional potentialities.

The **developmental** frame of reference tends to be both macro and microanalytic in nature. The peculiar character of this approach lies in its attempt to account for change in the family system over time as well as account for changes in patterns of interaction over time. The major conceptual tool for this time analysis has been termed the "family life cycle." Today, frequent reference is made to the "life course." This theory contends that, like the individual, families have tasks that arise at a given stage in the family life cycle.

The **feminist** frame of reference asserts that gender is basic to all social structures and organizations. The impetus for this frame of reference is the simple question: "And what about women?" Basic assumptions of this perspective are that *all* women are oppressed by virtue of their gender; that *every aspect* of women's' lives may impacted by gender inequality; and feminist scholars must be ever cognizant of the ramifications of gender inequality. "Rethinking the discipline" means moving beyond simply generating new concepts and theories—It means continually grappling with the questions *not* asked.

The turn of the Century may be a time of theoretical synthesis: an integration of macro and micro ideas, a joining of structural and exchange theories into a network theory, or a blurring of distinct theoretical boundary lines as theories borrow heavily from one another. There are two trends to watch for. **Critical social science** approaches societies and families in terms of both *what exists* and *what is possible in the future*. It questions what types of social change are feasible and desirable. **Feminist theorizing** is aimed at recognizing the absence of women in the history of social and political thought. It challenges patriarchal and sexist notions about the family, (such as the idea that it is "natural" or "biological," or that it has a single structure throughout time).

LECTURE AND DISCUSSION QUESTIONS

1.   **Just as theoretical approaches in family sociology are widely utilized and applied, they are also widely questioned. What are the major criticisms that have been directed against each of the six frames of reference presented by Eshleman?**
<u>Answer guidelines:</u>
The **structural-functional** frame of reference is criticized for supporting the status quo (including unfair power relationships within the family), by emphasizing system maintenance. For example, the notion that distinct and specialized husband and wife roles—he the breadwinner, she the nurturing homemaker—are efficient from a functional perspective is echoed by political conservatives, who wish to preserve the "traditional" family. This perspective is also criticized for failing to offer any exposition of the mechanisms of social change.

The **social conflict** frame of reference is criticized for over-emphasizing economic competition and exploitation (since family relations also display a high degree of cooperation and selflessness), and for failing to recognize that male dominance cuts across economic and class lines. Because it is largely a macro-level theory, the conflict perspective is also criticized for its lack of usefulness in explaining individual behavior.

The **symbolic interactionist** frame of reference is criticized mainly for the difficulty in applying objective research measures from this perspective, due to its emphasis on studying subjective meanings and internalized processes. Also, because the symbolic ineractionist approach focuses on micro-level phenomena, it typically fails to account for the impact of large-scale social forces, such as social movements, on individual and family behavior. Consider, for example, the impact of such movements as feminism and the Promise Keepers on families.

The **social exchange** perspective is criticized by those who have observed that people do not always necessarily attempt to maximize their rewards or minimize their costs within intimate relationships. People are not always as "rational" as exchange theory suggests—in fact, we often make inexplicable choices and sacrifices.

The **developmental** frame of reference is criticized because the processes of life are not often as neatly segmented as the perspective suggests. Secondly, the theory tends to be based on stable nuclear type families. What about other family types? There are actually many subgroup and individual exceptions to family-life event timing.

The **feminist** perspective is criticized for its tendency to blur class lines, thereby washing out the very important influence of socioeconomic status as a determinant of a wide range of behaviors. Another serious critique is that feminist research tends to primarily utilize *qualitative* research techniques, at the expense of *quantitative* methodologies. This is led some researchers and policy-makers to discount some findings—it is harder to generalize solutions based on the problems or experiences of individuals than based on large-scale studies with replicable methodologies.

The key point is none of the various family theories and approaches are "right" or "wrong," but each has some limitations in its application. No theoretical approach is adequate to frame all family behavior.

2. **What can the feminist perspective contribute to family studies that is neglected by the other major theoretical perspectives?**
   Answer guidelines: Feminist scholarship is forcing an ongoing questioning of concepts such as "truth," "reality," and "objectivity." It suggests that science--including family research--is a social activity embedded in sociohistorical context. It directs researchers to be cognizant of the *way* questions are asked, and, also, of questions *not asked*. It introduces the possibility of analyzing family life from a social justice perspective--a perspective in which individuals are regarded as being of equal worth, and in which differences are respected.

3. **One of the basic tasks of the structural-functional approach to the family has been to consider which family functions have been "replaced" by other social institutions (thereby supporting the idea of**

the "breakdown" of the traditional family). **What about the possibility of certain functions *increasing* in importance as the family moves toward modernization?**

Answer guidelines: Several kinds of functions are widely acknowledged to be increasing in importance with the emergence of the modern family. Marriage is increasingly regarded as the focus of sexual satisfaction for both men and women. The mutual provision of affection and emotional support between all family members is also regarded as an emerging function. The family has generally increased its role in the recreational activities of its members. Note: It is important to recognize that areas of expanded functions appear to revolve around *increasing intimacy* and *increasing intensity in personal relations* among family members.

CLASSROOM ACTIVITIES AND PROJECTS

1.   Read the title and synopsis of a sociological study on a family topic (preferably, this article should be interesting or even amusing). Challenge the students to come up with ideas for related studies on the *same topic*, but with *psychological* and *social-psychological* approaches. Or, the reverse strategy may be used, presenting an example of a psychology research topic, and asking the students to think how it might be tackled sociologically. This exercise should give the students a "feel" for how sociology is both similar to and distinct from both psychological and social-psychological approaches. Note: The instructor should be prepared in advance with good examples to illustrate this discussion, since students often take some time to become conversant with these distinctions.

2.   Theories about the family are sometimes translated into social policy— whether or not the theories are well grounded in fact or well understood. A good example of this is the recent trend toward overhauling federal and state welfare policies. Much if the change has been based on the idea that "the family" (or at least a certain segment of it) has been disintegrating, and that the welfare policies in place for decades have been to some degree responsible. Many of the changes implemented through federal and state legislation during the late 1990s were not recommended—in some cases they were *specifically contradicted*—by good social research. This could be a rich topic for class discussion, if the instructor is armed with the pertinent research findings.

A good resource to anchor such a discussion might be an article which appeared in *Footnotes*, the publication of the American Sociological Association, in 1997, "ASA Holds Congressional Briefing On Welfare to Work" (Vol.25, No. 4, April, 1997). This article ties several core questions *to actual research findings* and points to further resources. The core questions are, "What do we know about the patterns of welfare to work?"

7

"What are the realities of the labor market for welfare recipients?" "What is life like for families who leave welfare for work?" and, "What are the likely effects of welfare time limits?"

3.   Ask students to present a "theory" about some family subject, and write it on the board. Then ask the class to help evaluate it. Ask, "Is it a good theory?" "What would make it a good theory?" It is important to emphasize that a theory is far more than mere speculation or a collection of concepts. Students should be led to understand that, as Eshleman puts it, a good theory should be testable, abstract, have wide application, be cumulative, and serve as a basis for prediction. The students' original "theory" may be re-formulated or replaced with a new one. Note: It may happen that the students will not be able to present a theory at all...The best they may be able to come up with may be a proposition. If this occurs, it presents a good opportunity for the instructor to explain how difficult good theory formulation is, and the extent to which it relies upon accumulated knowledge and the diligent (often long-term) process of "theory building."

FILM AND VIDEO RESOURCES

Family & Household
This color video is part of the "Faces of Culture" series. It looks at the concepts of family and household from a cross-cultural perspective, and examines the basic functions of family units.
RMI Media Productions

Changing Knowledge, Changing Reality
This film makes the point that today's "truth" or "facts" will be superseded in the future as our scientific knowledge changes, and poses the questions: Is knowledge itself only what we make of it? Should we find room for tolerance of others' points of view?
University of Minnesota Film and Video, 52 min., color

Women and the American Family
The struggle of women for equal rights is examined from a historical perspective. Viewers are encouraged to discuss, explore, and develop ideas about the role of women in the next century, and the related changes that might occur with respect to the American family and its place in our society.
Video Knowledge, Inc.

CHAPTER 2

MARRIAGE, FAMILY, AND KINSHIP ORGANIZATION

CASE EXAMPLE
    Questions to consider
    Introduction to the chapter

FAMILY AS A SOCIAL INSTITUTION

FAMILIES AS GROUPS AND SYSTEMS
    Primary groups
    Secondary groups

CHARACTERISTICS OF MARRIAGE, FAMILY, AND KINSHIP GROUPS
    Boundaries of marriage
    Boundaries of the family
    Boundaries of kinship
    Family ambiguity

SUMMARY

OBJECTIVES

Based upon their reading and careful consideration of Chapter 2, students should:

1.   Be able to distinguish between the terms "institution" and "institutionalized," and be aware that some very common relationship and family behaviors are not institutionalized;

2.   understand the major functions of family as a primary group, and how the family compares to secondary groups;

3.   be aware that the absence or loss of familial support networks as primary sources of social support has negative consequences for individuals and families;

4.   recognize marital status and number of spouses as the two factors which provide the boundaries of marriage (and note that with variations in these two factors come substantial variations in patterns of marital interaction);

5.   be able to explain the status of monogamy in societies worldwide;

6. be familiar with the typology of family structures outlined in the text, and have a working knowledge of nuclear, conjugal, modified-nuclear, modified-extended, and extended families;

7. know something about the boundaries of the kinship system, including the incest taboo; and,

8. understand the kinship system as a pattern of social norms regulating family relationships, and be familiar with the functions of kin groups (property holding and inheritance, housing and the maintenance of residential proximity, obligation to help in time of need, provision of affection, emotional ties, and primary relationships).

OVERVIEW

This chapter explores conceptual distinctions made in the study of the family. The family is a social **institution**: a system of norms, values, statuses, and roles that develop around a basic social goal. In all societies, the family institution is organized around the management of sexual activity and the care of dependent children.

The term **family system** is used in sociology much in the same way physicists and biologists speak of solar or biological systems. The basic units of a marital or family system are the interrelated statuses (positions) and accompanying expectations (roles). **Family groups**, in contrast to family systems, are concrete realities, not abstractions. They are composed of real people.

Marriages and families are **primary groups:** small numbers of people who interact in personal, direct, and intimate ways. Much of the importance of marital, family, and kin groups lies in their function as primary groups. The polar extreme of the primary group is the **secondary group.** In a society dominated by secondary group relationships, the family provides the primary relationships that are vital to health and happiness.

Marriage, family, and kin groups are **institutionalized** social arrangements in all known societies. Marital status and number of spouses are two the major components of the boundaries of marriage. An increasing number of men and women are remaining single for longer periods of time, in comparison with the past. The legitimacy of singlehood as a life-style is becoming increasingly recognized. The proportion of the population never married has increased sharply over the past three decades.

To many Americans, the most traditional and proper form of marriage is **monogamy**, although a pattern of **sequential** or **serial monogamy** is emerging in our society. Distinct from monogamy is **polygamy,** which is the marriage of several or many. **Polygyny** refers to several or many wives. In actual practice, polygyny appears to be the privilege of the wealthy. Beyond prestige and status, polygyny may also be motivated by fertility considerations. **Polyandry** refers to several or many husbands. This practice appears to be quite rare. Multiple spouses, except in group marriage, are only found on a large scale when an unbalanced **sex ratio** (the number of males per 100 females) exists.

The terms **nuclear family** and **conjugal family** both refer to the family unit in its smallest form. The **conjugal** family must include a husband and wife, while a **nuclear** family may or may not include the marriage partners, but consists of any two or more persons related to one another by blood, marriage, or adoption, and who are of the same or adjoining generation. The **family of orientation** is the family where the first and most basic socialization processes occur. When an individual marries, he or she forms a new nuclear (and conjugal) family. A **family of procreation** is composed of self, spouse, and children. Where nuclear families retain considerable autonomy, and yet remain linked with their kin in other nuclear families, and they exchange goods and services, together they are referred to as **modified extended families.**

The term **extended family** refers to family structures that extend beyond the nuclear family. In the Unites States, the long-term downward trend in the percentage of **extended family households** was finally reversed in the 1980s. The term **joint family** refers to large family situations where at least two brothers live together in the same household with their wives and children. The smallest variety of extended family type is the **stem family,** which consists of two families in adjacent generations, and which is commonly a device for maintaining the family estate intact.

The **kinship system** involves special ties, bonds, and linkages among its members. Family groups and systems are units upon which the kinship system is built. Birth is the primary biological point of reference for kinship. Kinship relationships are also determined and defined by sex, birth order, time together, and seniority within the kin grouping. Kin groups tend to fulfill certain functions: property holding and inheritance; housing and the maintenance of residential proximity; obligation, or helping in time of need; and affection, emotional ties, or primary relationships.

There are several different types of rules of descent: **patrilineal** (through the father and his bloodline), **matrilineal** (through the mother and her bloodline), and **bilateral** (where power and property are transferred through both the mother's and father's line to both males and females). Rules of residence include **patrilocal** (the bride changes residence and lives with the parents of the groom), **matrilocal** (the newlywed couple lives with parents of the bride), **bilocal** (the couple live near the parents of either spouse) and **neolocal** (the couple live in a home of their own, which may be located apart from both sets of parents).

The range of kinship obligation patterns that have been identified includes obligations to keep in touch, the sharing of services and gifts, and helping kin in need. These patterns of obligation have been observed worldwide, with variations. Finally, kinship groups fulfill the important function of providing affection within primary relationships. Women seem to be the "specialists" in affective kin relationships.

The **boundaries** of marriage, family, and kinship are regulated by social norms. These norms vary widely from one society to another, but certain norms exist universally among kinship relationships. The most universal of these norms is the **incest taboo**. All societies forbid sexual relations between persons in certain kinship positions, particularly those within the nuclear family: father and daughter, mother and son, brother and sister, stepfather and stepdaughter, etc. Violations of these norms arouse strong feelings within both the kinship group and wider society. In the United States, incest occurs in all social classes. The most frequent target is a daughter; the most frequent perpetrator is a biological father.

Family ambiguity (not knowing who is in or out of the family system) is a rather new variable in understanding family stress.

LECTURE AND DISCUSSION QUESTIONS

1.   **What are the real biological effects when people reproduce in violation of the incest taboo?**
     Answer guidelines: This seems to be an area of confusion. When asked, students typically give silly answers such as, "Three eyes," or "The kid will be a half wit." It is standing joke that mentally retarded persons might be the products of "inbreeding." It is important that students know a little about the actual biological realities of close-relative reproduction—they will probably be surprised. There is a very slightly increased risk of birth defects among close-relative reproduction, but the general effect is the *enhancement or amplification* of characteristics both parents share. In some cases this might even be a positive outcome! If both parents share a positive trait, the offspring is likely to have this trait as well. This is not to say that society should *encourage* close-relative reproduction. The risk of defects is particularly high when siblings reproduce, since they share a great deal of genetic material (substantially more than is shared by parent and child). However, the actual occurrence of sibling-sibling reproduction is very low. In terms of actual occurrence, it appears that close-relative reproduction is most often the result of father-daughter incest, and it is more a social problem than a biological one. It is typically a matter of sexual exploitation and social inappropriateness, as Eshelman details clearly in this chapter.

2.   **How much of a problem is kinship "*boundary ambiguity*" in our society?**

Answer guidelines: Some extended family relationships have become very tenuous, particularly because of our high rates of divorce, remarriage, and parent nonmarriage. Some instances appear to involve genuine confusion as to who is in and who is out of the family system, particularly where stepfamily relationships are concerned. In other cases, individuals deliberately decide who will *not* be counted as kin. For example, research has shown that it is a common occurrence for children to be "cut off" from kin (most often paternal aunts, uncles, and grandparents) on the "side" of their noncustodial parent. Although kinship relations have traditionally been regarded as bilateral in the United States, divorced people may be less willing to serve as "kinkeepers" for the "other side" of their children's' extended family.

3.   **What do recent trends such as women keeping their own family names when marrying, children being given surnames consisting of hyphenated versions of both parents' names, and the very high recent rate of out-of-wedlock births (with the offspring very often not taking their fathers' surnames at all) tell us about the direction of change within our family system, particularly in our system of descent?**
Answer guidelines: We don't know! Social scientists are generally being very cautious about the significance of these phenomena. The normative ideal of descent in the United States remains that of a bilateral system of inheritance and power. Property is transferred through both the father's and the mother's line to both their male and female offspring. What the above-cited changes mean is not entirely clear. Anthropologists have traditionally regarded high rates of out-of-wedlock birth as indicative of social change that is too rapid, creating distress within a given population. However, it is too early to say whether these trends portend any shifts toward matriarchy or matrilinearity within our society. The patterns social scientists generally *do* regard as quite firm (and which are very dramatic in their own right) are *pluralism within our family institution*, and, to a greater or lesser extent, the *breakdown of norms related to patriarchy*.

CLASSROOM ACTIVITIES AND PROJECTS

1.   Try familiarizing your students with the term "fictive kin." Eshelman discusses the concept of fictive kin at two later points in the text, in the chapter on African American families and the chapter on aging families. This is a term students of family sociology should be conversant with. It might be interesting to first explain the concept—that fictive kin are nonrelatives who are accepted as part of the family, and then go on to explore what the students' own experience with fictive kin might be. List on the backboard all the roles that the students' fictive kin actually fulfill in the lives of their families ("grandfather," "aunt," etc.). Then see if there is a pattern. Tell the students that it wouldn't be surprising to note a prevalence of elderly persons listed as

fictive kin, since research has shown that old people often substitute for missing relatives by converting close friends into quasi-kin. These nonrelatives provide meaningful social networks—and as valuable resources—to help meet the needs of the elderly person. Let your students know that a similar function has been noted among families in poverty.

Make sure the students are aware of the key "lesson" with regard to fictive kin: that the family system is normally characterized by familiarity and intimacy—these are "must haves" for people everywhere. Moreover, if kin aren't available to provide the services and interaction patterns we need, we tend to *create* them.

2.   Present some specific examples of societies that exhibit marriage rules very different from our own, in order to "flesh out" Eshleman's presentation of the variations in norms concerning marriage and number of spouses. Many introductory-level anthropology texts offer highly interesting accounts of non-Western marriage practices and consanguinity rules, placing these phenomena within sociohistorical contexts. Exposure to such information should help students go beyond simply memorizing terms such as "polygyny" and "polyandry," to imagining what it might be like to be born into a very different culture with very different marriage practices.

3.   Ask the students to list some of the widespread, but *noninstitutionalized* family behaviors occurring within our society. Let them know that various theorists have listed divorce, cohabitation, and even adultery as fundamental elements of our marriage and family system. Students might be asked to consider when--if ever--these behaviors might become *institutionalized*. When a large minority practices them? When a majority practices them? When mass media present them as acceptable? When religious organizations appear to accept them--or accept them in policy? When government policy seems to acknowledge them? The instructor should use the criteria already provided by Eshleman in the text to guide this discussion.

FILM AND VIDEO RESOURCES

Kinship and Descent: Parts I and II

Part of the "Faces of Culture" series, this video focuses on the thesis that every society is based on an integrated culture which satisfies human needs and facilitates survival. It includes information on names and inheritance patterns. Part II identifies six major systems for classifying kin.
RMI Media Productions, Inc., preview booklet available

CHAPTER 3

THE FAMILY AND OTHER SYSTEMS: A FOCUS ON WORK

CASE EXAMPLE
> Questions to consider
> Introduction to the chapter

LINKAGES BETWEEN THE FAMILY AND OTHER SYSTEMS
> Mass media and the family
> Religion and the family
> Politics and the family
> Education and the family
> Economy and the family

WORK ROLES OF FAMILY MEMBERS
> Women as full-time homemakers
> Employed wives and mothers
> Employed husbands and fathers
> Men as full-time homemakers
> Dual-employed and dual-career marriages

SUMMARY

OBJECTIVES

Based upon their reading and careful consideration of Chapter 3, students should:

1. understand how the mass media influence our attitudes toward marital and family structures;

2. understand the linkages between family and the other basic social institutions: religion, politics, education, and the economy;

3. be familiar with the role of housewife and the current research findings related to this status in American society;

4. be familiar with relevant data concerning the employed wife and mother, and the relationship of employment of the wife and mother to marriage and offspring;

5.   be conversant with what is known about the employed husband and father, including the new status of "househusband;" and,

6.   be able to describe dual-career marriages in our society, the dilemmas associated with such arrangements, and with commuter marriage as a nontraditional lifestyle.

OVERVIEW

This chapter deals with the linkages between the family and other social institutions, including religion, politics, education, and the economy. Special emphasis is placed on the relationships between marriages and families and the world of employment, work, and the economy. It appears obvious that linkages exist between family systems and other systems, yet such macro-level analysis linkages are frequently ignored in family studies.

The **mass media** constitute an emerging social system and social institution that influences our attitudes toward marital and family structures. Television is now a primary agent of socialization. Many families use television as an "electronic babysitter," and this exposes children to repeated portrayals of violence. Feminists and scholars are concerned over the gender **stereotyping** which appears in the mass media. A stereotype is a widely held belief about the character and/or behavior of a group that seldom conforms to the facts.

Cross-culturally and historically, the relationship between the **religious system** and the family system has been reciprocal. In most societies, many family celebrations are also religious ones. In the United States, Lenski found differences in family practices between religious groups. More recently, an increasing body of evidence suggests a convergence of values and behaviors among major religious groups. What has not changed, is the general linkage between the family and religious systems.

The state or **political system** influences families through laws that regulate and support families. The extent to which the state has responsibility for supporting families is a matter of ongoing controversy. Most governmental programs and laws that affect families are not actually established for or directed specifically at them. Often in subtle and even deceptive ways, families take on an importance in the political arena.

The family and **educational systems** tend to supplement one another in teaching selected cultural values, norms, and skills. One intended function of education is to supplement family socialization. The close relationship between these two systems appears in many studies that show educational training in the home to be directly linked to the success of training in the school.

The **economic system** influences family organization and interaction at the at both the micro and macro levels of analysis. Marxian conflict theorists view economic relationships as the key to understanding inequality within, as well as outside of, the family. The dominance-suppression issue raised by Marx and Engels is at the heart of gender role discussions. Conflict theorists link the male-female division of labor to economic specialization and domination.

Traditionally, few roles of women have held a higher priority than to be wives and **homemakers**. However, the role of the housewife is generally categorized as a low status position, with both low prestige and low economic value. Without such services, most families' standard of living would be drastically lower. Around the world, women do most of the housework. The involvement of husbands is influenced by time availability, relative resources, ideology, and the power relationship between the marriage partners.

Men's involvement in the traditional "women's sphere" is lagging considerably behind women's entry into the traditional "men's sphere." From the conflict and feminist perspectives, housework serves as a prime example of the division of labor between men and women--it generates tension, conflict, and change. The literature suggests that when wives are compared with their husbands, "his" marriage is considerably better than "her" marriage. Career-oriented homemakers have been found to be more dissatisfied with their lives than homemakers who had never wanted careers. There is a widening fertility differential between housewives and employed wives.

Although the total number of women in the labor force, the proportion of mothers in the labor force relative to the total female population have both increased dramatically over the past several decades, the distribution of women in the workforce has changed very little. The largest percentage of employed women today occupies positions in technical, sales, and administrative support settings. The labor market is still sex-segregated, and women are paid less than men are in virtually all job categories. Research indicates that the best predictor of a wife's employment is her husband's support for her working. Employed wives and mothers work for a variety of reasons, but, interestingly, a direct relationship exists between economic attainment and being unmarried: the higher a woman's income, the more likely she is to be or remain single.

Employment of married women before childbearing is associated with lower fertility levels, later first-birth, longer intervals between births, and earlier uses of birth control. On the other hand, there has been a dramatic increase in labor-force participation among women with school- and preschool-aged children. Although it is often assumed that maternal employment has bad effects on children, research in the last several decades has seriously challenged this view. Mothers who hold high status, complex jobs tend to teach their children self-direction and nonconformity. The behavior of children of working mothers seems unaffected in any negative way, except in the area of **compliance** with parental directions. More important than maternal employment, per se, is whether the childcare is sensitive and responsive.

The effect of female employment on marriage, on the marital relationship, and on other family relations varies, depending upon a number of factors. Women holding nontraditional jobs have been found to be more likely to divorce than those holding traditionally "women's" jobs. Greater numbers of hours worked also appears to increase the probability of marital instability, divorce, or both. Wife's employment affects the marriage positively, to the extent that the husband is supportive of her working outside the home.

The number of employed husbands and fathers is increasing, but the proportion of men working relative to the total male population is decreasing. Husband's unemployment has well-documented negative effects on men. Not only does husband/fathers' unemployment affect the family members, so does employment where there is stress on the job, and job insecurity. Househusbandry is rarely a full-time job, unlike housewifery. Some evidence for greater change is seen in subgroups such as single fathers, but the extent to which contemporary husbands relinquish traditional male roles is not known. Their doing so appears to be tied to temporary conditions, in most cases.

The increasing employment of women, combined with the continuing high employment of men, is resulting in many **dual-employment** and **dual-career** marriages. Couples in these marriages may experience stress, role strains, and work overloads as they try to simultaneously work and meet family obligations. Childcare is a significant problem for many dual-career families. Employers that offer supportive policies and benefits are few in number. The difficult choices couples face include lowering career aspirations, consciously rejecting parenthood, one spouse withdrawing from the top professional tier.

For some couples, **commuter marriage**, a lifestyle in which the husband and wife live separately, is the compromise between giving up the marriage or careers. Although the occurrence of this lifestyle is not new, it has been stimulated by the emerging pattern of women having career aspirations. The commuter option has little social support, and brings difficulties of its own.

Childcare is another serious concern for many dual-career families. **Latchkey** ("self-care" children who are at home in houses without adults, usually after school) are perceived to constitute a major problem. Fortunately, there are fewer children in this category than is widely believed, and they are not necessarily the children of low-income, single parent households. Their lack of adult supervision is frequently a problem, however. The high cost and poor availability of childcare is prominent concern among dual career families, as well as single parent families.

LECTURE AND DISCUSSION QUESTIONS

1. **Eshleman suggests that there are macro level economic influences on family systems. What *are* the macroeconomic changes currently affecting the family?**

   Answer guidelines: It is very important to recognize how the family is being impacted by the impoverishment of the middle and working classes of our society. The term "impoverishment" is not use here for dramatic effect, but to describe a decades-long trend with several well-established features.

   The key trend is that of unequal income distribution among American families. Unequal income distribution among families has actually *increased* since the 1960s. This may be summed up with the expression, "The rich are getting richer, and the poor are getting poorer." The expression is true. Government data show that the richest 20 percent of households take in nearly half of the nation's total family income. At the same time, the middle class is shrinking, due to the loss of millions of higher-paid jobs, and to technological advances which allow increased productivity without concomitant payouts in wages.

   Students should be aware of the terms "real wages," and "real income." Real income refers to income adjusted for inflation. Real income has largely declined over the past four decades. The working class (blue-collar workers) has been hard hit. The restructuring of the economy—particularly the elimination of much of the "smokestack industries" has seriously jeopardized the earnings potential of blue-collar families. In 1979, a 30-year-old man with a high school diploma could expect to earn $27,074. By 1992, a man with the same profile would have earned only $20,000.

   Not only have such factors as inflation and the concentration of wealth in the hands of a few led to income inequality and the relative impoverishment of families. Changes in the types of households making up our population of families have also contributed to the problem. There has been an increase in the types of households that tend to be poor. There has been a dramatic increase in the proportion of single-parent households, and the latter generally earn much less than two-parent households. There has also been an increase in households headed by young workers with low salaries. Although there have been much-touted increases in the minimum wage, we should note that between 1970 and 1990 the minimum wage lost 40 percent of its real value because of inflation. Another household type that has been increasing is that of elderly women with small fixed incomes.

   The poor have been hardest hit of all by the macroeconomic trends. According to the Census Bureau, over 14 percent of the population now live below the official government "poverty line." "There is tremendous movement in and out of poverty every year—millions live *near* the poverty line, and are in jeopardy of falling into the category "working poor." About one fifth of all full time workers now fall into this category.

It is essential that students be aware of the actual character of the wage and income structure of our economy. Since there is a widespread assumption that we live in a "middle class society," it is possible that college students may not be aware of the major shifts that have occurred, and the consequent impact upon families.

2. **What should sociology students know about the interface between work and the family?**
Answer guidelines: As Eshleman points-out, there is a widespread expectation that men should be employed, and that a man's work is a key source of his identity and success--or failure. Students should be led to consider how men's work can "carry-over" into the lives of their entire families. In an older, but still instructive book (*Work and the Family System: A Naturalistic Study of Working Class and Lower Class Families*, Free Press, 1978), C.S. Piotrowski reported findings that the working conditions of male wage earners influenced the emotional lives of their families. Fathers who found enjoyment and gratification in their work brought a "positive carry-over" of "warmth and energy" into their households. In the "negative carry-over" pattern, fathers/husbands were subject to stress and poor working conditions, and the researchers found that their frustrations tended to "spill over" into family relationships. The third (and most common) carry-over pattern was that of the "energy deficit." Those father/husbands found their work monotonous and physically draining. Their tiredness led them to withdraw from other family members when they arrived home.

More recent research has continued to demonstrate that when fathers have developed a "bad attitude" during their workdays, it has a "trickle-down" effect within their families. A recent series of articles in the Journal of Marriage and the Family has suggested that the domino effect of negative emotions tends to be most pronounced in traditional nuclear families where a man is the primary breadwinner.

Beyond these "carry-over" patterns, the instructor may wish to mention Sennett and Cobb's idea of the "hidden injuries of class" (*The Hidden Injuries of Class*, Random House, 1974). Their thesis is that, in our society, a man's self-esteem, as well as the social status and material well being of his family, are tied up with his success in the job market. Men who are bruised in the job market often lose the respect and cooperation of their families as well. The vulnerability of low status fathers/husbands to unemployment may also place severe strains on the psychological health of their family relationships.

Students may be interested in considering how negative "carry-over" effects impact upon wives/mothers who are forced to act as "gatekeepers"--keeping children quiet and away their fathers, fending off displaced anger, acting as "both parents" when the father is emotionally exhausted and unavailable. Moreover, the extra burden borne by wives/mothers who are often *themselves* workers, and *themselves* often subject to negative working conditions, should be part of this discussion as well. According to recent research by David Almeida, a psychologist at the University of Arizona, women/mothers who are employed tend not to trigger the sort of negative chain reaction within the family when they've encountered tension on the job. The researcher speculated that this might stem from the different ways men and women are taught to process their emotions. We might ask if there is also another reason: perhaps the power differential within the nuclear family allows men to "share" their burdens with other family members more than it allows women to do so.

3.   **What have been the basic political responses to change in the family institution?**

      Answer guidelines: According to Arlene Skolnick (*The Intimate Environment*, Scott, Foresman and Company, 1987), there appear to be three major points of view in the debate over family change. One perspective is held by conservatives who claim the "profamily" label for themselves. They argue for a return to traditional family values and behavior. The second outlook is that of family scholars who insist that the notion of crisis in the family is largely a myth. A representative of this perspective, according to Skolnick, is Ben Wattenberg, who holds that there has been less change in the family than generally assumed, that many of the changes that have occurred have been positive, and (to the extent that harmful changes have occurred) they are correcting. The third viewpoint is held by scholars and others who see the family as a durable institution, but one currently beset with serious problems.

      It is important for students to realize that (as Eshleman points out) families are regulated and supported in a number of controversial areas by legal action and policy implementation. Students should be encouraged to apply the knowledge they gain in this and other family-related classes to what *they* think might actually be considered "profamily" action...As students of "the family," they may be able to join the debate at some time in their professional careers--and make valuable contributions.

CLASSROOM ACTIVITIES AND PROJECTS

1.   It is common in American society for the housewife role to be taken for granted. Ask your students to consider this fact, and to discuss how what housewives do tends to be devalued. Then ask the students to think about

the skills a "better-than-average-housewife" possesses. Examples of such special skills might include such things as chef, interior decorator, hostess/entertainment coordinator, counselor, or nurse. Pose the questions, "How much is a housewife (or househusband) worth?," Ask students to try estimating how much it might cost a family to contract special-skill services in an average year.

2.	Ask your class to consider whether housework should be an assumed responsibility of one spouse (either the wife or the husband), or whether both spouses should equally share these tasks. Many modern marriages are dual-earner or dual-career situations, which makes sharing household responsibilities the most viable option. As the research has shown, however, spouses may *vocalize* the notion that household chores are being shared, but the *woman* typically ends-up doing more of this kind of work. Ask the members of your class *why* this is the case, and *why* there tends to be this major discrepancy between what is believed and actual behavior.

3.	Ask the female students in your class to state why they are going to college. See how many of them specify that they are training to have careers, rather than to earn money. Encourage those who vocalize a preference for a satisfying career to say whether they want to do this *rather* than quit college, marry, settle down, and have children--Chances are, most of them will express a strong preference for *both* career and motherhood. Ask the students who hope for both career and family how they plan to avoid the pitfalls associated with doing both...How will they avoid the "supermom syndrome?" Be sure to also elicit the reactions of the men in the class.

FILM AND VIDEO RESOURCES

Work vs. the Family
This video examines the effect of employment of mothers and fathers on the family, and offers solutions for common problems.
PBS Video, 30 min., color

Who's Watching Your Kids?
This video is devoted to a thorough discussion of the kinds of difficulties working parents have in trying to find good childcare. It looks at the various kinds of childcare available, what kind will be the most comfortable for different types of families, and what families must do to arrange the best possible care.
Meridian Education Group

Pretend You're Wearing a Barrel
This video follows a divorced mother from the time of her 35th birthday, as she decides to get a job, sees an employment counselor, accepts an

apprenticeship in a "nontraditional field," and becomes an engineer.
Phoenix/BFA Films, 10 min., color

Women, Work and Babies: Can America Cope?

Jane Pauley reports on the "latest American revolution" brought about by the wholesale move of married, middle-class, upwardly mobile (even affluent) mothers, back into the workplace almost immediately after childbirth. The complications and challenges created by this relatively new phenomenon in American society are examined.
NBC, 48 min., color

Can Working Women Have It All?

Can women combine successful home lives with employment and not die of exhaustion in pursuit of "superwomanhood?" Panelists Kate Rand Lloyd of *Working Woman* magazine and Sylvia Hewlett, author of *A Lesser Life: The Myth of Women's Liberation in America*, join Phil Donahue in exploring the issues confronting today's women and the choices they must make.
Films for the Humanities and Sciences, 28 min., color

Men and Women: Balancing Work and Family

Part of the "Your Life's Work" series, this video explores the changes that are occurring in the economy and the workplace, and how these changes affect both men and women. The past, as well as the future is considered.
JIST Works, 23 min., color

Heroes and Strangers: A Film About Men, Emotions, and the Family

Directed by Lorna Rasmussen, this video explores whether men are heroes or strangers to their families--whichever, their roles are changing. This award-winning documentary portrays father/daughter and father/son relationships, revealing the complex social and economic forces affecting the role of men in their families.
Documentary Resource Center, 29 min., color

Beyond Macho

This program provides a powerful portrait of the "househusband," and explores the new roles that have evolved for men as a result of the economic and social changes resulting from new attitudes toward women.
Films for the Humanities and Sciences, 24 min., color

Problems of Working Women

This video examines the pressures facing working women with small children: salaries too low to pay for proper care and supervision of their children during the work day, the inadequacy or unavailability of child care facilities, and inadequate or absent help with household maintenance.
Films for the Humanities and Sciences, 24 min., color

The Double Burden: Mothers and Work
> This film vividly portrays the lives of three families, each with three generations of women who worked outside the home while also raising families. Their stories provide insights into the tasks of employment and childrearing.
> **New Day Films, 57 min., color**

The Global Assembly Line
> This film examines the emerging global economy and the consequences of corporate relocation on workers and families in the U.S. and abroad.
> **New Day Films, 59 min.**

Joyce at Thirty-four
> Directed by Joyce Chopra and Claudia Weill, this film presents the means by which a woman faces the conflict of work versus family.
> **New Day Films, 28 min., black and white**

The Family Established: Working Husbands, Working Wives
> This film explores some common aspects of marriage...First, how work, both inside and outside the home, affects marital relationships. What are the rewards, what are the costs of work in both arenas?
> **RMI Media Productions, 30 min.**

From Pregnant Worker to Working Mother
> This video explores the attitudes and emotional reactions of the future mother, and her employer and co-workers, during pregnancy. The typical concerns of a mother who returns to work after childbirth are featured.
> **Perennial Education, Inc., 22 min., preview available for rentals**

Families in the Balance
> A documentary of the day-to-day struggles of four families, as they try to balance work and parenting with the aid of child care, this video demonstrates that it is possible to provide quality, nurturing child care. However, when we do, there is a high cost to employers, parents, and children.
> **Cornell University Audio-Visual Resource Center, 23 min., color**

CHAPTER 4

PATTERNS IN THE SELECTION OF INTIMATE PARTNERS

CASE EXAMPLE
> Questions to be considered
> Introduction to the chapter

DEFINING HOMOGAMY AND ENDOGAMY
> Intermarriage

SOCIAL/STRUCTURAL CHARACTERISTICS
> Age at marriage
> Residential propinquity
> Social Status
> Religion and intermarriage
> Race/ethnicity and intermarriage

SUMMARY

OBJECTIVES

Based upon their reading and careful consideration of Chapter 4, students should:

1.   Be able to define homogamy, assortive mating, endogamy, exogamy, and heterogamy;

2.   understand the factors influencing rates of intermarriage, including how intermarriage rates are calculated, the difference between mixed marriage rates and marriage rates for individuals, and the distinction between a group's actual and expected rate of intermarriage;

3.   be familiar with the factors that foster intermarriage;

4.   understand age homogamy and the concept of the marriage squeeze;

5.   be conversant with the relationship between the law and the age at first marriage, and society's concern about young marriages;

6.   be able to define residential propinquity, and be familiar with the relationship between propinquity and mate selection, including norm-segregation theory;

7.   understand class endogamy and be able to define mesalliance, hypergamy and hypogamy, the mating gradient, and the relationship between class heterogamy and marital conflict;

8.   be familiar with the implications of interfaith marriage, including its frequency and major consequences; and,

9.   be acquainted with interracial marriage, including its frequency, male-female differences, the likelihood of success in these marital relationships, and the trends in intermarriage.

OVERVIEW

This chapter examines five normative structures shaping mate selection in the United States: age, residence, class, religion, and race. The terms generally employed to describe mate selection among those who share similar characteristics are **homogamy**, which denotes something about the likeness or similarity of married couples; **endogamy**, which refers to in-group marriages of almost any kind; and **assortive mating**, when people marry those like themselves more often than by chance. **Exogamy** refers to rules requiring members of society marry outside their kin group. **Heterogamy** denotes differences in mating patterns.

Factors influencing rates of intermarriage include who is included or excluded, how rates are influenced by the reporting of them (particularly in using figures of marriages as opposed to individuals), and what social and cultural factors are likely to affect the likelihood of intermarriage (including size of a group, heterogeneity, sex ratio and group controls, cultural similarities, romantic love complex, and psychological factors).

Most couples in the United States are relatively **homogamous** in terms of the age at which they marry. Although a person is "free" to marry someone considerably older or younger (within legal limits), most single persons select a member of the opposite sex from a closely related age group. Age homogamy is in itself a function of the age at marriage. Age differences in marriage are the smallest at the younger ages, and increase as age goes up.

The "**marriage squeeze**" is used to describe the effects of an imbalance in the sex ratio or an imbalance between the number of males and females available for marriage. Any shortage of marriageable males (a low sex ratio), for whatever reason, will produce a marriage squeeze. Age is the dimension considered most often in examining the marriage squeeze. Race is also a factor: black females are more affected by the marriage squeeze than are whites.

The legal control of minimum age for marriage, and of divorce in the United States lies with the states rather than with the federal government, and most state laws specify the minimum age at marriage (with and without parental consent). There is concern over young marriages because people who marry young may be less prepared for the mate-selection process and marital-role performance.

Consequently, they experience comparatively low marital satisfaction and higher divorce rates.

Residential propinquity refers to the tendency for people to select mates based upon proximity of geographic residence (same community, neighborhood, etc.). In addition to the greater likelihood of meeting and interacting with people who live close by, another explanation of this phenomenon lies in the **norm-segregation theory**, which suggests that we marry people who adhere to similar cultural norms, and that these people reside in segregated clusters.

Class endogamy refers to the tendency for people to marry persons from within their own socioeconomic grouping. Marriage with a person of an inferior position has been termed "mesalliance." Special cases of mesalliance are **hypergamy** (denoting the pattern wherein the female married upward into a higher social stratum), and **hypogamy** (where the female married downward into a lower social stratum).

When men and women date or engage in intimate types of personal interaction, it can be expected that women will seek out similar or higher status men, and men will seek out similar or lower status women. This tendency has been referred to as the **mating gradient**. One interesting consequence of mating gradient choices is an excess number of unmarried men at the bottom of the socioeconomic ladder, and an excess number of unmarried women at the top. While there appears to be some relationship between class heterogamy and marital conflict, the findings are inconclusive.

Studies have found that the number of people who marry within their own religion is far greater can be explained by chance occurrence. The frequency of interfaith marriage is determined in most investigations by checking religious affiliation noted in public records, or by asking people directly. Recent studies suggest that in the recent past in the United States, norms of religious endogamy have weakened, and that there has been a decrease in religious homogamy. The general opposition to interfaith marriages stems from the widespread belief that they are less stable, and affected by problems that intrafaith marriages do not experience. There appears to be some support for these observations, but the findings must be interpreted cautiously.

Of all the norms involving intermarriage, few are more widely held or rigorously enforced than in the area of race. Despite scientific findings disputing the "purity" of races, and the removal of legal barriers, the restrictions concerning interracial marriage still remain the most inflexible of all the mate-selection boundaries. Although the trend over several decades has been toward greater approval of interracial marriage, the strength of the prohibition--particularly against black/white marriage--remains high.

Since 1960, the Census has been tabulated to show the number of husbands and wives who have the same or different racial backgrounds. These marriages are sociologically important because they serve as an indicator of the relationships among various racial and ethnic groups. Most interracial marriages in the United States occur between Native American, Japanese, and Filipino women, and white men. In black/white marriages, black males marry white women more frequently than white men marry black women. There is a lack of consensus on the differential incidence of interracial marriage by sex. Success in racial intermarriage appears to depend upon the particular situation involved. One way or the other, the trend in interracial marriages is upward, although the total incidence is low.

LECTURE AND DISCUSSION QUESTIONS

1. **What do all the statistics about interracial marriage really *mean*?**
   Answer guidelines: In 1999, the Census Bureau reports that there are 1.3 million interracial marriages currently in existence. As Eshelman suggests, this represents an increase. Still, it's hard to get a "feel" for how many interracial couples there really are. It may be helpful to look at what proportion of all marriages interracial marriages make up. In 1996, 27 percent of Latinos were married to non-Latinos. Only 10 percent of African Americans were married to persons of other races. Less than 3 percent of whites were married to non-whites. The occurrence of black-white intermarriage seems especially low when we take into consideration the fact that the majority of white marriages to non-whites involve partners who are Asian or of some other race. These proportions suggest that, despite the popular perception that interracial marriage is making a real "jump" in numbers, the actual occurrence remains very small—particularly in relation to relatively large size of the African-American population in the United States.

2. **Eshleman is clear about the poorer expectations for teen marriages, compared with marriages entered into at later ages. What are the current projections for the actual occurrence of such marriages, compared with the past?**
   Answer guidelines: There are variations over time, but the rate of childbearing among adolescents has long been high in the United States compared with other Western industrialized nations. The rate of teen pregnancy started to accelerate in the early 1970s, and peaked in 1990. It has dropped significantly during the decade of the 1990s, hitting a 26-year low in 1999. Note, however, that a distinction must be made between adolescent *sexual activity*, which is *much more prevalent* than in the past, and teen *birth*, which has not increased for the childbearing population as a whole).

What is really important to realize is that, currently, premarital pregnancy among teens, when it does occur, *does not necessarily lead to marriage*. Young couples are much less willing than in the past to be forced into early marriage by the prospect of having a child out-of-wedlock. Thus, the most important issue is not so much the success or failure of teen marriages, but the social cost of their *not marrying*, and "keeping their babies" nevertheless. Within roughly a decade, there was a startling reversal: away from *most* young mothers (90%) *giving up* babies born out-of-wedlock for adoption, to the current situation (90% *kept* by the mother). This represents a tremendous value shift within our family institution.

3. **How might the idea of "homosexual marriage" be analyzed in terms of the concepts presented in this chapter?**
   Answer guidelines: Although "homosexual marriage" does not fit within the traditional sociological usages of the concepts of homogamy and endogamy, it is fascinating to apply these terms to the issue of homosexual pairing.

   Homogamy pertains to elements of "sameness" in the paired couple. Obviously, homosexual couples may be assumed to be "the same" in important characteristics. Moreover, it might even seem that the type of same-sex couple most motivated to "settle down" in a marriage-like arrangement might very well be those who are part of a meaningful community of friends and relatives--suggesting a parallel with the sort of social acceptance and support implied in the term "endogamy." In fact, just as many ethnic groups exhibit high levels of endogamy based on shared subcultures, many gay persons see themselves as part of a real and worthwhile subculture.

   Certainly, homogamy "works" (that is, it results in stable marriages and families) because the partners share important values and expectations, and because they enjoy social approval. However, *endogamy is fundamentally a social phenomenon, not a matter of individual need or design.* It is also very much a matter of social control, associated with societies (or, in the case of ethnic subcultures, relocated *parts* of societies) where the individual typically bends to the will of the whole. In America, we see the opposite: ours is a wide-open, heterogeneous society...A society truly without consensus on the meaning of marriage. Perhaps the intensity of the fight over "same sex marriage" in the United States is related to our lack of consensus. It is interesting to note that Denmark, Norway, and Sweden now recognize same-sex marriages as legal.

   The meaning of marriage is really the crux of the matter. What *is* marriage? Using the framework provided by Eshleman on the meanings of marriage, it would seem that the fight over "same sex marriage" is a particularly intense indicator of the clash among the individual, social, and sacred meanings of the marriage institution. Gay individuals and groups who want full social approval of their unions continue to push hard against what they see as discrimination. At the same time, persons and groups that adhere to the social and sacred meanings of marriage continue to push back, fearful that the legitimization of same-sex marriage would jeopardize the future of marriage altogether.

Gay people have won protection against discrimination in some municipalities and states (such laws allow for cohabitation and other same-sex activities without discrimination). There has also been a clear backlash. In the State of Colorado, for example, a majority of citizens have recently voted in a referendum to prohibit the implementation of local statutes protecting gay rights. In Hawaii and elsewhere, gays have failed in court tests to obtain marriage licenses been based on the argument of constitutional equal-protection provisions (of the rights of individuals).

However, in the business sector, gay people are making significant inroads. Over 350 companies, including IBM, Microsoft, Apple Computer, Eastman Kodak, Lotus, The GAP, and Walt Disney now offer medical, dental, and other benefits to domestic partners in same-sex couples. Dozens of other major companies are studying the issue, and some have promised to implement such benefits in the future.

The "sacred" institution may prove much more difficult to penetrate. No major religious denomination in the U.S. allows same-sex marriage ceremonies...Although some *individual* clergy perform ritual "blessings" of same-sex unions, and some clergy have performed traditional marriage ceremonies secretly or publicly (in defiance of denominational canons, sometimes with the backing of *individual* leaders), even the most "liberal" denominations (such as the Episcopal and United Methodist churches) have recently affirmed in their national conventions that gay "marriage" is specifically prohibited.

CLASSROOM ACTIVITIES AND PROJECTS

1. Students may be interested in considering why people hold relatively strong values concerning the principle of age homogamy for marriage. What are the real costs to society, if any, of "May-December" marriages? Using Eshleman's discussion as a baseline, encourage your class to discuss the consequences of age-discrepant relationships.

    This is an ideal issue for illustrating stereotypical beliefs that linger within our values about such marriages. For example, ask students whether they approve of much older men marrying much younger women, versus much older women marrying much younger men. What are the motivations attributed to such marriages? It is often assumed that a younger woman's motives for marrying an older man (and a younger man's motives for marrying an older woman) must involve *money*. At the same time, we often assume an older man's motives for marrying a younger woman (and an older woman's motives for marrying a younger man) must involve *sex*. Students might consider why we don't view these relationships as we would their age-consistent counterparts (that is, they love each other and want to be together).

2. Remind students that in many societies the mate selection process is still very much controlled by parents and other adults (such as "matchmakers"). Such practices both *result from existing norms of homogamy*, and *perpetuate continuing high rates of homogamy*. In the United States, we pride ourselves in having a "participant run" courtship system. Still, students could be encouraged to list ways in which external forces--other people and various social pressures--control the mate selection process in American society, ultimately resulting in considerable homogamy.

3. Try to engage students in a discussion of the "propinquity factor" as an influence in their own lives. Over several decades, research showed consistently that a majority of people chose mates who lived within a short distance of their homes. It is not clear if place of residence is as powerful a factor in mate selection today, but it is an interesting question. Ask students to state whether their parents were residentially propinquitous at the time they met (if there are enough responses, you may want to tally them on the blackboard). Next, ask students where they are meeting their "significant others." Students may be surprised to find a number of responses such as, "I met him in the laundry room of my building," and so forth, even in this age of Internet communications and video dating services!

FILM AND VIDEO RESOURCES

Interracial Marriage
This program examines how and why couples of different colors, religions, and ethnic roots are drawn to one another, how their differences affect their marriages, how they deal with their friends, and how their parents make peace with the children-in-law they wish were of their own race or background.
Films for the Humanities and Sciences, 52 min., color

When Shirley Met Florence
This video examines the lifetime partnership of two lesbian women who have spent a lifetime together.
Carousel films, 28 min., color

CHAPTER 5

EXPLATIONS OF PARTNER SELECTION

CASE EXAMPLE
Questions to consider
Introduction to the chapter

ARRANGED MARRIAGE VERSUS FREE CHOICE OF MATE
The social construction of love

INDIVIDUALISTIC EXPLANATIONS OF PARTNER SELECTION
Instinctive and biological theories
Parental image theory
Complementary needs theory

SOCIOCULTURAL EXPLANATIONS OF PARTNER SELECTION
Value theory
Role theory
Exchange theory
Sequential theories

PROCESSES OF STATUS CHANGE: SINGLE TO MARRIED
Dating
Steady dating: narrowing the "field of eligibles"
Engagement

NONMARITAL COHABITATION
Prevalence of cohabitation
Comparing cohabiting and noncohabitating couples
Cohabitation and marital stability
Cohabitation among people who are elderly
Cohabitation and the law

SUMMARY

OBJECTIVES

Based upon their reading and careful consideration of Chapter 5, students should:

1.   Be familiar with the range of variation on the continuum of arranged marriages versus free choice of mate, the functions of arranged marriage, and the factors constraining choice of spouse in the United States today;

2.   be able to explain the three individualistic explanations of partner selection;

3.   understand the four sociocultural explanations of partner selection;

4.   be familiar with the processes of status change as people move from singlehood to married life (including dating, steady dating, and engagement); and,

5.   be conversant with the phenomenon of nonmarital heterosexual cohabitation (particularly its prevalence in the U.S.), be able to compare and contrast cohabiting and noncohabitating couples, and know something about cohabitation and the law.

OVERVIEW

All societies have systems of norms and specific rules about who may marry whom, and how marriage partners are selected. The processes followed in the selection of specific marital partners vary widely from one society to another, and are different for first marriage and remarriage, males and females, wealthy and poor. On an ideal-type continuum, these methods vary from totally arranged marriages at one extreme to totally free choice of mate at the other. Total free choice is practically nonexistent anywhere in the world.

Most **psychological** and other **individualistic explanations of mate selection** are based on a variety of subconscious drives and needs. One of the oldest and most extreme explanations of mate selection suggests that **instinct** guides the process, but existing evidence does not support this point of view. Closely related to the instinct theory is the Freudian notion that a person tends to fall in love with and marry a person similar to his or her opposite sex parent (**parental image**). Again, no clear evidence exists to support this psychoanalytic theory.

The theory of **complementary needs** proposes that mate selection tends to be complementary, rather than homogamous. Tests of this hypothesis have failed to support it.

Age, residential propinquity, class, religion, and race are the **sociocultural factors** that influence mate selection. This approach specifies that the couple likely to marry is likely to share similar role definitions and expectations. A **value theory** of mate selection suggests that interpersonal attraction is facilitated when persons share or perceive themselves as sharing similar value orientations. **Role theory** appears to be conceptually more justifiable as an overall explanation of marital choice than any of the individualistic explanations. **Exchange theory** proposes that some type of social exchange is basic to the mate selection process. Although single factors are often stressed as significant in the process of mate selection, most explanations take into account factors implied in other explanations. **Sequential theories**, such as the "filtering" concept of Reckerhoff and Davis, the process or development idea of Bolton, and the SVR (*stimulus-value-role*) idea of Murstein, place in sequence selected single factors such as role, values, needs, and exchanges.

The **mate selection** process is the manner in which an individual changes status from single to married. All human societies have some socially approved and structured procedure to follow in getting married. Remarriage, an increasingly common event in industrialized societies, appears to have fewer established norms controlling it. In the United States, the mate selection process, particularly for first marriages, is highly youth-centered and competitive, and can be compared to a male/female game that has rules, goals, strategies, and counterstrategies.

One form of mate selection-related behavior experienced by most adolescents in the United States is **dating**. Young people make the move from an uncommitted relationship to a premarital relationship involving some commitment to one another and exclusion of others. **Engagement** in some form has existed in almost every society in the world, and serves a variety of functions for both the couple and the society.

An alternative to marriage (and an increasingly prevalent nonmarital arrangement) is **nonmarital heterosexual cohabitation**. Such arrangements are increasingly common in the United States. Their prevalence signals that a new normative pattern in courtship and marriage rituals may be emerging. Cohabitation prior to marriage may become institutionalized as a new step between dating and marriage for many couples. Compared with noncohabiting couples, cohabiting couples display lower levels of commitment, lower levels of happiness, poorer relationships with parents, and lower desire to marry. According to research investigations, unmarried cohabitation is not a panacea for preventing marital problems. The laws are changing as a consequence of increased cohabitation in the United States. The trend is toward granting legal protection for the "spouses" and offspring of cohabitors.

LECTURE AND DISCUSSION QUESTIONS

1. **Our society places great emphasis on "love" as a necessary condition for mate selection. How does Western culture compare cross-culturally, in this respect, with other cultures?**
   Answer guidelines: Historically and cross-culturally, many societies have featured romantic love--sometimes placing great importance upon it. The anthropologist Ralph Linton observed about sixty years ago that virtually all cultures recognize extreme emotional attachments, but only Western cultures--particularly American society--emphasize love as the proper basis of marriage.

People in many non-Western societies expect that a strong attachment normally develops between married partners through time. Yet, the expectation focuses upon congeniality, rather than passion. It is assumed that any well-socialized young people will be able to live contentedly with each other. Our culture, on the other hand, teaches that practically all of us will eventually "fall in love"--an experience we recognize as far beyond congeniality.

2. **Eshleman offers a detailed presentation of the process of status change involved in moving from singlehood to marriage, including male-female differences within this process. Why are women usually considered more "commitment oriented" than men?**
<u>Answer guidelines</u>: The family sociologist Willard Waller noted in 1938: "A man, when he marries, chooses a companion and perhaps a helpmate, but a woman chooses a companion and at the same time a *standard of living*." Although gender roles before and after marriage have changed considerably, married women still tend to derive their social status from their husband's occupational prestige. Women have more to lose than men in mate selection, and perhaps tend to be more practical--even "managerial" of their own feelings--than men. A series of studies have found, indeed, that men feel free to be more romantic than women in premarital relationships.

3. **Eshleman raises an important question: Does a "new set of rules" exist today for couples moving toward intimacy and commitment?**
<u>Answer guidelines</u>: Contemporary theorists offer a variety of opinions on the extent to which males seek to move toward sexual intimacy, while females seek commitment.

The men's liberationist Warren Farrell (*Why Men are the Way They Are*, Berkeley Books, 1986) takes a pessimistic stance on the continuing "battle of the sexes." Farrell suggests that men and women are moving *away* from a convergence of interests, and, in fact, there has been a backlash against the "sexual revolution." Farrell goes so far as to suggest that women "withhold sex" in a conscious manner to obtain resources and commitments from men, much as women of older generations did.

Lillian Rubin (*Erotic Wars*, Farrar, Straus & Giroux, 1990) surveyed nearly a thousand men and women, and found that "the sexual revolution which freed women to say 'yes' also made it difficult for them to say 'no.'" Rubin concludes that the rules and customs of dating and intimacy *have* changed, but intimacy is still a "meeting of intimate adversaries."

CLASSROOM ACTIVITIES AND PROJECTS

1.   Most students tend to exaggerate the degree of "free choice" that they have in intimate relationships, and, ultimately, in selecting a marriage partner. In order to illustrate the socially imposed limitations, first draw a funnel on the board. Then, beginning at the top (the widest part) of the funnel, write in "all eligible partners." Moving from the top to the narrowest part of the funnel (the bottom), write in the following considerations, "propinquity," then "ethnicity and race," then "age," then "physical attractiveness," then "social class and income." After doing this, have students assess how small their individual "pool of eligibles" really is.

2.   Well-known family sociologist Willard Waller spoke of "rating and dating" in describing how certain elements of socioeconomic status are taken into account in dating behavior among college students. If you teach at a college or university where fraternities and sororities are commonplace, the "rating and dating" complex should be familiar to students. If not, you can ask students to discuss how important levels of physical attractiveness really are, in terms of who dates whom. In any event, students will benefit from discussing this "rating and dating" process, because it typically shows just how pragmatic the process of finding a mate is in American society.

3.   Students may tend to view cohabitation as a strategy for avoiding the problems associated with marriage. Ask your students: "What are the advantages of living together in comparison to marriage?" After the class has aired their views, ask: "What are the advantages of being married in comparison to cohabiting?" Encourage students to be objective in evaluating these lifestyles. Students may be interested in speculating about the higher rates of domestic violence occurring among cohabiting couples.

FILM AND VIDEO RESOURCES

The Familiar Face of Love
This film provides a study of love and mate selection, taking historical and cross-cultural factors into account.
Filmmakers Library, 27 min.

The Marriage Market
Part of the "Portrait of a Family" series, this video explores various aspects of choosing partners and falling in love.
RMI Media Productions, 30 min., preview kit available

A Hero is More Than a Sandwich

Featuring Dr. Sonya Friedman, this video explores the wide range of "Junk Food Heroes," helping women learn to recognize and protect themselves against dangerous cultural images that crop-up in the search for a mate. **J2 Communications, 30 min.**

CHAPTER 6

SEXUAL NORMS AND RELATIONSHIPS

CASE EXAMPLE
    Questions to consider
    Introduction to the chapter

SOCIAL REGULATION OF SEXUAL RELATIONSHIPS

BIOLOGICAL VERSUS SOCIOLOGICAL APPROACHES TO SEXUAL BEHAVIOR

THE SOCIAL DIMENSIONS OF SEXUALITY
    Social network theory
    Choice theory
    Sexual script theory and sexualization

NONMARITAL SEXUAL BEHAVIOR
    Family antecedents of sexual behavior
    Relevance of formal sex education

PREMARITAL SEXUAL INTERCOURSE
    The incidence and prevalence of premarital intercourse
    Changes in premarital sexual activity
    High-risk sexual behavior and AIDS

SEX AND MARRIAGE
    Changes in marital sexual activity
    Factors related to marital sexuality
    Sexual adjustment in marriage

EXTRAMARITAL COITUS
    Incidence of and attitudes toward extramarital sex

SUMMARY

OBJECTIVES

Based upon their reading and careful consideration of Chapter 6, students should:

1.   Be familiar with the major biological and social forces that control human
      sexuality;

2.   understand the effort to construct a more comprehensive theory of the social dimensions of human sexuality, using the social network theory, choice theory, and scripting theory;

3.   be able to discuss the antecedents of sexual behavior;

4.   be aware of the social consequences of sexual behavior;

5.   understand the relevance of formal sex education to premarital sexual behavior;

6.   be familiar with the research findings on the frequency of premarital intercourse over the past several decades; and,

7.   be familiar with the impact of AIDS on premarital sexual behavior.

OVERVIEW

All societies have social norms that grant approval to certain sexual behaviors, and disapproval to others. In American society, as well as in virtually all others, the most pervasive sexual interest is in heterosexual behavior and relationships, both marital and non-marital.

Socialization theories have frequently been used to explain sexual attitudes and values. **Social control theories** assume that humans generally have a strong predisposition to sexual activity, and. In the absence of social constraints, would engage in undesirable sex. Social controls regulate sexual activity. Sociobiologists tend to claim that male-female differences are biologically determined, while sociologists are more likely to claim that differences are cultural in origin.

Efforts to construct a more comprehensive theory of the social dimensions of human sexuality include **social network theory**, **choice theory**, and **scripting theory**. Social network theory emphasizes that the couple is part of a larger social network and culture, and that this environment greatly influences their sexual behavior. Choice theory focuses on sexual decision making and how individuals make sexual choices: choices are made on the basis of goals we have in mind, and on the resources available to meet them. Scripting theory explains sexual content. This perspective assumes that humans have no biological instincts dictating our sexual behaviors—rather, our sexual self-concepts, values, and behaviors are internalized through a process of sexual socialization.

Sexualization, (sexual socialization), is the process by which persons learn and internalize their sexual self-concepts, values, attitudes, and behaviors. According to symbolic interaction theory, we become sexual beings through the process of social interaction, and sexual behavior can be understood only in terms of internalized symbolic meanings. **Sexual scripts** designate the who, what, where, when, and why of sexuality. **Cultural scenarios** are the instructional guides that exist at the level of collective life. **Interpersonal scripts** transform the person trained in cultural scenarios and general social roles to context-specific behavior. These cultural scenarios and interpersonal scripts result in **intrapsychic scripting**: an internal dialogue--a personal self that is in reality a social self. Sexual scripts include both attitudinal and behavioral components. It is important to recognize that attitudes, behaviors, and the relationship between them must be viewed within a cultural/social context.

Antecedents of sexual behavior are factors that have preceded sexual activity. Many antecedents are family related, such as parental influence in the sexual socialization process and parental discipline. Formal sex education is another very important antecedent. Research indicates that family communication does not account for very much in terms of either teen sexual behavior or teen contraceptive use. There is a curvilinear relationship between parental disciplinary patterns and sexual permissiveness--the lowest level of permissiveness tends to be among adolescents with *moderately* strict parents.

The term **premarital sexual intercourse** indicates that at least one of the partners is single and has not been previously married. Cross-culturally, it appears that most societies permit or even encourage premarital relationships, particularly for the males. Premarital sexual permissiveness increases as a couple approaches marriage or a committed relationship. A significant difference exists between **incidence and prevalence**. Incidence is the occurrence or nonoccurrence of an experience; prevalence refers to frequency. Both incidence and prevalence appear to have increased significantly over the past several decades.

Many social forces have led to changes in premarital sexual activity in the United States over the past few decades. The incidence of premarital coitus has increased, especially for females, and there has been a movement in the direction of increased permissiveness. However, in contrast to the social forces that have supported sexual permissiveness, there has more recently been an emergence of new conservative political and religious movements, as well as new and serious health epidemics related to sexual activity. These can be expected to modify the sexual activities of people of all ages.

Many young people in the United States engage in **high-risk sexual behavior**, sex with multiple partners and/or the failure to protect against the transmission of disease. Factors associated with sexual risk taking among adolescents include low GPAs, more frequent alcohol consumption, low levels of parental monitoring, lack of communication with mothers about birth control, more frequent contemplation of suicide, history of sexual and physical abuse, and more troubled relationships with parents.

Changes are taking place in the area of sexual risk taking, but not as dramatically as one might think. Nationally representative data reveal that about one-third of sexually experienced unmarried women have changed their sexual behavior in response to the treat of AIDS.

LECTURE AND DISCUSSION QUESTIONS

1. **Does, or does not, school-based sex education work?**

   Answer guidelines: One of the main arguments used against school-based sex education is that it doesn't work because it shouldn't be taught in the school, anyway. This argument should be familiar to students; "Sex education is the responsibility of parents, since it's a private matter." Another major argument centers on the feeling that sex education will "corrupt" youngsters, making them more prone to experiment.

   The great difficulty with the first argument is that parents generally *don't* teach their children much about sex. The patterns shown by research in this area are that children report little sex information from parents, that parents tend to feel uncomfortable talking about sex with their children, and that parents overestimate the role they play in the sex education of their children. Thus, it is not surprising that the responsibility for real sex education has fallen to schools, despite the popular idea that sex education is basically a matter of *moral* education and therefore, best left to the family.

   Actually, it may be the case that more parents want help with sex education than is generally thought. A 1995 study found 65 percent of adults approving of schools giving sex education. A very vocal minority, led by conservative religious groups, has been able to override the will of the majority on this issue. Those opposed to sex education typically emphasize that abstinence should be taught in its place. Unfortunately, "the jury is still out" on the effectiveness of teaching abstinence *in place of* all other sex education. Most experts now agree that teaching abstinence alone is ineffective, if the goal is to reduce teen pregnancy and disease rates.

   What *does* work? Research by Kirby, et al. in 1994 uncovered six common elements in successful sex education programs. Programs that taught students to resist peer pressure had some impact, since there is generally a high level of peer pressure to engage in sexual activities. Effective programs also provided very specific "technical" information. A third, somewhat surprising, technique the researchers deemed effective was the inclusion of experiential activities, such as role playing, small groups discussions, games, and brainstorming. A fourth strategy that characterized effective programs was that of identifying media pressures to have sex. Successful programs also reinforced norms against early and unprotected sex. For the first time, research suggests that positive group and peer pressure may be stronger than the negative pressures parents fear so much. Finally, the researchers found that the best programs developed students' skills in communication about sex, and included elements of negotiation and refusal to bow to pressure.

One known weakness of school-based sex education is that it generally starts way too late, in relation to when youngsters actually reach puberty and begin experimenting (this seems to refute the notion that formal sex education "corrupts" youngsters). Girls' breast development occurs around age nine, on the average, and menses begin around age twelve. This means girls may need sex education to begin in the fourth grade, in contrast with most current programs, which focus on ninth or tenth grade students. It is not difficult to imagine, given the controversy over having sex education at all, how opponents might respond to initiating it in the fourth grade!

2.   **Has there actually been a "sexual revolution?"**
     Answer guidelines: A few writers have suggested that there has not been anything quite like a sexual revolution. Some have gone so far as to say that there *was* a sexual revolution, but it has *reversed* itself. It appears that those theorists have been responding to short-term trends, such as the "baby boomers" settling down into family life, a backlash to AIDS (which has led some to reconsider promiscuity), and the shallow (in terms of numbers of people involved), but well-publicized "chastity movement."

Two or three decades are a rather short time span to conclude that there has been a "revolution" in *any* area of social life. Still, a majority of sociologists appear to agree that there *has been* a sexual revolution. What has it entailed? It has entailed detectable changes in actual behavior.

First of all, there has been a decline in the "double standard." As Eshleman points out, premarital sex has always been a generally accepted part of the male role in Western society, but never before has it been acceptable for women. Now, a majority of women have experienced sex by the time they marry. Second, there has been an increased emphasis on sex for pleasure (this may not sound revolutionary in the contemporary setting, but never before in Western society has such an emphasis on sex for pleasure been observed--especially where women are concerned). Third, people now become sexually active at a younger age than in recent history. A study conducted in Michigan by the Centers for Disease Control found that 16 was the median age of first intercourse for women, and that 98% had experienced intercourse by the age of 21. Fourth, an important feature of the "sexual revolution" is the tendency toward multiple sexual partners over the life span. This is made possible by earlier sexual activity, casual sex while dating, later age at first marriage, and periods of singlehood after divorce and before remarriage.

42

Aside from the changes in sex roles and sexual values that have made a "sexual revolution" possible, there have also been technological supports for behavioral changes. Highly reliable contraceptives (when used properly) have become widely available. Moreover, safe, legal abortion has been available since January, 1973. It is nearly impossible to overestimate the importance of these factors: This is the first time in the history of mankind that sexual activity has not necessarily carried with it the possibility of parenthood! At the very least, pregnancy may definitely be prevented. We should understand that contraception is a key sexual issue, since it affects how people perceive sexual freedom, it affects decisions about whom people are willing to have sex with (now not only those necessarily regarded as potential marriage partners), and, because pregnancy can be prevented, sex tends to be more removed from marriage altogether.

3. **How do Americans compare with other countries in contraceptive usage and sexual sophistication?**
   Answer guidelines: As Eshelman points out, research has indicated a broad tendency toward unprotected sexual activity. Unfortunately, Americans are also *less competent* in contraceptive usage, on the average, than others in developed countries. Apparently, despite the "sexual revolution," and our relaxed actual sexual behavior, we have a counterproductive approach to protecting ourselves against pregnancy and disease.

   A recent study by the Alan Guttmacher Institute, a nonprofit corporation focusing on reproductive health issues, found that there had actually been a *decline* in utilization of contraception. Nearly 57% of American pregnancies were found to have been unplanned.

   The Guttmacher report cited several reasons for our poor use of contraceptives: ambivalent, puritanical attitudes toward sex (women most likely to report being "swept away" before intercourse were the *least* likely to have used contraceptives), irrational fear of adverse side affects with birth control devices, and a large, economically deprived underclass. The researchers recommended large-scale sex education and the expansion of availability of contraceptives.

   Other research has noted that even those who intentionally use contraceptives tend to be haphazard and/or ill informed in the usage of such products. For example, one study discovered that an alarmingly high 98 percent of birth control pill users had, at some time, used the pills incorrectly!

   Apparently, not only are we ill informed and self-defeating in contraceptive usage, Americans are also somewhat ignorant about sex itself. A 1990 report released by the Kinsey Institute went so far as to call us a nation of "sexual illiterates."

The authors, June Reinisch and Ruth Beasley, concluded that the sexual revolution had been "vastly overrated." What the authors found particularly alarming was the fact that many of the survey questions respondents answered incorrectly dealt with vital health issues--of which misunderstanding could put lives in jeopardy.

CLASSROOM ACTIVITIES AND PROJECTS

1.   The optimistic attitude of many students seems to produce a nonchalant attitude toward AIDS, such as, "We will come up with a cure soon," or "There will be a vaccine." Have students think about what may happen if a cure is *not* soon found for AIDS, in particular whether people will be able to continue to accept sexual permissiveness.

      Good strategies for teaching about AIDS may be found in several older, but still accurate, journal articles. One is Rose Weitz's "Confronting the Epidemic: Teaching About AIDS," which appeared in the July, 1989 issue of *Teaching Sociology* (Vol. 17, No. 3: 360-364) Another is the series of five articles on AIDS which appeared in the October, 1989 issue of *Social Problems*, which covered a broad range of concerns.

2.   As you discuss premarital and nonmarital sexuality with your students, ask them to think about the mixed messages we receive concerning sexual behavior: On the one hand, we are told that sex is a "natural" matter of biology and emotional need, which we have a *right* to express. On the other hand, we are taught that our sexual feelings must be controlled--only under certain conditions are we permitted to have sex. Using Eshleman's presentations of biological predisposition and of "sexual scripts" as points of departure, encourage students to vocalize their own impressions of the apparent contradictions surrounding expression of sexuality in our society.

3.   Engage students in a "thinking exercise" of how we learn about sex. Ask students to think about (but *not* share with the class) the youngest age at which they remember having sexual feelings or curiosity. Next, ask students to think about (but *not* share with the class) the earliest information they obtained about sexual questions they had. Explain that most early "sexualization" (a term students should be familiar with, from Eshleman's presentation) occurs at a very early age, within the home. Parents exert a great deal of *control* over the types of cultural influences pertaining to sex the young child is exposed to—and then parents *interpret*, to a great extent, the meaning of those influences.

      Next, ask students to think about (*not* share with the class) how they continued to learn about sex as older children and as adolescents. Ask them to consider how their parents' *attitudes* may have affected them, versus any real *information* they may have obtained from their parents.

The objective of this exercise is for students to see that although parents play a vital role in shaping our sexual attitudes and sexual self-concepts, most of us have obtained very little information about sex from our parents. Research in the United States has shown consistently that parents seldom serve as the primary source of sexual information. Ansini, et al. 1996, found that siblings were *twice as likely* to provide vital information on reproduction, anatomy, and other sexual topics as parents were . An earlier study of 8000 college students found less than 15 percent of them reporting that they'd obtained meaningful sex information from their parents.

If you discuss with your class the issues surrounding school-based sex education (see number 1, above in the "Lecture and Discussion" section for this chapter), it is important that they have this background awareness of how youngsters actually obtain sex information.

FILM AND VIDEO RESOURCES

Safe Sex

AIDS is not just a plague that afflicts gay men--a staggering number of heterosexuals have fallen victim to the virus. This video points out that most educators agree it is better to discuss safe sex frankly with teenagers, and even with children, than risk contracting AIDS.
Films for the Humanities and Sciences, 28 min., color

Preventing Teen Pregnancy

Phil Donahue hosts this program focusing on teen pregnancy. Some controversial recommendations are made, including formal sex education beginning in the preteen years. The issues of contraception and sexual abstinence prior to marriage are also examined.
Films for the Humanities and Sciences, 28 min., color

AIDS: The Women Speak

The AIDS epidemic is affecting more women. This program tells the stories of the many ways AIDS has affected individual women.
Films for the Humanities and Sciences, 28 min., color

AIDS: The Changed Face of America

This specially-adapted two-part Phil Donahue program provides examples of how AIDS has dramatically changed the face of America: changes in the dating scene and in sexual practices, greater openness about homosexuality (and more attacks upon homosexuals), social and job discrimination, health care crisis, and new tests of human character.

The Sexual Brain

This program shows some startling effects of hormone injections on brain structure and raises provocative questions about the sexual and reproductive roots of structural differences between males and females.
Films for the Humanities and Sciences, 28 min., color

Love and Sex

As this Phil Donahue program suggests, falling in love, having sex, and making babies are easy enough, but understanding human sexuality is much more difficult. This program examines different topics relating to sexuality, including comments by Dr. William Masters and Dr. June Reinisch (Director of the Kinsey Institute).
Films for the Humanities and Sciences, 52 min., color

Men, Women, Sex, and AIDS

Hosted by Tom Brokaw, this program discusses sex in the age of AIDS...What is responsible and safe behavior? How early, and how explicitly should young people be informed about AIDS? Is enough money being devoted to AIDS research? What effect is the rapidly growing number of victims having on health care facilities and insurance programs? Brokaw discovers some starting answers.
Public Media, Inc., 49 min., color

Men Under Siege: Life With the Modern Woman

This video is a lively appraisal of changing sex roles in America, and the impact of these changes on work, marriage, and sexual relationships.
Coronet Multi-media Co., 33 min. prevail available for rental

CHAPTER 7

THE MARITAL SYSTEM

FUNCTIONS OF MARRIAGE AND MARRIAGE-LIKE RELATIONSHIPS
Marital status and well-being

MARRIAGE TRENDS AND CHARACTERISTICS
Reasons people marry
Variations in marriage rates

POWER IN CONJUGAL AND INTIMATE RELATIONSHIPS
Characteristics of power
Power and decision making in conjugal and intimate relationships
Theory of resources issue
Egalitarian ethic

MARITAL QUALITY
Dimensions of marital quality
Evaluating marital quality
Marital conflict
Marital quality over the life course

SUMMARY

OBJECTIVES

Based upon their reading and careful consideration of Chapter 7, students should:

1.   Understand the functions of marriage and marriage-like relationships;

2.   be familiar with marriage trends and characteristics discussed in the chapter, including major variations;

3.   understand the characteristics of conjugal power, and its processes in relation to decision making;

4.   understand how the theory of resources issue might be applied in evaluating decision making processes within the intimate relationship;

5.   be able to describe the egalitarian ethic;

6.   be familiar with the dimensions of marital quality;

7. know how the Dyadic Adjustment Scale is used to evaluate marital adjustment;

8. understand the relationship between marital quality and marital conflict; and,

9. be familiar with what is known about fluctuations in marital quality over the life course.

OVERVIEW

Marriage and sexually bonded relationships fulfill various functions for the individual and society, including basic personality formation, status ascription, nurturant socialization, tension management, replacement of members, economic cooperation, reproduction, stabilization of adults, and the like. Within the social and cultural context of the United States, we are currently witnessing a variety of marital forms in addition to the traditional monogamous, sexually exclusive marriage pattern for the fulfillment of individuals' perceived needs. The additional forms include serial monogamy, adultery, and non-marital cohabitation.

It has been suggested that marital and intimately bonded partners provide companionship, interpersonal closeness, emotional gratification, and support that buffer individuals against physical and emotional pathology. This is referred to as the **marriage protection hypothesis**. Married people are less likely to engage in risk-taking behavior, and they lead more stable lives. Married women tend to be healthier than single women are, and marriage and marriage-like relationships have been shown to be particularly rewarding for men. However, the differences between married and unmarried people may be declining.

Marriage is viewed very favorably in the United States. The **marriage rate** is the proportion of people in a given population who marry. Marriages have a distinct seasonal pattern. Marriage rates show distinct differences by geographic region, and state laws are also related to the incidence of marriage in a particular location.

One important aspect of the marital system (a conjugal relationship) is the *power* positions of husband and wife--as individuals and in relationship to each other. Conjugal power refers to the ability of the husband and wife to influence each other. Power involves the crucial dimensions of **authority** and **influence**, and refers to a capacity or ability rather than the exercise of that ability. The use of power within marriage is a dimension often overlooked. One of the ways in which conjugal power has traditionally been measured is to determine which spouse makes the major decisions, and how the husband and wife decision-making patterns vary by area of concern. The **theory of resources** contends that the more a partner controls resources of value to him- or herself and the mate, the greater his or her relative power, but data show mixed and inconsistent results. It is necessary to examine the meanings couples give to the material and structural conditions of their lives.

48

The extent of the **egalitarian ethic** found in a marriage appears to be related to its quality. Joint decision-making, sharing of marital power, perceptions of both self and spouse as doing a fair share of family work, and a feeling of equity appear to be positively related to marital satisfaction and negatively related to depression. However, there are differences for husbands and wives where patterns of egalitarianism are concerned, depending upon the individuals' orientation to traditional values.

Marital adjustment, **happiness**, **satisfaction**, **quality**, **well being**, and a number of other terms are applied in the study of marital quality. Some terms are applied in the psychological sense, while others are used in the social sense. The **adjustment** of married mates is unlike any other human relationships. Marital **quality** is a varied concept that lacks a general consensus of definition. Marital **success** is distinguished from marital **happiness**, in that the former refers to the achievement of one or more goals, such as permanence, while the latter is an emotional response of an individual.

According to Jessie Bernard, the major dimensions of any human adjustment problem are: (1) the degree or extent or nature of the differences between or among the parties involved, (2) the degree or extent or nature of the communication between or among the parties, and, (3) the quality of the relationship between. The most widely used measurement of marital or interpersonal adjustment in recent years has been the Dyadic Adjustment Scale, developed by Graham Spanier. The scale consists of thirty-two items centering around four basic components: *satisfaction, cohesion, consensus,* and *affectional expression*.

From the point of view of the social conflict frame of reference, marital **conflict** is natural and inevitable. The "question" is how the couple manages conflict. Failure to engage in conflict when an injustice is perceived may result in a less beneficial marriage. The *lack* of conflict may actually lead to the dissolution of a marriage, if issues of injustice or inequitability are not brought into the open. The management of conflict should not be confused with the management of externally produced adversity, such as economic loss--such stressors are less related to interpersonal qualities than to disruptions of patterns of social interaction.

When marital is examined throughout the life course, satisfaction appears to be highest at the beginning of marriage, and low points come when families have school-aged children and teenagers. Studies indicate a curvilinear relationship throughout the cycle--the beginning and the end of marriage are points of highest satisfaction.

LECTURE AND DISCUSSION QUESTIONS

1. **How have the underlying value shifts concerning marital "satisfaction" contributed to marital instability?**

   Answer guidelines: Although "Till death do us part" has long been the *expressed* standard for marriage, there is no question that, in actual practice, American couples believe in permanence only as long as they meet each other's needs and the marriage remains happy. Otherwise, if they grow apart or fail to meet each other's needs, it is expected that they may-- and perhaps *should*--divorce and find new partners who will.

   Intimacy expert James Coleman (*Intimate Relationships, Marriage and the Family*, Macmillan, 1988) has suggested that most young people in our society have probably accepted the idea of serial marriage, even though they realize that the price is "living their marriage in the shadow of divorce." The willingness of couples to consider the possibility of marital impermanence, even while they are ostensibly married for life is related to several major trends: the **sexual revolution** (which leads people to expect sexual fulfillment as an entitlement in marriage, and the lack of such fulfillment is grounds for ending the marriage), the **longevity revolution** (which makes it possible to evaluate marital quality far into the future, and embark on new marriages even late in life), and the **psychological revolution** (which leads people to insist upon satisfaction in the inner experience of their marital relationships, and feel justified in moving on to new relationships, if necessary, to experience those relationship qualities).

   There is some "good news" about marital instability: the worst may be over. In 1999, the Census Bureau reported that the proportion of households made up of families has stabilized—a reversal of a downward trend begun in the 1970s, when the "baby boomers" were reaching adulthood—a time of substantial tumult of various kinds within marriages and families.

2. **What problems might be encountered with the "egalitarian ethic" described by Eshleman?**

   Answer guidelines: Arlene Skolnick (*The Intimate Relationship*, Scott, Foresman, and Company, 1987) has suggested that the sex role changes associated with the egalitarian ethic have been difficult and confusing for many people because both sexes are sometimes ambivalent about the changes. Skolnick says women feel that men want them to be self-reliant, but still feminine and "nice." In turn, men feel that women expect them to be gentle and sensitive. Yet, the man who is emotionally expressive risks being labeled a "wimp."

   In her book *Intimate Strangers* (Harper and Row, 1983) Lillian Rubin also notes these "mixed feelings." As examples, Rubin describes a staunch feminist who admits she sometimes feels angry that her husband does not solely support his family the way her father did. Along similar lines, the husband of a working wife appreciates his wife's contribution to the family income, yet longs the "good old days" when "a man was a man, and a woman was a woman."

3. **Eshleman makes the very important point that the quality of a marriage is not based on whether conflict exists, but on how conflict is *managed*. What are some of the ways couples can manage conflict?**
    Answer guidelines: James Coleman (*Intimate Relationships*, Macmillan, 1988) offers some guidelines for resolving marital conflict. First, the couple may need to pinpoint the problem. This may necessitate recognizing that a problem exists, then focusing on the *actual* problem (often, couples quarrel over seemingly trivial issues, while avoiding the core problem). Coleman notes that in pinpointing the problem, it is important to first focus on needs, feelings, and concerns--not solutions.

    The second step is exploring options. According to Coleman, the couple should consider alternative options, even when some of them may seem impractical (the important thing is not to belittle one's partner's ideas). After all options have been considered, the ones that are best for the relationship should be selected.

    Finally, Coleman suggests that the couple evaluate change, using feedback. Even if the feedback is unfavorable, corrections can be made. Feedback eventually becomes a vital part of the overall process of conflict resolution.

Psychologist John Gottman, who has devoted twenty years to studying the management of conflict in marriage, insists that here are several acceptable patterns or styles. What matters, according to Gottman (*Why Marriages Succeed or Fail*, Fireside, 1994) is that the couple has many more positive responses to each other than negative ones. In fact, Gottman offers a very specific formula: No matter what style the marriage follows, the couple must have *five times as many positive as negative moments together*. If the couple is unable to achieve this balance, the prospects for satisfaction (and survival of the relationship) are not good.

CLASSROOM ACTIVITIES AND PROJECTS

1. A companion concept to the theory of resources is the "*principle of least interest*." Have students think about relationships in which one person is more interested in maintaining the association than another. Then, encourage them to discuss how the person who has the least interest is placed in a position of some power.

2. Over ninety percent of the adult population marries, at least once. A majority of those who divorce remarry eventually. Clearly, marriage is widely regarded to be the most appropriate state for adult living. Ask the members of your class to comment on why they think marriage is so popular. What are the advantages to being married in American society? What are the disadvantages? You might also want to pose the question more broadly: "Are humans *naturally* monogamous?"

3. Americans seem to compare their own marriages with some sort of ideal. Married couples often speculate about how their marriages "stack up" in comparison to other marital relationships (how many times per week they have sex, how well they communicate, whether they are they doing a good job serving as each other's best friend, and so forth). These comparisons can lead to unrealistic expectations of potential happiness and satisfaction. Ask your students to think about whether the way marriage is portrayed in our culture causes couples to question too much whether their marriages are successful, and, if so, whether this tendency ultimately damages marriages.

FILM AND VIDEO RESOURCES

Men Are From Mars, Women Are From Venus

John Gray narrates this video, which deals with why men and women are different, and why they approach relationships differently. It presents means of improving partners' abilities to communicate with each other, and discovering how to cope with difficult feelings and avoid arguments. The

video emphasizes how partners may learn how to build fulfilling relationships that increase self-esteem and meet the needs of both partners.
Wishing well distributing Co., 180 mins.in three volumes, color

Why Men Don't Talk to Their Wives

Research shows that men and women communicate differently; they tend to talk about different things and in different ways. In this specially adapted Phil Donahue program, several couples talk about their problems in communicating, and a marriage therapist offers exercises to improve communication.
Films for the Humanities and Sciences, 28 min., color

Married Lives Today

This video makes the point that marriage is more varied and subject to change than in the past. This sensitive documentary film juxtaposes a young couple operating a business together who see themselves as completely equal; another couple, more traditional in outlook; and a third couple who, though separated, continue to share the responsibilities of their daughter. As different as they all are, all three couples continue to function creatively in their married lives.
Phoenix/BFA Films and Video, color, 19 min.

CHAPTER 8

U.S. FAMILIES: CHARACTERISTICS, CHANGE, AND ISSUES

CASE EXAMPLE
> Questions to consider
> Introduction to the chapter

CHARACTERISTICS OF U.S. FAMILIES
> Numbers of families and households
> Sizes of families and households
> Marital status
> Family income

TODAY'S FAMILIES: SIGNIFICANT CHANGES

ISSUES IN U.S. FAMILIES
> Meaning of marriage and the family
> Family organization
> Family functions
> Marital- and gender-role differentiation
> Social class and social mobility
> Partner selection
> Love
> Sexual relationships
> Family size and family planning
> Aged family members
> Violence and abuse among intimates
> Family permanence
> Other contemporary issues

SUMMARY

OBJECTIVES

Based upon their reading and careful consideration of Chapter 8, students should:

1.   Be familiar with the basic characteristics of U.S. families;

2.   be aware of the dramatic demographic changes in family organization that have occurred over time, and of the great diversity among families within our society;

3. be able to cite many of the major issues affecting the family in the U.S., including the meaning of marriage and the family, family organization, family functions, how changes in family life are altering family law, social mobility, mate selection, sexual relationships, family size, family planning, old age, and family reorganization;

4. be comfortable with the use of ideal-type constructs;

5. be able to discuss the three mutually incompatible meanings of "the family" presented by Eshleman, showing awareness of how the simultaneous existence of these very different meanings is related to conflict within our basic social institutions;

6. be able to name the primary functions of the contemporary family;

7. understand what is meant by gender-role differentiation;

8. be familiar with Eshleman's basic points regarding the social class mobility of families, the meaning of various approaches to partner selection, the issue of love, the significance of sex in relation to marriage, the issues surrounding family planning, and the role of aged family members; and,

9. be aware of research into family issues such as violence and abuse among intimates, family impermanence, and other contemporary issues.

OVERVIEW

The U.S. Census serves as a primary source of information about the changing characteristics of families. The term **family**, as used in Census reporting, refers to a group of two or more persons related by birth, marriage, or adoption who reside together in a household. A family is different from a **household**. A household consists of all persons who occupy a housing unit—not all households contain families. **Family size** refers to the number of persons who are living together and are related by birth, marriage, or adoption. U.S. households had fewer persons per unit than did families in 1997. The number of persons per household has decreased considerably since the earliest census reports. The social impact of this decreasing size is unclear, due to conflicting research findings.

As for **marital status**, the Census identifies four major categories: single, married, widowed, and divorced. The data show that marriage continues to be popular in the U.S.

Family income refers to the total amount of earnings reported by related persons who were members of the family during a specified time. Median income varies widely by social categories.

Demographics refer to the social statistics of a population. In the U.S., the Census data illustrate the pluralistic and changing nature of the U.S. family.

Many of the concepts, illustrations, and ideas used in the text are treated in "**ideal-type**" terms. Ideal types are *not* what is implied in common usage. They are hypothetical constructs based on "pure" characteristics; they always represent the end, the extreme, or the pole of a continuum. Ideal-type constructs perform several basic functions. They provide limiting cases with which concrete phenomena may be contrasted, they provide for the analysis and measurement of social reality, and they facilitate classification and comparison. Ideal-type constructs are used in the text to illustrate the conflicts between traditional social values and nontraditional marital and family values. The use of these ideal-type classifications is not meant to perpetuate traditional myths, but to contrast the emerging "variations" or "alternative" patterns with the traditional patterns.

Some social scientists argue that the family in America is not merely changing, but declining. The perspective of this chapter is that family change does not necessarily mean decline or breakdown. Patterns of family life that predominated in the past are compared with present patterns. The author shows how traditional and nontraditional norms exist simultaneously, giving rise to major issues in the area of the family.

The **meaning of marriage and family** depends upon how the institution is viewed: as a sacred phenomenon, as a social obligation involving conformity to societal demands, or as existing for the satisfaction of the individuals involved. The **family organization issue** centers on the "proper" form of marital and family organization. The **family functions issue** has to do with arguments over the meaning of the loss of functions in the family institution. The increasing specialization and complexity of modern society has led to a dehumanizing and fragmenting process, and many in our society insist that the traditional functions of the family should be maintained. The **marital- and gender-role differentiation issue** pertains to the confusion and uncertainty over "proper" role definitions for the sexes, as contemporary American marriages are shifting from the complementary type to the parallel type. The **social class and social mobility issue** centers around the extent to which it is desirable to have tremendous variations in wealth, status, and power, and the extent to which it is possible to move from one status to another. The **partner selection issue** centers around two questions: who chooses and who is chosen. Around the world, and traditionally in the United States, the most prevalent pattern is that of arranged marriages rather than free choice. The **love issue** has to do with whether love is even necessary in marriage, how intense it should be, and the extent of exclusiveness that should be expected in love relationships. The central question surrounding the **sexual relationships issue** is whether sexual relations should be limited to marriage. The trend has been away from traditional norms and from double standards that differentiate sexual norms for men and women. The **family size and family planning issue** focuses on limitations on the number of children, determination of when and if to have them, and selection of the appropriate means to accomplish these ends. The **issue of aged family members** has to do with how changes in the overall social scene, together with changes in the family, have combined to change the role of the elderly in the American family. The **issue of violence and abuse among intimates** focuses on physical violence within the family. The **family permanence issue** raises the question whether marriages and families are permanent, life-long, until-death commitments, or temporary, until divorce or separation arrangements.

There are a number of **other contemporary issues** that are not ordinarily classified as marriage or family issues per se, but which may extensively impact on family life. At the most general level, every social policy and social problem is family-related.

LECTURE AND DISCUSSION QUESTIONS

1.	**What are "marriage contracts" (in some instances called "prenuptial agreements"), and how might they affect marital success?**

2.	Answer guidelines: First, it is necessary to realize the distinction between a prenuptial agreement and a marriage contract. A prenuptial agreement is a legal document, most often spelling out how property will be distributed in the event of a divorce. Such agreements are not recognized as valid in a number of states, the rationale being that the state should not encourage the possibility of divorce—to do so would undermine the sanctity of marriage (by weakening the potential for permanency).

The marriage contract is quite another matter, when it is construed as a personal agreement between husband and wife. Such agreements cover such areas as how disagreements and conflicts should be handled, how money should be handled, how household chores will be apportioned, what methods of contraception the couple will use, how many children the couple will have, and how children will be raised. They are particularly useful when the couple (or one partner) has concerns about how responsibilities will be shared. It should be noted that such "lifestyle clauses" are not generally enforceable in court, even in states where prenuptial agreements are recognized.

In states where prenuptial contracts are honored, couples should be aware of the language in the existing law of their state. States vary significantly in how property may be distributed, should divorce occur. Some major areas that may be covered include the disposition of premarital property, the use of income and assets, the manner in which businesses or investment partnerships will be owned, what type of insurance coverage the couple shall have (and who will be beneficiaries), and, in the event of divorce, how child custody and support will be handled.

2. **What is the significance of the movement for "covenant marriage?**
<u>Answer guidelines:</u>   This movement seems to represent a potential shift in public policy as to the meaning of marriage. In 1998 two states, Louisiana and Arizona, passed laws allowing couples to opt for more strict "covenant marriage" vows, with compulsory premarital counseling and tougher standards for divorce. Those covenants will presumably be enforced by the court in the event of divorce—although this has not yet been tested, given the newness of the laws. Seventeen additional states have considered covenant marriage provisions.

Ironically, the lobbying for these laws has been carried out by many of the same political conservatives who argue for *less* government in other arenas of social life. On the other hand, a few conservatives have worried that creating, in effect, two types of marriage will open the door to other options—such as same sex marriage.

The covenant marriage movement apparently stems from dissatisfaction over the prevalence of divorce (although—another irony—the divorce rate in the United States has actually been declining since the 1980s). There is also a "save the family" backlash involved, since evidence has emerged that liberalized attitudes toward divorce and no fault divorce have probably had deleterious effects upon children. It is not only political conservatives who are concerned about the toll of divorce on children and on the rest of society…Divorce is costly for state and local governments as well, so there is a strong economic incentive for public officials to reduce the incidence of divorce.

Sociology students should be encouraged to ponder whether the marriage covenant movement could unintentionally produce two strata of marriage, the *married* and the *really married*.

3. **How well does Bernard Farber's pluralistic model of the family fit contemporary family life?**
Answer guidelines: One of the greater challenges in the field of family sociology is to differentiate shallow, short-term trends from the kind of fundamental, long-term change which transforms the social landscape. The core of the pluralistic model of family organization--acceptance of multiple family forms and considerable variety in family life--is firmly entrenched among the majority of people in our society (although some ethnic and religious groups provide striking exceptions).

Farber's "universal permanent availability" concept appears well supported by long term trends such as high divorce and remarriage rates, extensive cohabitation, small families, married women in the workforce, love and interpersonal competence as the bases for marriage, and reduced emphasis on premarital chastity.

It is important to realize that other "trends" which, at times, *appear* at times to be taking hold, such as communal living, childlessness, non-marriage, and swings back to chastity, eventually prove to have been based upon period or generational effects. Students should be made aware that family sociologists use caution when evaluating trends. The instructor should also emphasize that students themselves will be able to evaluate "trends" critically once they have mastered the basics of "what is going on" in contemporary families.

CLASSROOM ACTIVITIES AND PROJECTS

1. Use a few minutes near the beginning of class to have the students write down their responses to one or more of these questions: "What is a family?," "What is required of a family?," or "What would you like your family to be like, and what will you (or do you) expect from your mate?" Their answers may be used later in the class period to review Eshleman's key question, "Is the word *family* a meaningful concept?" Or, their responses may be utilized to discuss one or all of the family issues presented by Eshleman. An alternative might be to save their responses until the last day of the course to explore how their ideas about the family may have changed.

2. Put the elements of Eshleman's ideal-type love continuum on the board. Ask students where they think most college students or most people in our society fall on the elements of this continuum. It is essential that students understand how unique North American society is in relation to other cultures in relation to the idea of romantic love. Students might be encouraged to consider the question: "Are we setting ourselves up for failure due to our (relatively) extreme emphasis upon romantic love (in conjunction with tremendous freedom in courtship practices), in view of the rather consistent research findings that romantic love seems to fade quickly in the majority of relationships?" This exercise can be used to illustrate how strongly people adhere to their own preferred meanings of marriage and family, even in the face of objective evidence that such meanings may not function well. This is an excellent time for the instructor to briefly review the terms "norms," "values," and "ethnocentrism."

3. Most students may be unfamiliar with the term "common-law marriage." Discuss with your class the fact that marriage may either be established *ceremonially*—by marriage ceremony—or *nonceremonially*, by cohabitation (in some states).

    When a marriage is established by ceremony, the couple follows a series of procedures sanctioned by law: they get blood tests, obtain a marriage license, take part in a ceremony performed by an official who is authorized to do so, sign the marriage certificate (together with the marriage official and witnesses), and then file the certificate with the proper local registry. Note that some localities now also require a prerequisite first step of premarital counseling.

Students may not know that thirteen states and the District of Columbia also recognize bona fide marriage *by cohabitation*. Just as in ceremonial marriages, common law couples must meet basic characteristics: they must be legally divorced if previously married. Additionally, they must meet minimum age requirements. To establish common-law marriage, they must also demonstrate that they have been living together, and that the relationship has been consummated.

When children are born of common law marriages, they have the same legal rights as those born to parents in ceremonial marriages. Even where common-law marriage is recognized, however, ceremonial marriage conveys more rights (such as access to health care benefits).

FILM AND VIDEO RESOURCES

The Family
Few American households fit the profile of the traditional nuclear family. Broken homes, battered wives, estranged children, corporate nomads, and the like, are commonplace. In this segment of a popular series, Phil Donahue explores the many social changes that have affected the institution of the family.
Films for the Humanities and Sciences, 52 min., color

A Family To Me: Redefining the American Family
This program portrayals of four unique families: two brothers who discovered new identities as "househusbands;" a black single parent who shares her philosophy of childrearing and being on her own; a lesbian couple who share their experiences mothering twin boys; and a divorced couple who have created a joint custody arrangement congruent with their Jewish values. Recommended by *Teaching Sociology*.
New Day Films, 28 min., color, study guide available

Inside Life Outside
This video provides a powerful and intimate look into the world of the homeless. Depicting life for homeless Americans on New York City's Lower East Side, this presentation helps the viewer to understand the plight of the homeless, and the implications this problem have for family life in our society.
New Day Films, 57 min., color

The American Family: It's Not Dying, It's Changing

Featuring Delores Curran, this video addresses various aspects of today's family, outlining changing functions of the family in society, and assessing shifting family value systems.
Tabor Publishing Co., 90 min., color

Abortion: Personal Portraits

The anguish and the reasoning on both sides of the abortion controversy are presented through the portraits of five women who have made hard choices.
Films for the Humanities and Sciences, 26 min., color

Abortion: Desperate Choices

Behind the headlines, behind the explosive debate between pro-choice and pro-life groups, ordinary women's lives are being changed forever by abortion. The program encounters unmarried teens, married women who choose abortion, mothers who decide to give up their babies for adoption, and women who remember the danger and stigma of illegal abortions. Each tells her private, heart wrenching story, resulting in a balanced, highly personal look at this controversial subject.
Ambrose Video Publishing. Inc., Discussion guide included

When Abortion Was Illegal: Untold Stories

Directed by Dorothy Friedman, this documentary presents information about a largely undocumented era of medical history. First-person accounts reveal medical, legal, and emotional consequences of abortion when it was a criminal act. Health care workers, women who had illegal abortions, and others share their experiences.
Bullfrog Films, Inc., 28 min.

AIDS: Our Worst Fears

This program explains what we do and do not know about AIDS, who is most susceptible and most at risk, and what preventive actions and precautions can be taken. The video was updated in 1988 with the latest statistics available at that time.
Films for the Humanities and Sciences, 38 min., color

CHAPTER 9

AFRICAN AMERICAN FAMILIES

CASE EXAMPLE
    Questions to consider
    Introduction to the chapter

SIGNIFICANT SOCIAL TRANSITIONS OF AFRICAN AMERICANS
        From Africa to the United States
        From slavery to emancipation
        From rural/southern areas to urban/northern areas
        From negative to positive social status
        From negative to positive self-image

PATTERNS OF African American FAMILY LIFE
        Matricentric female-headed family pattern
        Middle-class two-parent family pattern
        Patriarchal affluent family pattern

SUMMARY

OBJECTIVES

Based upon their reading and careful consideration of Chapter 9, students should:

1.   Be able to describe in detail the five major social transitions that have shaped African American families in America;

2.   be able to summarize the controversy concerning the impact of slavery on African American family patterns and norms;

3.   be able to describe the old and new models of African American families;

4.   be familiar with the Moynihan Report and subsequent interpretations of its findings; and,

5.   be able to describe the three patterns of African American family life (matricentric female-headed, middle-class two-parent, and patriarchal affluent);

OVERVIEW

There are various ways in which **African American families** are unique and different from white families in U.S. society. Many of these differences can be traced to selected historical factors unique to African American families. Changes center on these transitions: (1) from Africa to the United States; (2) from slavery to emancipation; (3) from rural and southern areas to urban and northern ones; (4) from negative to positive social status; and, (5) from negative to positive self-image.

Three factors in the transition from Africa to the United States have profound relevance: **color**, **cultural discontinuity**, and **slavery**. *Color* is the most influential characteristic of African American people in society. Darker skinned blacks are at a continuing disadvantage, and experience more discrimination than lighter-skinned blacks in contemporary United States. Second is *cultural discontinuity*. The system of behavior that was socially learned and shared by members of African society was not applicable to the social conditions faced in the United States. Third is *slavery*. For decades, family sociologists accepted uncritically the interpretations of African American family life which emphasized the instability of marriages and family ties, the disruption of husband-wife and kin networks, the extent of matrilocality, and the lack of authority of fathers. A number of studies have raised questions about the conclusions of those earlier reports, noting that the slave family was stronger and tended more typically to be characterized by two-parent households than previously thought. Still, most scholars would agree that slavery had a major impact on African American family life.

The significance of the migration patterns of African Americans revolves around their selectivity: Not all ages or complete families were caught up in the movement to urban areas and to the North, since the industrial pool preferred young men. Both the community left behind and the migrating community were affected. However, not all the consequences of migration were negative. City life offered better schools, better social welfare services, better medical and public health facilities, more tolerance for racial minorities, as well as occupational opportunities. Research has shown differences in family patterns between African Americans with "southern origins" and "northern origins," but caution is advised in drawing conclusions about the differences.

Some argue that the single most important variable in understanding the African American family today is social class. The *traditional*, and old model of the African American family projected a negative stereotype, whereas the *emerging*, or new, model challenges those negative views, stressing that the African American family consists of a variety of types at different social-class levels. The old model was portrayed in the **Moynihan Report**, which contended that there had been a serious weakening in the African American social structure, and a trend away from stability within families at lower socioeconomic levels. More recently, Billingsley and other researchers have refuted Moynihan's ideas. They contend that the African

American family is not a "tangle of pathology" as alleged by Moynihan, but, rather, an adaptive and flexible mechanism for the socialization of children.

It is important to consider the implications of progress--and lingering disparities--in the areas of *employment*, *income*, and *education* for family life among African American families. Although an increasing number of African Americans have entered positions of professional leadership, continuing high levels of unemployment continue to threaten family life. In the area of income, African Americans lag significantly behind whites. About one third of the black population lives below the official poverty line. Since marital satisfaction and stability are generally associated with a family's financial well being, it is not surprising that blacks, on the average, display a higher rate of marital disruption than whites. Generally, as economic conditions improve, the incidence of family disorganization decreases. In the area of educational attainment, African Americans have experienced a dramatic improvement in recent decades. There is one unfortunate side effect, however: Black women, on the average, complete higher levels of education than black males. This makes it increasingly difficult for black women to find mates with education levels equal to or better than their own.

At least three distinct patterns of African American family life have emerged from the social transitions described: the **matricentric female-headed** pattern, the **middle-class two-parent** pattern, and the **patriarchal affluent** pattern. The matricentric female-headed pattern is the least stable of the three.

The **matricentric** family is the most commonly appearing family pattern among African Americans. Black families living below the poverty level are most likely to fit this pattern. Eshleman notes that it is debatable whether the family structure of the female householder with no husband present explains the family's poverty, or whether the poverty explains the family's structure. Regardless, according to sociologist Robert Staples, the increase in female-headed households has probably been the most significant change in the black family in the last thirty years. One reason is the dramatic increase in out-of-wedlock births. Another, less visible, reason for the increase in female-headed households is the shortage of men relative to the number of women during the marriageable years (a low sex ratio).

The **middle-class, two-parent** African American family pattern has been relatively neglected by social scientists, perhaps because such families are stable, conforming, and achieving. These families are noteworthy for producing African American leaders.

The **patriarchal affluent** family pattern features two parents, typically professionals, who are "affluent conformists." In these families, husband/father dominance is often the ideal or goal (even when social discrimination prevents the husband/father from actually achieving high status and earnings). This family type is quite stable. It tends toward strict patterns of socialization and social control. Particularly at high socioeconomic levels, patriarchal affluent families differ little from many white families. This is not to say there is no difference--all African American families are impacted by the unique role of race in American history and culture.

LECTURE AND DISCUSSION QUESTIONS

1.   **What does the historical fact of black-white race mixing under slavery mean to contemporary Americans?**
      <u>Answer Guidelines:</u> At the turn of the Century, there seems to be a strong interest in understanding and coming to terms with the fact that most of the mixed ancestry between African Americans and Caucasians occurred during the time of slavery—and resulted largely from the rape of black women during that time.

      How do we know this? Somewhere between 74 and 90 percent of African Americans have white ancestors. An estimated one percent of white Americans—a small percentage, but still representing millions of people—have black ancestors without even knowing it. Since laws against intermarriage existed in the U.S. as late as 1967, and the actual rate of intermarriage, though increasing, has remained small (it has increased from 0.7 percent in 1970 to 6 percent in 1996), we can say with some certainty that the vast majority of mixed race ancestry originated in the time of slavery—when African Americans and whites lived in close proximity, and when there was a tremendous power imbalance between white men and black women.

      The national best-selling book, *Slaves In the Family* (Ballantine Books, 1998), by Edward Ball, is one of several efforts to explore the intertwined ancestry of blacks and whites from a single plantation system into the 20th Century. Ball did this by challenging generations of silence within his own former slave-owning family. He interviewed dozens of his own family members—white *and* black—and scoured historical records, to assemble a vivid and complex picture of racial intermingling.

2.   **The relative health of "the black family" is likely to remain a controversial issue far into the future. What is the absolutely essential information sociology students must know about this issue?**
      <u>Answer guidelines:</u>   If students are confused about this issue, they are not alone--It takes considerable effort to sort-out the theories and research findings that have followed the "Moynihan Report."

      The "Moynihan Report," itself, took rather extreme positions on the black family. The report advanced the thesis that the black family had been broken up by slavery, and had never since taken on a viable form. Moynihan's most controversial argument was that even ending black unemployment would not cure the "tangle of pathology" of the black family.

65

The report concluded that the black family was so damaged and untenable that black children would not be able to profit from opportunities offered them in school and in the job market. Moynihan claimed that until the "damage" to the black family was repaired, "all the effort to end discrimination and poverty and injustice will come to little."

In order to respond to Moynihan's arguments, the instructor should refer to Eshleman's point that after the Civil War most blacks apparently *did attempt* to adhere to norms prevailing in the dominant society that households should be couple-headed. Herbert Gans' classic *The Black Family in Slavery and Freedom, 1750-1925 (Pantheon, 1976)*, is still an excellent resource on black family history). Then, as now, departures from the two-parent family appear to be strongly influenced by shifts in the economic opportunity structure--for both black and white families.

Research has suggested that when the effects of both income and race on family structure are examined, income differences emerge more strongly than race. Poverty among *whites* is *also* correlated with illegitimacy and family instability, while high income, high status blacks tend to have more stable and conventional family arrangements.

The "big question" is whether the structure of the family--black *or* white--*leads to* destabilization and poverty. The "jury is still out" on the causal mechanisms involved. We could just as easily insist that poverty leads to destabilization within the institution of the family, ultimately leading to a high incidence of poor, female-headed household units. One logical approach to studying this question might be to examine high income female-headed households...Are they inherently "tangled by pathology," and downwardly mobile? Unfortunately, the research among high income female-headed households has been limited, because it is such a small category among families in our society. However, it does suggest that such families are comparatively stable and healthy.

As for the "black family," it is important to remember: (1) that it is not monolithic, since class differentiates family behavior among blacks; and, (2) black people in our society continue to face the hardships generated by discrimination, and this fact "spills over" into their families in ways researchers have scarcely begun to measure. Moynihan's notion that blacks--due to their "pathological" family structure--could not take advantage of new opportunities seems particularly unfair in light of the continuing discrimination African Americans face in the arenas of employment, housing, and education.

3. **Eshleman states clearly how important the family is in shaping African Americans' attitudes about themselves. How can the black family**

imbue its children with a positive identity in the midst of a racist society?

Answer guidelines: The evidence suggests that black parents have a unique burden in helping their children come to terms with the persistent external message of white superiority. Research suggests that all children are aware of racial differences at a very young age (perhaps age two or three). So, black children, like white children, are at risk of internalizing biases quite early. Despite the "black is beautiful" movement, African American children pick up subtle, but psychologically damaging messages of inferiority in media messages and advertising for products intended for the white mainstream. African American parents must be prepared for coping with the inevitable occasion when their child, overwhelmed with the pervasive "whiteness" around him, announces "I want to be white."

Black psychologists James Comer and Alvin Poussaint, authors of *Raising Black Children* (Plume, 1993), point out that even black children from affluent homes in integrated settings need constant parental reassurance of their own worth, because from their earliest days they sense that their lives are "viewed cheaply by white society." Darlene Powell-Hopson and Darell Powell-Hopson (also black psychologists) who have written *Different and Wonderful: Raising Black Children in a Race Conscious Society* (Fireside, 1993), say that African American families must guard against negative messages at home (such as showing preference for lighter complexions or straight hair). The Powell-Hopsons recommend that black parents take an aggressive approach to displaying preferences for black images--thereby "inoculating" their children at an early age. For example, the parent might choose a black doll or action figure, then do everything possible to convey that it is the parent's favorite toy.

Comer and Poussaint emphasize that black parents who use a calm and straightforward approach can help to neutralize racial identity crises in their children. Still, racism and discrimination take their toll, and African American individuals' protection of self-esteem is an ongoing process at any age. Two excellent sources of information on self-esteem maintenance in black adults are *Cool Pose: The Dilemma of Black Manhood in America*, by psychologist Richard Majors and sociologist Janet Billson (Lexington Press, 1992), and *In the Company of My Sisters: Black Women and Self-Esteem*, by psychotherapist Julia Boyd (Dutton, 1993).

CLASSROOM ACTIVITIES AND PROJECTS

1. The adoption of black children by white families is a controversial area of family policy. Advocates of the practice maintain that white parents provide homes for black children who would otherwise languish in the foster care system. Critics of such adoptions claim that white parents are ill equipped

to prepare black children against racism. Encourage students to debate whether interracial adoptions are a good idea, focusing especially on the self-esteem and identity needs of minority children. Since the National Association of Black Social Workers has consistently opposed such adoptions, it may be possible to invite a representative of NABSW to speak to the class.

The article "Multi-colored Families," which appeared in *Time* magazine, May 3, 1999 (it is special section without page numbers) is an excellent, up to date resource for discussing both cross-racial adoptions and the general challenge of raising biracial children and/or children of color in biracial families. The article notes that despite wide opposition, nearly a third of the children adopted from the public foster-care system are placed with families of a different race. This, together with the 1.3 million interracial marriages in the U.S., is producing a significant number of households in which children are of a different race than at least one of the parents. The article includes many topics, including insensitive public behavior toward interracial families, the reactions of extended family and friends, and the experience of white parents/partners losing "white privilege" when they become partners of African Americans and/or parents of mixed race or different race children.

2. Ask students to discuss the phenomenon of the single-parent black family beyond its linkage with poverty. For example, your college-age students might be interested in discussing how the particular "marriage squeeze" on black females is experienced by individuals. Or, a more macro-level question might be considered: In view of Eshleman's point that black leaders tend to emerge from two-parent families, what might the increasing proportion of single-parent families among blacks mean for the future of African American communities?

3. Ask students to evaluate images of the black family in the media, TV in particular. If the instructor prefers a rather structured discussion, the three patterns of African American family life detailed by Eshleman ("matricentric female-headed," "middle-class two parent," and "patriarchal affluent') may be written on the blackboard, and examples listed under those categories. An alternative approach might be to ask students to consider the rather extreme examples of black family life portrayed in the "sitcoms" (comedic characters living in poverty, or, conversely, comedic characters living in upper middle-class affluence). The students might be asked to consider why there are few realistic dramas portraying blacks coping with ordinary family issues, as opposed to specifically racial issues.

FILM AND VIDEO RESOURCES

Black Mother, Black Daughter
This firm is a moving testament to African American women who have struggled over 200 years to maintain family and community life in predominantly white America.
National Film Board of Canada, 29 min., color

Developing Positive Self-Images in Black Children
This video explores the sociological implications of raising black children in a racist society.
African American Images, 60 min., color

Just Black? Multi-Racial Identity
This provocative video presents several articulate young men and women of mixed racial heritage. They share their struggles to establish racial identity.
Filmmakers Library, 58 min.

The Vanishing Family: Crisis In Black America
Narrated by Bill Moyers, this controversial film investigates the black family in America today, in which a high proportion of children are growing up without fathers in their homes. It explores some very basic race and ethnic relations issues. [Note: Use cautiously, since it features "deficiency" notions about minority families.]
Carousel Film and Video, 64 min., color

A Singing Stream: A Black Family Chronicle
Directed by Tom Davenport, this video features interviews, stories, and scenes from daily life, reunions, gospel concerts, and church services, tracing the history of the Landis family of Granville County, North Carolina.
Davenport Films, 58 min., color, study guide available

Goin' to Chicago
Directed by George King, this film chronicles one of the most momentous, yet least heralded sagas of American history--the great migration of African Americans from the rural South to the cities of the North and West. History is traced through the personal stories of a group of older Chicagoans born in the Mississippi Delta. They share their bitter recollections of sharecropping, and recall moving stories of their journeys on Hwy. 61 to Chicago.
California Newsreel, 71 min., color

The Family Way

A dramatic production about a strong black nuclear family that learns of the pregnancy of its teenage daughter, this video portrays how each member of the family deals with the problem, and provides a basis for discussion about teen sexuality, family communication, and the ways pregnancy can be handled within the family context. Although the program focuses on an African American family, the production is applicable to all ethnic groups.
New Dimension Media, Inc., 26 min.

On My Own: The Traditions of Daisy Turner

This film explores the family traditions passed through generations of a rural black family in Vermont, through the memories of an old woman dating almost back to the Civil War.
Filmmakers Library, 28 min.

Homecomin'

This video feature a re-enactment of a true-life experience, in which Jason, a black father, comes to grips with his responsibility to his son, while coping with separation from his family.
Phoenix/BFA Films and Video, 27 min., color

Family Across the Sea

Directed by Tim Carrier, this video shows how scholars have uncovered the connection between the Gullah people of South Carolina and the people of Sierra Leone. The video demonstrates how African Americans have kept some of their ties with their homeland, through centuries of oppression in their speech, songs, and customs.
California Newsreel, 56 min., color

CHAPTER 10

HISPANIC AMERICAN, ASIAN AMERICAN, AND NATIVE AMERICAN FAMILIES

CASE EXAMPLE
- Questions to consider
- Introduction to the chapter

HISPANIC AMERICAN FAMILY SYSTEM
- Social status characteristics
- Marital status
- Mexican American families

ASIAN AMERICAN FAMILY SYSTEM
- Social status characteristics
- Marital/family patterns
- Birth characteristics

NATIVE AMERICAN FAMILY SYSTEM
- Social status characteristics
- The Native American experience
- Marital/family patterns

SUMMARY

OBJECTIVES

Based upon their reading and careful consideration of Chapter 10, students should:

1. Have a good understanding of the correct use of the terms "*ethnic*" and "*minority*;"

2. be aware of the diversity that exists between and within the ethnic groups covered;

3. be familiar with the social characteristics of the category of Hispanic Americans, and with the Hispanic American family;

4. be aware of the historical derivation of the term "Chicano," of the distinction between Mexican Americans and Mexican nationals, and of the consequences of misperception of identity for persons of Latino/Hispanic origin;

5.	be familiar with the social characteristics of the category of Asian Americans, and with the Asian American family;

6.	be able to describe some of the distinctions in historical experience and culture that exist between groups in the Asian American category, and how these factors have influenced family patterns; and,

7.	be aware of the unique experience of Native Americans, and of the strengths and difficulties expressed within the family patterns of this category.

OVERVIEW

Each of the three populations covered in this chapter is **ethnic** in that they share a sense of identity based on common national origins and cultural traditions. They are **minorities**, not merely in numbers of persons within their categories, but also because they lack the power and prestige of more dominant groups.

The **Hispanic American** population is a fast growing category. While the United States population has increased by about 10 percent over the past decade, the Hispanic American population increased by 48 percent. As noted in Chapter 9, in reference to the African American family, Hispanic American families can be better understood by examining unemployment, income, and educational information. For Hispanics, unemployment tends to fall between the rates for whites and blacks. The Hispanic poverty rate (26 percent) is about two and one-half times that of non-Hispanics. Most national policy discussions fail to address poverty issues relevant to the Latino/Hispanic experience. The reasons for this include misperceived identity (even though a large proportion of Latinos are native-born, they are often perceived as immigrants and competitors for resources and jobs), failure to address the difficulties of the "working poor," geographic concentration of Hispanic populations (which directs remedies toward local efforts, rather than national efforts), low rates of political participation among Hispanics, and important subgroup differences.

Poverty rates vary by groups. For example, the poverty rate among **Puerto Rican** -origin families is very high. Puerto Ricans have traditionally been concentrated in cities, where job opportunities have been limited and inconsistent. Also, Puerto Ricans are characterized by female-headed families to a greater extent than other Latino/Hispanic families. Research has indicated that the combination of parental employment patterns and female-headed households account for a serious child poverty problem.

Just as poverty rates vary by Hispanic group, so do infant mortality rates. Puerto Ricans, Mexicans, and Cubans have the highest rates of infant mortality. The factors related to higher infant mortality rates are high nonmetropolitan residence, high rates of birth to teens, late onset of prenatal care, low mean education, and high percentage of births to teens. The average educational attainment of Hispanic Americans is lower than that for both whites and blacks.

About 68 percent of all Hispanic-origin family households consist of married couples. Another one-fourth of households is maintained by females with no husbands present. Both the married couple and female householder rates for Hispanics fall between those for whites and blacks. Considerable differences can be seen by country of origin.

Strong family ties characterize the traditional Mexican American culture. The extended family has long been recognized as the most important institution in the **Chicano** community ("Chicano" is another term identifying persons of Mexican American descent). **Familism** (where the needs of the family collectively supersede individual needs) appears to be a more typical feature of Mexican American families than non-Hispanic families. Compared to non-Hispanic families, husbands still exert more power over wives. Mexican men have traditionally adhered to an ideal of manliness called **"machismo,"** and women still fulfill the majority of childcare and household tasks. However, husbands/fathers have been shown to have considerable interest in their children, and, when compared to their Mexican American parents and grandparents, change is very real among contemporary families.

Hispanic American families are continually changing and adapting to new conditions. This change causes numerous conflicts between one class and another, the foreign born and the native born, new immigrants and old ones. Vestiges of tradition remain, while new patterns emerge. Therefore, it is difficult to characterize *the* Hispanic American family.

Like Hispanic Americans, **Asian Americans** are a diverse collection of ethnic minorities, including Chinese, Filipino, Japanese, Asian Indian, Korean, Vietnamese, Laotian, Cambodian, Thai, and Hmong. The category also includes the subcategory Pacific Islanders, who are a Census classification rather than an ethnic group. These groups vary tremendously in ancestry, language, culture, and recency of immigration. Some have sizable numbers in the United States. Most are concentrated in urban areas. Asian Americans tend to be better educated than the population as a whole, and have a higher median level of family income. Asian American families are less likely to fall below the poverty level than many other groups, but the rate of poverty is increasing as factors such as job discrimination and exclusion from high-earning occupations give them a lower return on their educations than that enjoyed by their European American counterparts.

Most Asian American populations have entrenched norms and role expectations pertaining to family and kinship matters. Asian and Pacific Islanders have a married couple rate similar to the white population. Particularly among Chinese, Japanese, and Filipino marriages, there is a high level of family stability and permanence. Divorce rates are low, and kinship ties are strong. Some traditional cultural norms such as speaking the native language, patriarchal authority, rigid role expectations for wives and children, and heavy emphasis on obedience and loyalty to parents, bring strains between older and modernizing generations. Second and third generations tend to pick up dating and mate selection patterns that are at odds with the expectations of their parents and grandparents. There has been a significant increase in the extent of intermarriage between persons of Asian American origin and others nationalities. The ethnic identity of the offspring of these mixed marriages depends upon a number of factors. The Asian American population has more than doubled recently, making it the fastest-growing population in the United States. Most of this growth has been due to immigration.

The **Native American** population is increasing dramatically as well--Census data indicate that the Native American population is increasing at about four times the national average. This increase is due to a jump in the birthrate, a reduction in infant mortality, and a greater number of persons now identifying themselves as having Native American ancestry. More than half of Native Americans live on reservations, trust lands, or in tribal-designated areas.

It is a mistake to view Native Americans as a homogeneous people. They share many values in common, but have distinct languages, tribal customs, family forms, life-course rituals, patterns of lineage, and kinship relations. They share a history of struggling to maintain their culture and independence. Assimilation has often meant genocide for Native American peoples--unlike most other minorities in the United States, which have typically sought a place in the "melting pot." In the early 1800s, Native American peoples were stripped of their religious heritages, as specific reservations were relegated to various churches. Children were frequently removed from their families, until the Indian Child Welfare Act of 1978 was put in place to stop this practice.

The Native American experience has placed great stress on their family institutions. A very high rate of interracial marriage with non-Indians has further weakened cultural identity in many instances. Future changes within the Native American minority are expected to be in the direction of increased diversity. Still, kinship ties are of great importance to Native Americans, and family networks remain, regardless of changes in life-style patterns.

Native Americans have one of the lowest median family incomes of any ethnic minority in the United States. Low educational achievement, combined with a large proportion of household heads relegated to low-earning jobs, has contributed to this high incidence of poverty. The median age of the Native American population is young, compared with the overall American population, and their life expectancy is dramatically shorter--less than 50, compared with a life expectancy of about 75 among whites.

LECTURE AND DISCUSSION QUESTIONS

1. **Eshleman's presentation captures the tremendous diversity of experience that has characterized ethnic and minority groups in our society. How might we assess the future prospects for minority families in the decades ahead?**

   Answer guidelines: After a period in which we celebrated ethnic diversity, and broad social acceptance of individuals and families "finding their roots," it appears that our society has settled into a more uncertain and perhaps more uncomfortable mode of scant tolerance. A number of scholars have pointed to broad evidence of "backlash" in race relations, and a slowing of objective measures of improvement in life opportunities for minorities. It is far from clear how much real acceptance persons of color and/or ethnicity can expect in the time ahead. Thus, it is also far from clear how easily minorities will achieve the "American dream" for their families.

   Sociologists are sometimes able to learn by examining emerging patterns in situations that are *not* modal. For example, gerontologists have gained important clues for predicting what life will be like in an "aging America" by studying social relations in Florida and Arizona, which have unusually high populations of senior citizens. A similar principle might be applied by examining the experience of California, which has unusually high numbers of ethnic minorities compared with the rest of America. Some have pointed to California as a "test case" of race and ethnic relations for the whole country, since the diversity of its population is what our nation as a whole may expect in the next century. In California, minorities--together--are rapidly becoming the majority.

   The perspective provided by the California experience is not entirely rosy. Many of the social issues that have arisen suggest not continuing integration, but a hardening of boundaries by color, race, ethnicity, culture, and class. Many people live in highly segregated communities, rather than "mixing" with other racial and cultural groups. Competition for resources, services, and opportunities is steep. Some complain of feeling generally "crowded." The pressures of rapid growth have been exacerbated by the discomfort many of the white majority feel in finding themselves becoming a "minority"...During the decade of the 1980s, fully 85 percent of the 7 million persons added to the California population (births and immigrants) were Hispanic or Asian. According to the 1990 Census, 57 percent of the population was counted as white, but this was thought to be an overestimate, due to the undercounting of minorities. It is estimated that, even if California were to close its borders today, the birthrate among young immigrants is so high that the state's population would still grow by 4 million by the end of the 1990s.

Students should be challenged to consider what social change similar demographic shifts elsewhere in the country will bring, and how sociological knowledge of resulting strains could ease the way. What might be some "profamily" policies, given the tightening of resources and persistent atmosphere of competition? A good background resource is *Time* magazine's special cover issue of Nov. 18, 1991, entitled "California: The Endangered Dream."

2. **What is known about the real experience of people who enter into cross-racial and cross-ethnic marriages?**
   Answer guidelines: As Eshleman points out, some of the ethnic minorities in the United States, such as Japanese Americans and Native Americans, have very high rates of intermarriage with members of the white dominant culture. The trends suggest that an increasing proportion of Americans is willing to enter into marriage with persons of other racial and cultural origins, and that the general social tolerance toward such marriages is growing.

   There is a substantial body of research findings on mixed marriages, some of it highly specialized. However, here are some of the general findings on mixed marriages and families: Interracial marriages are more fragile than are homogeneous marriages (Glick, 1988); As with homogeneous marriages, mixed marriages with children are more likely to last (Rankin and Maneker, 1987); Motives for marrying a person of another ethnic or racial group are typically the same as homogamous marriages--"love and compatibility" (Porterfield, 1982); Interracial and intercultural marriages are more accepted within urban areas and multicultural settings, and the children of such marriages fare better in multicultural settings (Johnson and Nagoshi, 1986); Some of the difficulties in mixed families are in the areas of establishing consensual parental roles, contradictory parental expectations for children, and coping with a hostile external environment (McDermott and Fukunaga, 1977); Patterns of coping may employ either "*complementary adjustment*" (in which one parent assumes the role of primary leader), or "*additive adjustment*," (in which the parents try to take elements from each of their cultures that they define as desirable for their family life) (McDermott and Fukunaga, 1977).

3. **What is the state of the Native American family in regard to the impact of intermarriage?**
   Answer guidelines: Some have expressed concern, since the Native American population is so small in elation to the larger U.S. population (0.8 percent, as of 1990), that the Native population could be obliterated culturally by intermarriage. This is not an unreasonable fear, since small indigenous populations other places in the world have been, at times, largely absorbed by intermarriage into the dominant group. Further, Native Americans are marrying outside their group at a faster pace than all other racial-ethnic groups. About half of all Native American men marry non-

Indians (compared with about 1 percent of whites men, and 2 percent of black men marrying outside of their own race-ethnic groups).

However, it is interesting to note that—*possibly* in part due to the reservation system, which has been so harmful to Native Americans economically, and in other respects—some Native Americans are making a point of *not* intermarrying. Olson and Wilson (*Native Americans in the Twentieth Century,* Brigham Young University Press, 1984) have found that members of some major tribes such as the Navajo and the Sioux, confine most of their social contacts to members of their own group, and tend to marry within their own group. The Hopis in Arizona rarely marry outside their tribe. Similarly, the Hanos, Zunnis, Acomas, and Lagunas tend not to marry outside their groups, and are loyal to their traditional clan systems, native tongues, and religious customs.

This strong tribalism is also *familism*, since the Native American cultures emphasize close ties, shared activities, mutual loyalty and mutual protection among family members, as well as close ties with and respect for elders.

CLASSROOM ACTIVITIES AND PROJECTS

1. Depending upon the region in which your university or college is located, your student population may or may not show ethnic diversity. If there is little representation of ethnic or cultural variety in your setting, it may take a real effort on the part of students to imagine family life among ethnic minority families. For example, students who have grown up in a principally rural Midwestern setting might have little more familiarity with Chinese American family life than portrayed in books and movies such as *The Joy Luck Club*. Ask students how much they think they know about the family life styles of ethnic groups outside the mainstream of American culture, and identify sources of good information. If the students prove not to be very knowledgeable, the instructor should guard against any "blaming" tone, of course. The objective should be to cultivate as much positive curiosity as possible.

2. A sizable proportion of Mexican American families with rural roots has had some contact with the large-scale agricultural production industry. For decades, farm workers have struggled--often against powerful corporate interests--for safety protections in the field and more decent living conditions for families involved in this type of work. Some students may be able to share experiences about this. All the students should be reminded that, although there has been progress, farmworkers still get low wages for terribly hard work, and opportunities for their children to break out of this lifestyle are still surprisingly limited. At minimum, students should be able to cite some of the difficulties faced by farmworker families. Even better, if

possible, would be an awareness that the majority of Americans still get our food at a cost to the families who help pick and pack it.

3. Eshleman makes the point that the Census grouping of Asian and Pacific Islanders as a population masks discrepancies among the subgroups. For example, about half as many Japanese live below the poverty level as persons of Chinese, Asian Indian, or Vietnamese descent.

This tendency to "lump together" various minority groups happens a lot, in various contexts. In the case of Asian and Pacific Islanders, it happens even though they speak different languages and represent different cultures. Ask students if they think this might reveal, in the dominant culture, insensitivity to, or a lack of interest in knowing about, individual subgroups. If there are students of minority groups in your class, allow them an opportunity to describe the experience of being "lumped together" into a category.

This often happens when we refer to "Latinos." Sometimes we seem to forget that the term encompasses many different Spanish-speaking groups. People who trace their roots to early Spanish or Mexican settlers in the American Southwest may have very different family experiences than recent immigrants from the Dominican Republic. The family experience of a rural Mexican American whose family has lived in the Midwest for several generations is probably very different than an urban Puerto Rican whose family was headed by a single mother.

Another category for which "grouping" is convenient, but where doing so masks tremendous cultural variation, is "Native American." This category includes people speaking 300 different languages and dialects, practicing different religions and social customs, and experiencing greatly varying lifestyles.

The point is not that researchers should not group populations. It is a valid thing to do in an informed manner, in some instances. Certainly, the groups mentioned do share characteristics in some categories. What is important is that students be aware that such groupings can also hide important differences—and, if we're not careful—lead to stereotyping when approached casually.

FILM AND VIDEO RESOURCES

More Than Words
This video portrays a small Native American tribe as it struggles to retain and revive what is left of its culture. The focus is on a 77-year old woman who is the last of Alaska's Eyak Indians to speak the language of her forebearers.

Cinema Guild, 60 min., color

Honoring Our Voices

This video features six Native American women, who share their stories about recovery and healing, as they overcome hardships and family violence. Through the far-reaching changes in their lives, they reveal the rewards of empowering themselves and their families, as well as the strengths of counseling based in Native healing strategies and traditions.
Women Make Movies, Inc., 33 min., color

Hopi: Songs of the Fourth World

This story of the Hopi captures their deep spirituality, and reveals their integration of art into daily life. Amidst the beautiful images of Hopi land and life, a variety of people--a farmer, religious elder, grandmother, painter, potter, and weaver--speak about the preservation of the Hopi way.
New Day Films, 58 min.

The Divided Trail: A Native American Odyssey

Directed by Jerry Aronson and Michael Goldman, this intensive emotional journey follows two Chippewa Indians, who, with their friend, migrate from their Northern Wisconsin reservation to the slums of Chicago.
Phoenix/BFA Films and Video, 33 min., color

The Culture of Poverty

This film explores emerging strategies for meeting the needs of poor Latino children. It profiles an independent effort to keep them off the street and instill in them a sense of pride.
Films for the Humanities and Sciences, 26. min., color

AIDS, Teens, and Latinos

This program traces the major factors contributing to the fact that a high proportion of minority women infected with the AIDS virus are Hispanic, and focuses on the cultural factors that may underlie the extraordinarily high--and rising--number of teenage pregnancies among Latinas.
Films for the Humanities and Sciences, 28 min., color

CHAPTER 11

SOCIAL-CLASS VARIATIONS IN U. S. FAMILIES

CASE EXAMPLE
    Questions to consider
    Introduction to the chapter

MEANING OF SOCIAL CLASS

DETERMINATION OF SOCIAL CLASS

CONSEQUENCES OF SOCIAL CLASS TO FAMILIES

SOCIAL CATEGORIES OF FAMILIES
    Wealthy families
    Middle-class families
    Blue-collar families
    Families living in poverty

SOCIAL MOBILITY: CHANGING FAMILY LIFE-STYLES
    Likelihood of social mobility
    Extent of social mobility
    Consequences of social mobility

SUMMARY

OBJECTIVES

Based upon their reading and careful consideration of Chapter 11, students should:

1.   Understand the meanings of the terms social class and social stratification;

2.   be familiar with the contrast between functionalist and social conflict views of stratification;

3.   be familiar with how social class is determined, and the consequences status has for family members;

4.   be familiar with the characteristics of the wealthy, and the ways in which the wealthy differ from middle-class and blue-collar families;

5.   be familiar with the characteristics of middle-class and blue-collar families;

6. be familiar with the methods through which families in poverty survive;

7. understand the concept of an entrenched underclass;

8. understand the feminization of poverty in American society;

9. be conversant with what is known about mother-absent and father-absent families; and,

10. be familiar with the concept of social mobility, including its extent in American society and its consequences for family members.

OVERVIEW

The concept of "**social class**" refers to an aggregate of individuals who occupy broadly similar positions on scales of wealth, prestige, and power. "**Social stratification**" refers to a differential ranking of people into horizontal layers (strata) of equality and inequality. Functionalists view stratification as both inevitable and necessary in society. Conflict theorists see stratification as leading to dissatisfaction, alienation, and exploitation in society.

Social class is determined by a combination of variables, including occupational prestige, employment and occupational prestige of the husband, wife, and other family members, as well as income, wealth, education, and self-rankings. Given the number of women and wives in the paid labor force, current evidence makes it clear that class identification must be gender specific.

Social class both determines and results in important differences in influence, power, and opportunities. Class also determines the age at which one is likely to marry, the success of that marriage, the meanings attached to sexual behavior, the size of the family, the recreation engaged in, the type of food eaten, the discipline and care given to children, sleeping arrangements, and contraceptive usage.

From a Marxian perspective, the middle class is comprised of the **bourgeoisie**, those people who own small amounts of productive resources and have control over their working conditions in ways not found among the **proletariat**. The proletariat is working-class people who work for wages. Middle-class families are likely to receive salaries, rather than the hourly wage prevalent among blue-collar or working class families. Blue-collar or working class families consist of workers who generally have some sort of manual skill. Most women would fit in this category. Since members of this class are almost completely dependent upon the swings of the business cycle in our wage-price-profits system, blue-collar families are less stable.

In 1997, more than 35.6 million persons in the United States lived below the poverty level. For white families the poverty rate was 8.4, compared with 47.6 percent for Hispanic-origin families, and 39.8 percent for African American families. The United States leads industrialized countries in the rate of poverty.

The demographic and socioeconomic trends associated with the *feminization of poverty* are: female headedness of household, decreasing marriage rate and continuing high divorce rate, the rise of teen parenting, and inadequate support from combined sources. Not all one-parent families are poor, but the vast majority holds a disadvantageous position in society relative, to other family groups.

Strong evidence exist *against* arguments that welfare benefits and governmental programs make simply living in poverty a meaningful option for the poor: the "welfare trap" is less one of behavioral dependency than one of economic survival. The solutions to the feminization of poverty include expanding benefits or increasing income through jobs that provide a living wage.

The survival of families in poverty currently depends to a great extent upon exchange patterns among kin and "**fictive kin**" (friends who serve as family). How well mother-only families manage seems to be closely linked with their living arrangements: those in which the mother-headed families lived alone fare the worst, compared with other arrangements in which families share households. The majority of persons and families in poverty at any given time typically live below the poverty level intermittently. Although poverty is not a persistent condition for most families, for the "**underclass**" it is.

Although family **mobility** is often thought to mean improvement, it can be **upward, downward**, or **lateral**. Upward or downward mobility is referred to as *vertical social mobility*. Lateral social mobility is referred to as *horizontal*. The likelihood of vertical social mobility depends upon opportunity structure, the individual him/herself, and the "*frictional factor*" (chance, luck, or fortune). It has been estimated that one of every four or five persons moves upward at least one social-class level during his or her lifetime, and it is among blue-collar workers that the greatest amount of upward mobility occurs. However, despite a growing economy, a substantial minority of Americans experiences downward mobility. Women who separate or divorce face the greatest risk of downward mobility. Not all social mobility has negative consequences. In an open-class system, social mobility may have positive aspects for families whose members are able to advance.

LECTURE AND DISCUSSION QUESTIONS

1. **What will be the impact of the extensive welfare reform now occurring on poor families?**
   Answer guidelines: In August, 1996, President Clinton signed the Personal Responsibility and Welfare Reform Act. Now, at the turn of the Century, all

50 states have some sort of welfare reform programs under way. What will the impact ultimately be on poor families? We can make good predictions based on what was known about poverty and about welfare *before* welfare reform was implemented.

In this chapter, Eshleman makes a prophetic statement about the federal "Contract with America" that has allowed states to implement sweeping welfare reforms: "There was emphasis not on getting people and families out of poverty, but rather on getting people and families off welfare."

The states certainly have been successful at getting people off the welfare rolls. In Idaho, for example, the welfare caseload dropped 76 percent between 1997 and 1998. Unfortunately, the states are not keeping data on *why* people have moved off the rolls. The states have wide latitude to determine eligibility guidelines, and they often use punitive measures such as "failure to comply." Federal statistics from 1997 showed that 38 percent of those who left welfare had been ordered off for "infractions" of tight welfare rules. In Tennessee, only 20 percent of those who left welfare actually left for employment. In Indiana, more than half of the cases examined in the federal study was not the result of people finding work, but of sanctions. Evidently, a sizeable proportion is not willing or not able to comply with the new requirements.

What are those who leave welfare moving *to*? Ironically, those who move on to work may be in approximately as bad shape economically as those on welfare—or worse. This was to be expected, prior to welfare reform: work alone is not a cure for poverty. Millions of working parents are not able to lift their families out of poverty.

Some of the earliest outcomes of welfare reform were predicted in advance by welfare experts: the rapid movement of parents into the workforce has created a "daycare crunch." In the State of Michigan alone, there was an immediate influx of 12,000 parents into the workforce, creating a shortage of 200-400 day care centers.

Another predicted outcome: African American families have been hurt disproportionately. Black families have lingered on the rolls longer, and are facing worse prospects for getting off and making good progress. On the average, minority families face significantly more disadvantage. They have less education, more children, and less work experience. They are also hampered by geography to a greater extent than are whites—they are much more likely to live in poor central cities where transportation to good jobs is lacking.

Plans to "crack down" on welfare dads have met with little success. The "Parents' Fair Share" program, operated in selected cities around the nation until 1997, targeted the fathers of children on welfare. The program was able to get some increase in child support payments from fathers who'd previously been *unwilling* to pay, because it located such fathers and forced them to begin paying. The program had little success, however, with fathers who were *willing*, but *unable* to pay more. Overall, the program was unable to help participants get longer lasting or better-paying jobs, even after job-search skills training. This suggests that even when men are willing to take responsibility for their children, they may not be able to earn enough to lift them out of poverty. Again: *work is not necessarily a cure for poverty*.

Welfare reform has come at a time when the typical young family saw its income drop by one-third over two decades. Even the conservative Karl Zinmeister, of the American Enterprise Institute, said in 1997 that "moving back to two-parent families wouldn't help very much because the absent father often makes so little money that he would do little to lift the family out of poverty" (Zinmeister was not making "a case" for single parent families, but rather reacting to Census data on the sudden increase in poor young families).

The child poverty rate for the nation was at 20.5 percent in 1998. This phenomenon is not *caused by* welfare reform, but the wave of welfare reform is not improving the lives of poor people. In 1998, Tufts University's Center on Hunger and Poverty released a report on the practical impact of welfare reform in all 50 states. Basing their research on the existing body of social science research as to what was *actually needed* to lift families out of poverty and make them self-sustaining, the Tufts group reported that the *majority of states had "adopted policies that, on the whole, made it more difficult for people collecting welfare to rise above poverty and support themselves."*

We have long had information that women head the majority of poor families. Therefore, the lower earnings-potential of women will be a continuing problem, even when the welfare rolls are reduced.

The actual impact of poverty—on welfare, or off welfare—on the daily lives of families is not becoming more visible to the majority of us. It is borne mostly in silence by families. Children, who have no voice in the matter, are at the greatest risk. Poor families that have lost welfare benefits are reported to be "doubling and tripling up: in housing, according to David Liederman, Director of the Child Welfare League of America, "And when they can't do it any longer, their kids will come into the foster care System." The League for Human Services in Michigan has stated that the "stress these families are under is nothing short of incredible." The coalition has reported that "Everywhere in Michigan, more families are becoming homeless" (*Ann Arbor News*, May 14, 1998), and blames the welfare cut-offs. In Michigan, families were considered by the State to be "self-sufficient" at 27 percent below the federal poverty level (the federal poverty line was set at $12,516 in 1996 for a family of three).

2. **How has the "feminization of poverty" developed?**
   Answer guidelines: As Eshleman points out, the reasons for single parenthood, and related poverty, vary by race and ethnicity. Among whites, the majority is divorced. Black children are more likely to have been born into a single parent situation because their mothers have not married. Spanish-origin one-parent families are about equally likely to find themselves in such circumstances through divorce, not marrying, or abandonment by father.

   It must be remembered that "poverty" is a relative term. Women make significantly lower salaries in the workplace: about 74 cents on the dollar, compared with the earnings of men. This translates to about $5,000 per year, on the average, in actual dollars. This is enough lower that their families are provided with noticeably lower standards of living than those enjoyed by male-headed families. Single parents are also "doubly" disadvantaged relative to the much higher average incomes enjoyed by married-parent families in which *both* work.

   Not only are more limited employment opportunities and lower salaries to blame. As the primary child-care providers in our society, many single mothers who head families are out of the workforce due to their inability to obtain or afford adequate child care help.

   Some theorists believe that no fault divorce laws have also contributed to the feminization of poverty. A series studies suggests that divorce generally reduces the assets available to wives and children. Prior to no fault divorce laws, judges typically divided family property in accordance with the needs of the mother and children. More recently, assets are split in half, the family home is sold, and the husband departs with key intangible assets (career assets, future earning power, education, pensions, and insurance). The wife departs--often poorly trained--to a highly discriminatory job market. Finally, fewer than half of fathers comply with court-ordered child support orders.

   David Blankenhorn has been one of the strongest voices among social critics who insist there has been a broad trend toward the legitimization of fatherlessness in America--with dire consequences. His 1995 book, *Fatherless America: Confronting Our Most Urgent Social Problem* (Harper Collins) presents a compelling case for the argument that fathers have been made "superfluous," and that the negative outcomes for children in particular are measurable...The feminization of poverty is foremost among these outcomes. Students may already be familiar with Blankenhorn's work, since this book is perhaps one of the most controversial in the area of the family in recent decades. Note: The instructor may wish to balance Blankenhorn's very powerful arguments against his rather weak final recommendations—Bkankenhorn's book demonstrates that it is easier to analyze social problems than to propose meaningful social policy.

3. **What are the fundamentals sociology students must understand about the interplay between social class and family life?**
    Answer guidelines: A very small number of families exist at the top income and social status strata. Families in these strata tend to associate with "their own," and intermarry. On the other extreme, the *officially* "poor" make up about 15% of the population. There is considerable movement of individual families in and out of this status--the actual population below the official "poverty line" is constantly changing.

    It is essential to also know something about a growing category, that of the "*near poor*." The "near poor" are those who are in danger of falling below the poverty line at any given time (the number in the "near poor" category is estimated to be roughly 35 million people). So, it is not just the "poor," but *also* the near poor who have real difficulty securing the essentials of family life such as decent housing, health care, transportation, and education. When we *combine* the categories of poor and near poor, it becomes evident that we are considering a really large segment of the American population who may, understandably, experience strain in their family lives due to inadequate resources.

    There is some "vertical mobility" between social classes in our society, and members of the lower strata share many key values of middle and upper class life, such as believing in the desirability of marriage. However, the poor and the near poor are typically set apart from the higher social classes by their lack of education, marketable job skills, and intangible resources such as career orientation and confidence. The circumstances of poverty produce adaptive behaviors. The adaptive behaviors may, in themselves, discourage marriage and marital stability.

CLASSROOM ACTIVITIES AND PROJECTS

1. Ask students to think about, and comment upon, what they believe are their individual chances for social mobility. Then, ask the class to evaluate the differences between a college student population and, say, a blue-collar group of people the same age. Students should be able to cite a number of differences in probable outcomes for family life.

2. It is important that students try to appreciate how poverty looks from the perspective of the poor. There are organizations (typically coalitions made up of labor representatives, church activists, social work educators, and welfare rights activists) that conduct "welfare simulations." These

simulations are very suitable for family sociology classes. They involve dividing-up participants into small groups representing fictitious families, then putting each "family" through experiences based on the actual experiences of welfare recipients. The simulations provide a very thought-provoking experience for participants. Another possibility might be to invite a guest speaker from the National Welfare Rights Organization (many states and cities have local chapters) to come to your class.

If you prefer to simply lead a discussion in your class about poverty, there are a number of excellent resources for this, including Ken Auletta's *The Underclass* (Random House, 1982), William Julius Wilson's *The Truly Disadvantaged; The Inner City, The Underclass, and Public Policy* (University of Chicago Press, 1987), and, also by Wilson, *When Work Disappears: the World of the New Urban Poor* (Random House, 1997. You might choose to present a summary of various passages from these books.

3.   Computer Assisted Learning (CAL) is becoming more popular a classroom device in the teaching process. Susan H. Gray has created a package for exploring poverty and public policy, called *The Poverty Game*. Suitable for use within 50-minute class sessions, the game involves students taking turns assuming the role of President of the United States at the beginning of a first, four-year term of office. In this role, the student is instructed to take actions designed to reduce poverty (and, hopefully, be reelected). Before the "next election," students must make ten social policy decisions, and consider potential public and political reactions.

In this exercise, students are sensitized to the implications of social policy for the problem of poverty. Additional details about *The Poverty Game* appear in Gray's article, "The Poverty Game: A Computer-Based Learning Package for Exploring Poverty and Public Policy" (*Teaching Sociology*, October, 1989: 489-492).

FILM AND VIDEO RESOURCES

Family in Crisis

This Phil Donahue Show focuses on the plight of poor children growing up in single-parent households. Senator Daniel Patrick Moynihan (NY) and Dr. Joyce Ladner, a Howard University sociologist, examine the problems faced by children who are growing up without fathers. The seemingly irreversible cycle of poverty that affects some minority families is also considered.
Films for the Humanities and Sciences, 28 min., color

Dreams on Hold

This documentary examines the growing gap between America's rich and poor, and highlights the nation's shrinking middle class. The major forces

of change related to this problem are noted: underemployment, the shift from a management to a service economy, the dependence of most families on two pay checks, and the employment of mothers outside the home.
University of Minnesota Films and Video, 20 min., color 1986

Children of Poverty

This powerful video profiles the struggles of female household heads to nurture children and survive against incredible odds.
Films for the Humanities and Sciences, 26 min., color

Children in Need

This video presents a detailed analysis of the report by the U.S. Committee for Economic Development on our society's neglect in the care and education of our children.
PBS Video, 60 min.

CHAPTER 12

THE PARENTAL SYSTEM

CASE EXAMPLE
    Questions to consider
    Introduction to the chapter

TRANSITION TO PARENTHOOD
    Mothers' roles
    Fathers' roles
    Parent's roles
    Value of parenthood

SOCIAL CONSEQUENCES OF PARENTHOOD

YOUNG AND UNWED PARENTHOOD
    Concern about young parenthood
    Concern about unwed parenthood

FAMILY SIZE AND RELATED FACTORS
    Birth rates and birth expectations
    Childless marriage
    Effects of family size on members
    Birth order and sibling relationships
    Sex control

SUMMARY

OBJECTIVES

Based upon their reading and careful consideration of Chapter 12, students should:

1.   Be familiar with the major shifts that occur with the transition to parenthood;

2.   be able to identify the values associated with parenthood;

3.   be familiar with the social consequences of parenthood, including changes in the employment patterns of women, and (short-term) improved marital stability;

4.   understand the facts relevant to the concern over young and unwed parenthood;

5.   know how out-of-wedlock birth affects children, parents, and society;

6.   be familiar with birth rates and birth expectations in the United States;

7.   be familiar with what is known about childless marriage, and the effects of large and small families;

8.   understand the significance of birth order and sibling relationships on family members; and,

9.   be familiar with the issues surrounding sex control and gender preference.

OVERVIEW

Becoming a parent is one of the most significant of family life-course transitions. The transition to parenthood requires a major reorganization of statuses, roles, and relationships. Children are found to be a major source of self-fulfillment, esteem, and affection for parents. However, while the value of children occupies a central place in the lives of married adults, changes are taking place in the perceived value of children, compared with other options and choices.

Theories of childrearing and socialization emphasize **mothers' roles**. The wife and mother is the primary caretaker. Although **fathers' roles** are often de-emphasized, studies show that fathers do exert influence in their children's lives, when present. Fathering is uniquely sensitive to contextual influences, such as mothers' expectations and behaviors, employment opportunities, and economic factors. Father absence is linked with lower academic performance, heightened risk of delinquency and deviant behavior, and greater likelihood of dropping out of school.

Parenting is becoming more difficult around the world, due to such social changes as unemployment, poverty, high rates of divorce and single parenting, reduced levels of parent-child activities, reduced emphasis on parental supervision, loss of traditional family structures and value conformity. Quality of the parents' marriage is a strong predictor of parental satisfaction; parents report higher parental satisfaction when they're in good marriages.

One major social consequence of parenthood is the withdrawal of women from the paid work force. Another consequence is (at least short-term) improvement in marital stability, compared with childless couples. Young parenthood and unwed parenthood are issues of special concern for both parents and the children involved. Young parents are at a disadvantage in many different ways. Unwed parenthood appears to make a difference in terms of children's' abilities to develop and mature.

While the birth rate within marriage is dropping, the number of births outside of marriage is increasing sharply, and the greatest of these increases are among women who are past their teenage years.

There is new research on the consequences of fatherhood outside of marriage. Such fathers were found to leave school earlier, have lower earnings, work fewer weeks per year, and be more likely to live in poverty. These disadvantages, in turn, hamper their abilities to help support their partners and children.

Most couples have children, or expect to have them. The rate of births varies according to a variety of social factors. Over the past few decades, women have delayed having children and have had fewer children, in comparison with the past. Some couples have no children by choice, and the rate of childlessness has increased over the past few decades.

Family size does make a difference. Certain life patterns develop according to the number of children a couple has. Most of the negative stereotypes about the small family or single child family have little, if any support. Differences do exist with respect to order of birth, but researchers warn against ignoring sex and family size in these considerations.

Some evidence suggests that gender preference for male children persists in many countries. The technological ability to determine the sex of children could result in dramatic changes in sex ratios, birth rates, and in family relationships in general.

LECTURE AND DISCUSSION QUESTIONS

1.   **What can be done about the problem of older men impregnating younger teenage girls?**
Answer guidelines: Recently, there seems to be a growing awareness that when a teenage girl becomes pregnant, it is not just "her problem," or her family's problem (or, of, course, "society's problem)—there is *always* a father involved. Given the overall social climate, we can expect this awareness to grow, and to spur new efforts to make young fathers functioning fathers and financial contributors to their children.

We are beginning to ask who these fathers really are. It is becoming apparent that a significant proportion of them is not made up of teenage boys, but older men. It is not clear whether this is a growing problem, or, whether it is simply a problem of which there is growing awareness. Possibly as a result of the "Personal Responsibility" movement, social workers and judges are generally tending to insist upon finding out "Who is the father of this child," and—when the father is an older man—considering the option of prosecuting him.

91

Recent studies have determined that teenage girls are very frequently impregnated by older—sometimes *much* older—men. Nationwide, an average of 400 teenagers *a day* becomes pregnant by men over the age of 25! Twenty percent of all teenage pregnancies involve fathers who are at least six years older than the mothers. Among black teenagers, the percentage is much higher. In California, which has the highest per capita rate of teenage pregnancy in the U.S., some judges are giving men who've impregnated teenage girls a choice: "Marry her, or be prosecuted for statutory rape." Statutory rape laws, which are used much less now than in the past, are based on the idea that a girl below a certain age isn't mature enough to legally consent to sex.

It is important to consider the social meaning of this phenomenon. Teenagers who become pregnant often have a history of sexual experience with older men. In California, nearly half of all teenagers who give birth are victims of prior sexual molestation or rape. Perhaps research is needed to determine how and why girls become involved with predatory older men, and how parents can protect them from doing so.

It may be that many of the older men in these cases are already married or unsuitable for marriage. Also, we should ask if a girl is too young to consent to sex, is she old enough to consent to marriage? Is it in the best interest of the teenage mother to be wedded to a man who is choosing her over jail (and/or a record as a sex offender)? This may be quite different from the "shotgun wedding" of the past, when both partners were typically young. This phenomenon may reflect a more serious social problem—sexual predation against a generation of young women, over which there is too little protection, by a category of men over which there is too little social control.

2. **Eshleman points out that the technological possibility of controlling gender in offspring has important implications for family life (it could even change the entire sex ratio of society, if carried to extreme). What are some other areas in which technology is entering into the parental system?**
   Answer guidelines: As Eshleman notes, the reproductive technology available today can decrease the number of involuntarily childless situations. In fact, about 20% of infertile couples can now be helped to reproduce.

   A closely related area is, of course, the *prevention* of births among couples who have potential genetic problems that could affect their offspring. The prenatal testing revolution has gone so far that reliable *prefertilization* testing (rather than testing after the pregnancy has already begun) is now available in some hospitals. This enables the prediction of some defects in a human egg even before it is fertilized, as well as uncovering even more genetic disorders in a test tube after it is fertilized. The technique is called "preimplantation genetic diagnosis." The couple is then offered the option of discarding the fertilized egg, and trying again.

An excellent resource on the growing power of prenatal genetic testing, and the thorny ethical problems emerging from it is *Time* magazine, Jan. 11, 1999, pages 56-60. The article, entitled, "Good Eggs, Bad Eggs," details the poignant personal issues the new technology creates, as well as the broader family and societal issues involved.

Another area of reproduction that has emerged in the news is, of course, surrogate parenting. Recent examples of surrogate parenting in the news suggest a possible trend of close relatives (such as grandmothers and aunts) serving as surrogates.

The area of the ownership and control over human body products, products of conception, and embryos is another emerging area. Judges have been forced to rule upon the use (and misuse) of sperm, fetal tissue, the continuation of pregnancy after the mother has become incapacitated--or brain dead--and on custody of embryos after divorce. It is interesting to note how technology has begun to affect the rights of men (married and single) who want to become fathers, as well as those who don't. In one recent case, a man who had not wanted to become a father sued a woman for "theft of sperm." Highly reliable paternity testing has only become widely available within the past decade. It is now sometimes utilized by *men* who want to *enforce* paternity, as well as by women.

3.   **What do the available research findings tell us about the process by which voluntarily childless couples decide not to have children?**
     <u>Answer guidelines</u>: According to Lloyd Saxton (*The Individual, Marriage, and the Family*, Wadsworth, 1990), who offers a comprehensive analysis of the phenomenon of childlessness, few couples plan at the beginning of their marriages to remain child-free. Rather, they reach the decision through a progression of steps. Initially, they may put off childbearing until a definite objective is achieved (such as being out of debt). Subsequently, they may still intend to have children, but become increasingly vague about when that will happen. Later, these couples typically begin to debate the specific pros and cons of parenthood. Finally, the couples make the definite decision not to have children.

CLASSROOM ACTIVITIES AND PROJECTS

1.   Your students may be interested in discussing what kinds of issues gay partners have to face when considering whether or not to become parents. In some respects, the decisions gay couples face are not unlike those of heterosexual couples; they have to consider how parenting duties will be

shared, whether one or the other parent will quit work to engage in full time child care (or use daycare); they have to consider whether their budget will allow for the addition of a child to the family, etc. Gay and lesbian partners have the added burden of discrimination to consider—discrimination against their children, as well as themselves.

Gay couples have to consider the legal issues pertaining to their rights to function fully as parents. Some jurisdictions allow the gay partner of a natural (or adoptive) parent to become the adoptive parent. In that case, the new parent has the same legal rights to make medical and other decisions about the child that any parent would have. The law is not uniform across jurisdictions, however, and such rights may not be in effect if the family should travel or move. In some states, gay couples (or gay partners of natural parents) are not allowed to adopt at all. Students should be aware that this is not an issues that affects only an isolated number of families: there are millions of families in the U.S. with at least one gay parent.

2. Most students are familiar with the perceived benefits of parenthood, but many may not have thought about the costs. In particular, the negative impact of children on marital satisfaction is a hard concept for many students to grasp. Because of our socialization, this notion "goes against the grain." It may be useful for students to explore the stresses and strains that children place on a marital relationship. Encourage students who are parents to contribute to this discussion.

3. Popular wisdom typically holds that one-child families should be avoided because "only children" are thought to be selfish, greedy, and encounter more problems in comparison with those who have siblings. As Eshleman points out, contemporary research suggests that "only children" are not automatically predisposed to difficulty, and that there may even be some distinct advantages to the one-child family. Ask the members of your class to evaluate the pros and cons of "only children." If possible, see if you can motivate a few students who *are* "only children" to contribute to this discussion.

FILM AND VIDEO RESOURCES

We Are Family: An Adoption Story
This video presents one dramatic case study of an adoption process that includes the birth mother and father , and their families, as well as the adoptive parents.
New Dimension Media, 24 min., color

Parental Scripts

94

Parents of handicapped children assume "roles" that will help their children to become more independent.
AGC Educational Media, 16 min., color

Life With Baby: How Do the Parents Feel?
Three families, including an unwed mother on welfare, and two couples, discuss the emotional adjustments related to contemporary parenting.
Filmmakers Library, 27 min.

Teenage Pregnancy
This program follows several teenagers through the births of their children and subsequent changes in their lives. It is a sobering look at the realities and responsibilities of teenage pregnancy.
Films for the Humanities and Sciences, 26 min., color

Teen Dads
This film portrays a group of teenage fathers--some have married and some have not, but all are accepting psychological and financial responsibility for their children, and are helping in their physical and emotional care.
Films for the Humanities and Sciences, 52 min., color

Being a Single Parent
This program focuses on three very different kinds of single parents: a divorced woman, a woman who chooses to be a single parent, and a man who raised his two sons. It shows how parents cope with their roles as parents and wage earners.
Films for the Humanities and Sciences, 19 min., color

Decisions
More than a million teens will become pregnant this year. This documentary portrays the decisions made by three pregnant teens.
Community Intervention, Inc., 26 min., color

The Decision for Nonparenthood
Hosted by Greg Morris, this video features couples who opt for nonparenthood.
Agency for Instructional Technology, 29 min., color, includes teacher's guide

The Decision for Parenthood
Hosted by Greg Morris, this video features couples who opt for parenthood.
Agency for Instructional Technology, 29 min., color, includes teacher's guide

Child in the Family
This compelling video shows the roles of parents and functions of the family, through interviews with parents. This focus on families provides insight that

will be significant to those who seek understanding of child and the family in child rearing.

Magna Systems, Inc., 27 min., color

CHAPTER 13

PARENT/CHILD INTERACTION AND SOCIALIZATION

OBJECTIVES

Based upon their reading and careful consideration of Chapter 13, students should:

1. Be able to define socialization, and be familiar with its preconditions;

2. be familiar with frames of reference used to explain socialization: including learning-behaviorist, psychoanalytic, child development, and symbolic interaction;

3. be able to distinguish between Erikson's and Piaget's theories of child development;

4. be familiar with the basic assumptions of symbolic interactionism;

5. be able to define "the self," and be familiar with Mead's stages of self-development; and,

6. understand the relationship between socialization and gender roles.

OVERVIEW

The central concept in dealing with parent-child relationships is **socialization**--the process by which infants and adults learn the ways of a given society and develop into participants capable of operating in that society. Socialization of the young infant may be the single universal function of the family, worldwide. An ongoing society and a biological inheritance appear to be the two preconditions for socialization.

Learning-behaviorist or **reinforcement theory** assumes that the same principles that apply to lower animal forms apply to humans (conditioning processes may be either classical or operant). In contrast, **classic psychoanalytic theory** claims that internal drives and unconscious processes are centrally important. **Child development** theories focus on the individual, and the manner in which motor skills, thought, and reasoning develop. Erikson focused on distinct stages of human development, with each one constituting a crisis. Piaget focused more on the cognitive development of the child as he moves through four major stages.

Symbolic interaction theory contrasts considerably with all of the previous theories. Infants are not born social, but rather develop through interaction with others: As interaction occurs, meanings are internalized and organized, and the self develops. A social being can take the role of others, and interpret, define, and use symbols. **Interaction**, the **social self**, **significant others**, **reference groups**, and the generalized **other** are all concepts that are basic to the socialization process under symbolic interaction theory. Socialization does not end at any given age, but is a lifelong process. Symbolic interactionism assumes that humans must be studied on their own level, that the most fruitful approach to social behavior is through analysis of society, that the human infant at birth is asocial, and that the human being is an actor as well as a reactor.

Gender identity and **gender roles** refer to identity and to the expectations associated with being masculine or feminine. Gender identity formation is a developmental process, but it does not always follow an orderly sequence that is the same for all persons. Male-female and masculine-feminine differences are universal, but vary from culture to culture and from society to society. Research has shown that not only do males and females differ in behaviors, but also in value patterns. Sex role socialization follows the basic of process of any type of social-ization. In interaction with others, children learn about gender and sex roles very early in their lives.

LECTURE AND DISCUSSION QUESTIONS

1. **Much of the current imagery of fatherhood is based upon what some have called the "deficit model," which emphasizes men's inadequacies as parents. Is it possible to develop a more positive model?**

   <u>Answer guidelines</u>: Some scholars who are studying fatherhood are trying to develop a more positive model, as well as a unifying theoretical framework. They are re-considering Eriksonian theory on the developmental tasks of fathers. Using Erikson's term "generativity," which refers to caring for and contributing to the life of the next generation, Alan Hawkins and David Dollahite (*Generative Fathering: Beyond Deficit Perspectives*, Sage, 1997) have brought together in an edited volume the work of scholars and practitioners to produce a new framework.

   Generative Fathering tackles the role-inadequacy perspective typically cast upon contemporary fathers (as absent, underinvolved, or even "deadbeat") and—assuming this is not what fathers want, and that it is possible under current conditions to change—proceed to a generative fathering framework. The authors contend that the role-inadequacy perspective is actually a cultural critique based on fear of the diminishment of a strong family culture. They point out that this is not an outlook that will help fathers improve their parenting. They urge use of the developmental framework, emphasizing personal transformations rather than sociohistorical transitions.

   The main focus of Hawkins and Dollahite's book is the stage identified by Erikson as middle adulthood. This is the time in his life when the father is challenged to overcome personal stagnation and self-absorption, in order to promote the development of the new generation and the broader community. This is a very complex stage, regardless of how well the father is actually performing.

   How can fathers be empowered (and inspired) to become generative fathers? The authors recommend starting with an "ethical call to fathers," based on the assumption that fathers are "called by" the next generation to meet their needs, and to labor for their well being. Secondly, they call for the development of a set of "generational ethics" or specific expectations for how fathers can devote themselves to the needs of the next generation. Third, the authors urge social scientists and practitioners to recognize "contextual agency." That is, recognize that fathers make choices within the context of a variety of factors. Finally, they urge we credit the "responsibilities and capabilities" of fathers—that men have the ability within themselves to be good fathers, and that most men want to be. The authors and contributors to their book provide considerable detail as to how this may be accomplished.

2. **Which fathers are most likely to be very involved in childrearing?**
Answer guidelines: Information provided by the U.S. Census Bureau and other researchers show some surprising patterns. When mothers work outside the home, fathers assume the role of primary caregiver much more often than childcare centers, in-home babysitters, preschool centers, or any relatives. Fathers in service occupations who have nontraditional work schedules are twice as likely to provide direct childcare than are fathers in other occupational categories. Fathers are more likely to serve as primary caretakers when there is more than one child in the family—presumably because of the need to save on the high cost of paying for multiple children by other means. Poor fathers are also more likely to provide direct childcare, because their families need to avoid costs. Also, it is probable that poor fathers are more likely to experience periods of unemployment, during which they assume major childcare responsibilities.

On a more individual level, there are few demographic predictors of which fathers will be more "involved" in their children's lives. There is a great diversity of fatherhood patterns across our society, and individual role fulfillment varies from man to man.

3. **We generally assume that the way we socialize our young is correct and good, not only for individual families, but also for society. Is this necessarily true? Is it possible to identify problems that flow from our ideas about child development?**
Answer guidelines: In America, as in other Western societies, we generally apply the developmental model to children, and assume that it is "natural"— that children develop through several stages, at particular ages, and that there are appropriate child behaviors and appropriate socialization practices—that follow the timetable of stages.

We choose to treat children as a distinct social category. We have established firm discontinuities between what is expected from children, as opposed to what we expect from adults. However, we go one step further. When these socially created discontinuities are not recognized, we assume the child's very nature is being violated. Arlene Skolnick (*The Intimate Environment*, Scott, Foresman, and Co., 1988) suggests that, "We find the fact that young children work in some cultures anomalous and distasteful" (p. 340). Skolnick believes that not only do we use our norms of child development as the measuring rod against which other cultures are to be judged (suggesting that our ideas are *ethnocentric*, but we may also be *chronocentric*. We are biased in favor of a particular historical period, since only in recent Western history have children been totally exempt from all work).

100

Skolnick continues that the paradigm of modern developmental psychology, in particular, has led us to believe that each child has an individual developmental process which "unfolds from within, and takes considerable time—up to about twenty years." This paradigm is not necessarily found in other cultural and historical contexts: "In premodern times, in our own historical past, and in groups outside the middle class, a different concept of childhood has prevailed. Children are seen as miniature adults—small or inadequate versions of their parents" (Skolnick, p. 339). In contemporary society, we think of this extreme (looking upon children as miniature adults) as tantamount to child abuse. But, it's worth asking whether we have gone to the *opposite* extreme.

The anthropologist Ruth Benedict warned over forty years ago that the way we think about children would eventually cause problems in our society. Her main concern was the extreme discontinuity between adult and child roles. Such discontinuity can cause youngsters particular difficulty in the adolescent stage. Because we make such sharp distinctions between what we expect of children and what we expect of adults, teenagers are required to "reverse themselves" rather suddenly. Consider the opposite role expectations we hold for children and adults: Children are not expected to be responsible in most areas of social life, while adults are expected to be totally responsible; children are expected to focus on playful self-indulgence, while adults focus on work; children are expected to be obedient, while parents are expected to be dominant; children are expected to be free of all sexual impulse, while adults are expected to be sexually active.

Benedict suggested that many people are subject to becoming fixated at immature levels of behavior, because they are not able to make the transition to roles that were forbidden to them as children. The potential for individual psychological maladjustment aside, there is also the possibility that we may be depriving children of important sources of self-esteem by totally removing them from the productive enterprises of society. Historically, children working on family farms or in apprenticeships could see evidence of their own competence, but modern children are dependent upon their parents to guarantee their self-esteem.

Our approach puts a huge burden on parents, too. It may be that the self-denying parent--who is totally responsible for building his/her child's self-esteem through unconditional love--together with the irresponsible, totally dependent child, are a bad combination. Perhaps a challenge of the future will be to find ways of developing children's abilities without exploiting their labor (as in the past) or ignoring their potential for involvement in the larger community (as in the present).

Another area of concern is the isolation and privacy of the nuclear and/or conjugal family, which are peculiar to America and a few other modern societies. It is important to understand that this pattern is quite unusual historically and worldwide. In most societies around the world, the nuclear family household is not so isolated from other kin and other households. The typical pattern is for the clan and/or community to both *assist* and *regulate* parents. As a result, parents do not have such total freedom in socializing their children as we have, but they do have greater social backing and help than American parents have.

CLASSROOM ACTIVITIES AND PROJECTS

1. Mead's stages of personality development provide a means of illustrating how play becomes more and more difficult for people as they move toward adulthood. For the adult, life is filled with rules and regulations--the "rules of the game." Nonpurposive behavior becomes more difficult to justify. Encourage students to think about how societal rules can stifle creativity-- and how each of us has been dealing with this process ever since perhaps Kindergarten (when we learned that at 2:00 p.m., everybody was to take a nap, whether we were tired or not...)

2. Ask students to think about ways in which males play instrumental roles and females play expressive roles. Have students explore how these role formations come into being, with particular emphasis on how males have come to occupy the powerful, decision-making positions in American society. This technique should help to clarify the relationship between socialization and gender roles.

3. Ask students to discuss the idea, "We require people to get a license to drive a car, but there is no special training for being a parent...People ought to receive real training for the tough job of parenting." Ask students to list the skills and types of knowledge required of parents in today's complex society (coping with our complex medical system on behalf of the child, teaching communication skills, interfacing with educators and a variety of other professionals, etc.). Discuss how parents obtain their knowledge about parenting, compared with parents in the past. Ask students for ideas about how society could better educate and support people with the vital "job" of parenting.

FILM AND VIDEO RESOURCES

Self Identity and Sex Role Development

This video examines the linkages between parenting and self, group, and gender identity. Theories of cultural and societal influences on the sex role concepts and behaviors of children are presented.
Film Ideas, 25 min., color

Context of Development

This video presents the unfolding of life as a drama within the context of inherited characteristics and the encompassing environment. Landmarks are development are presented within the fascinating interplay of heredity and environment.
Magna Systems, 27 min., color

The Developing Child: The Crucial Early Years

This video shows how mental growth in children can be assisted by parents helping and encourageing them, without creating stressful conditions.
Films for the Humanities and Sciences, 26 min., color

Understanding Sex Roles

Focusing on the meaning of sexuality and personality, this program will spark a stimulating classroom discussion of sex roles in modern society. Gender-related issues of romance, sex relationships, and marriage and career development are covered, along with the evolution of sexual stereotypes.
Insight Media, 40 min., color, videotape, 1988

Adolescence

Mental and physical developmental changes during adolescence are discussed, as well as techniques that encourage a teenager's desire for freedom while building a sense of responsibility.
Insight Media, 20 min., color, videotape, 1988

Heroes and Strangers: Men, Emotions, and the Family

This award-winning documentary explores a father/son and a father/daughter relationship, revealing the social and economic forces affecting the role of men in the family. The film raises provocative questions about love, work, and gender roles.
New Day Films, 29 min., color, all formats, study guide

Child Management

Through proven techniques, humor and dramatizations, this program addresses the issue of child discipline. It urges parents to think about managing their child's behavior before the fact, by developing a plan for behavior management. The differences between discipline and punishment are highlighted.
Community Intervention, Inc., 20 min., color

Spare the Rod
>Discipline is one of the most important responsibilities parents have. This video attempts to provide some perspective on the subject of discipline. It details some of the disciplinary options available to parents, and provides guidelines for choosing among them.
>**AGC Educational Media, 24 min., color**

From Risk to Resilience
>This series of six videotapes deals with changes in the way childen are socialized in our society. Drawing from research, information is provided as to how children may be strengthened to cope with complex society.
>**Marco Polo, range of lengths, color**

CHAPTER 14

THE AGING FAMILY

CASE EXAMPLE
    Questions to consider
    Introduction to the chapter

POSTPARENTAL PERIOD: THE MIDDLE YEARS
    Marital status and coresidence in the middle years
    Significance of the middle years

GRANDPARENT STATUS

FAMILIES OF LATER LIFE AND PEOPLE WHO ARE AGED
    Growth of the elderly population
    Marital status in the later years
    Intergenerational relationships
    Living arrangements among the elderly

COMMON PROBLEMS OF PEOPLE WHO ARE AGED
    Health and care
    Children's problems
    Income and standard of living
    Abuse and neglect

SOCIALIZATION IN LATER LIFE

RETIREMENT

DYING AND DEATH

WIDOWS AND WIDOWERS

SUMMARY

OBJECTIVES

Based upon their reading and careful consideration of Chapter 14, students should:

1.   Be familiar with the post-parental period (the middle years), and understand the relationship between marital status and the length of the middle years;

2. be familiar with the concept of mid-life transition;

3. be familiar with the grandparent status, and how its evolution has depended upon social context and demographic shifts;

4. be familiar with the characteristics of the family of later life, and the implications for marital and family relationships;

5. understand the problems facing the aged in American society, including those involving health and care, insufficient income, abuse and neglect, and difficulties in retirement;

6. understand how families deal with dying and death; and,

7. be familiar with the special circumstances encountered by widows and widowers.

OVERVIEW

This chapter focuses on two major periods of the life cycle: the middle years (post-parental period), from approximately age forty to retirement, and the later years, from approximately age sixty or sixty-five until the end of the life span. The middle years, after the departure of children and prior to retirement, is a period when most men and women are married. It is one of the longest periods of the marital life cycle, and covers a span of twenty to twenty-five years.

The significance of the middle years differs somewhat for men and women: Men may experience what writers have termed a "mid-life transition," while women may be affected by what is called the **"empty nest syndrome."** It appears that family and work changes reduce the potentially negative impact of this period for both sexes. Some parents are now experiencing a longer period of time with children in the home--demographic indicators show that more young adults reside with their parents than they did a few years ago.

The **grandparenting** period can be either a middle-age or an old-age phenomenon. The grandparent may play an instrumental role in family systems by linking generations. This period appears to be a positive status for most, although the roles vary considerably in terms of social class and cultural context. In the United States, later life is frequently viewed as an undesirable period marked by dependency relationships and declining productivity. These experiences stand in contrast to many other societies, where people gain in status and prestige as they age. Married couples comprise a high proportion of the over-65 group. Approximately 10 percent of the elderly are never married.

Intergenerational relationships encompass a wide variety of interaction patterns between family members of different generations. Elderly persons, on the average, have considerable contact with other family members. Relationships are characterized by reciprocal support, but not by *routine* exchange of resources.

Caregiving to elderly members is an important function of American families. Still, there exists a "myth of abandonment." The majority of those who require care receive it from family members. The closest caregiving arrangements are typically found between mothers and daughters. Adult children who need caregiving due to mental or physical handicaps pose a strain felt by the middle generation.

The problems facing the aged population tend to cluster around three issues: health, money, and abuse. Most health problems are addressed in the home rather than in hospitals, with primary care coming from spouses or children. Retirement, widowhood, and changing relationships all may create the need for resocialization to new roles and new definitions of self in relationship to society.

Retirement has been described as a process involving the periods of preretirement, retirement transition, and postretirement. The process appears to be generally positive for both sexes, with marital and household roles changing relatively little as a consequence. The increased employment of women appears to be decreasing any differences between the sexes in terms of the significance of retirement.

Dying and **death** involve very important processes and events for family members. The recognition of family members as supporters of dying persons has encouraged movements in treating terminally ill and dying patients in home settings, or in family-focused medical settings. Research suggests that the death of a parent adversely affects the martial relationships and well being of adult children.

More old women occupy a **widow** status than any other marital status. Given the unbalanced sex ratio among old people, remarriage is impossible for many women. Although the availability of a new spouse is more likely for men than for women, problems remain (suicides are high among widows of both sexes, especially among the very old).

LECTURE AND DISCUSSION QUESTIONS

1. **Eshleman devotes considerable space to the issues surrounding young adults becoming independent and leaving home—with some returning early in their adult lives, earning the label "boomerang kids." What is normative behavior in this area of intergenerational relations?**
    Answer guidelines: This is an area where norms are not clear. Some families expect young adults to leave home and establish independence early. Others allow young adults to remain at home (or return home), but under firm rules of conduct, and sometimes paying rent. Others of the

parental generation seem not sure what to do, and there is some difficulty negotiating the extent of support and emotional involvement the parental generation will provide. It has been noted that many of the current generation of young adults are not sure what they want, alternately asking their parents for help, then asking them to "butt out."

This confusion over the beginning of the postparent period can be very trying for the parent generation. Psychologist Francine Toder has produced a book dealing with this set of problems, called *Your Kids Are Grown: Moving On With Them or Without Them* (Insight Books, 1994). Toder presents a startling conclusion from her research: A healthy parent-child relationship does not necessarily lead to a healthy parent-adult-child relationship. The later stage calls for an entirely new set of parenting skills! Moreover, old parenting practices and "relationship rules" established earlier sometimes must be "unlearned." For example, the close supervision parents exercised over adolescent children must be replaced by a more "hands off" approach to the young adult. Meanwhile, young adults must develop new concern for the well being of their parents, who are becoming more vulnerable with advancing age. As Eshleman notes, there is evidence that adult children's problems tend to affect their parents in the form of stress and depression.

One notable problem introducing stress into the lives of millions of older adults currently is the phenomenon of "grandparents raising grandchildren." The Census Bureau has reported a sharp increase in this type of arrangement over the past decade. Millions of young adults are returning home (or never leaving home), and introducing grandchildren into their parents' households. The line between parenting and grandparenting is often blurred, as the older generation is called upon to help support their own children, and raise their children's children as well.

2. **Eshleman points out that middle-class grandparents are free to "construct" their own grandparent roles. What are the demographic and social changes that have made this possible?**
   Answer guidelines: In short, grandparents have more time to act as grandparents, and are more able to enlarge upon the grandparent role than in the past. Due to a dramatic drop in the middle age and old-age mortality rates, a much larger proportion of the population now *survives* to *be* grandparents. So, grandparents and grandchildren now have the opportunity to know each other over significant portions of their life spans.

   Several other factors make it possible for older people to "expand upon" a distinct grandparent role: the economic independence and self-reliance of both the nuclear family and the senior generation; the institutionalization of retirement (now spanning fifteen years for men, and even longer for women); technological improvements in travel and communications; and high standards of living, particularly for the grandparent generation.

In addition, experts on "grandparenting" have noticed that the emotional *content* of grandparenthood has apparently shifted so that it is now geared to intimacy with the grandchild. This appears to be a result of the increasing emphasis upon emotional investment in children across our society, and a general "search for sentiment" in intimate relationships.

3. **Eshleman mentions the emerging grandparent visitation rights issue. What has brought about this apparent increase in litigation by grandparents?**
   Answer guidelines: First, there has been an interesting reversal of earlier demographic patterns: While early in this century there were many grandchildren (due to high birth rates) and few grandparents (due to few persons living to old age), now there are relatively *few grandchildren* (due to low birth rates) to be shared by relatively *many grandparents* (due to the survival of many more people into old age). Thus, there are many more grandparents present in the population with whom the middle generation must manage relationships.

   Second, there has developed an emphasis upon sentimental ties and affection as the primary core of the grandparent/grandchild relationship. This sets the stage for over-involvement on the part of grandparents, and for parental jealousy.

   Third, divorce and remarriage are very common in our society, but behaviors in that area are not fully institutionalized. Kin control over the conduct of individuals has weakened considerably, making it possible for parents to remove access to grandchildren--without opposition or retribution. Also, our kinship system features considerable "boundary ambiguity" as to obligations between extended family members when divorce or out-of-wedlock birth has occurred. There are few clear rules for parents and kin (or *former* kin) to follow in such situations, and the majority of grandparent visitation disputes do arise within these contexts.

   Fourth, there has been a general increase in use of the legal system for assistance in all types of family problem solving.

   Fifth, the general mobility of our population and the isolation and privacy of conjugal family units make it possible for parents to remove grandchildren and keep grandparents at a distance.

CLASSROOM ACTIVITIES AND PROJECTS

1. In 1999, the Older Women's League announced plans to lobby Congress into action on the problem of elderly women living in poverty. This is not a

new problem. It has been recognized for decades that women generally lag in retirement funds. Current statistics portent a grim future for many old women: elderly women are three times more likely to live in poverty than older men are. Discuss with students why this might be. There are a variety of reasons; women are more likely to take career breaks to care for family; women receive less money than men for similar work; and women are more likely to work in lower paying jobs, for smaller companies, without pensions.

It may be that students are disinterested in this topic, since it may seem remote to them. However, they might become more interested if they realize that women continue to hold the same kind of low-wage, no benefit jobs their mothers and grandmothers worked at. The mothers of this generation of students are definitely at risk for poverty when they retire—and that will be soon. Also, it might benefit the female students, especially, to realize that this is a matter that ought to be considered as they plan their own careers.

2.   A growing number of men and women in American society are having to take care of their elderly parents, as well as their own children. The adult "children" who assume such responsibilities have been referred to as the "sandwich generation." Because more people are now living into old age, and because full-time professional care for the elderly is often unaffordable, this has become a serious problem for many American families. It is possible that one or more member of your class has felt the impact of this problem in his/her own family, and might be able to tell about the experience. A useful approach to this discussion might be to list the different difficulties faced by all three generations caught up in this sort of situation.

3.   Do women ever "retire?" Ask your students to consider how even those women who have worked and have earned pensions are less likely to actually retire, because they continue to have many of the same responsibilities (such as house cleaning, cooking, caring for grandchildren) as prior to retirement age. In comparison, when men retire, they are divested of a large set of work-related obligations. It might be useful to consider both the negative and positive consequences for both men and women.

FILM AND VIDEO RESOURCES

Legacy: America's Indan Elders
Elders from several Native American tribes speak about existing programs for older Indians, as well as the difficulties faced in providing serives to elerly Indians.
Terra Nova Films, 30 min., color

Grandparents Raising Grandchildren

This video presents the stories of four grandparents who are raising grandchildren, and examines the emotionaal and social issues involved. Support groups are portrayed.
Terra Nova Films, 30 min., color

Kicking High in the Golden Years

This award-winning documentary illustrates the rewards of aging with dignity and purpose, within the context of strong family, inter-generational, and community experiences.
New Day Films, 50 min., color

Parenting Our Parents

The "sandwich generation," staggers under the double burden of growing kids and chronically ill parents. As the size of the elderly population increases, the forecast is for a society of the old caring for the *very* old.
Films for the Humanities and Sciences, 26 min., color

Ageless America

Medical breakthroughs have increased longevity for elderly Americans. This has led to a host of new problems, caring for the elderly, the prospect of aging for a generation of the middle-aged with fewer children and many more single women, the "sandwich generation" of adults with responsibility for both children and aging parents, and the problems of aging.
Films for the Humanities and Sciences, 52 min., color

The Family Extended

Part of the "Portrait of a Family" series, this program centers on the increasing number of older people who have been married before, and are committing themselves to marriage again. Such reconstituted families are different from traditional nuclear families in some important ways.
RMI Media Productions, 30 min.

The Last Right

This dramatic production depicts how one family confronts the illness and death experience of an elderly family member. It raises the ethical issues that surround family caregiving and the right of the elderly to choose how to live or die.
New Dimensions Media, Inc., 29 min., color

Grandparenting

The complexities of modern living affect even the simple joy of grandparenting. Verl Rosenbaum, psychoanalyst and author, interviews grandparents who discuss the various facets of today's family life, as well as the grandparents' important contributions to the third generation.
Cornell University Audio-visual Resource Center, 30 min., color

Grandparents

This video explores the unique relationship shared by grandparents and their grandchildren. Noted psychiatrists Arthur Kornhaber reviews the important role grandparents have traditionally held in society, and stresses the need for linking generations together.

Cornell University Audio-visual Resource Center, 26 min., color

Constructing the Multigenerational Family Genogram: Exploring a Problem in Context

Directed by Stephen Lerner, this video teaches how to construct and use the multigenerational family genogram. It illustrates how the idea of the genogram is used, particularly in family therapy. Available in Spanish.

Menninger Clinic, 31 min., black and white

I Want to Die at Home

In this remarkable portrayal of loyalty and love, Elizabeth discovers she has incurable cancer. Her strongest wish is to die in the familiar surroundings of home, close to the people she loves. This documentary is not so much about her death, but about her loyal friends and family, who share in her care and steadfastly keep her company throughout this critical stage of her life.

Filmmakers Library, 46 min.

I Never Planned On This

This reassuring video examines normal, healthy aging, showing that it is part of the gradual biological process that begins at birth.

Filmmakers Library, 46 min.

Beyond Retirement

A profile of six individuals, all well over sixty-five, this video emphasizes that activity, growth, creativity, and self-discovery can continue to enrich older persons' lives, maintaining vital lifestyles into the retirement years.

Journal Films and Video, Inc., 27 min.

CHAPTER 15

FAMILY VIOLENCE

CASE EXAMPLE
> Questions to consider
> Introduction to the chapter

SOCIAL STRESSES ON FAMILIES
> ABCX model of stress
> Variations on the ABCX model

VIOLENCE IN FAMILIES AND AMONG INTIMATES
> Myths of family violence
> Causes of family violence
> Child abuse and violence
> Parent abuse and violence
> Wife and female-partner abuse and violence
> Husband and male-partner abuse and violence
> Mutual abuse and violence between couples
> Sibling abuse and violence
> Elderly abuse and violence
> Violence among other intimates
> Treating and preventing family violence

SUMMARY

OBJECTIVES

Based upon their reading and careful consideration of Chapter 15, students should:

1. Understand the nature and content of stressor and/or crisis-provoking events affecting the family;

2. be familiar with the ABCX model of stress and crisis;

3. be acquainted with the nature and extent of violence in families and among intimates, including the myth of the U.S. family as non-violent;

4. be aware of the myths regarding violence within the family;

5. be well-acquainted with existing data pertaining to child abuse and violence, wife or female-partner abuse and violence, husband or male- partner abuse

and violence, sibling abuse and violence, and abuse and violence against elderly family members; and,

6.   be familiar with the methods for treating and preventing family violence.

OVERVIEW

Marital and family crisis and violence are not unique to any given stage of the family life cycle, or to any particular family structure. Stressor or crisis-provoking events are situations that threaten the status quo and well being of the system or its members. These events may come from sources either within or outside of the family. Certain events solidify the family unit, while others are very disruptive.

The **ABCX model** refers to some event: (A) interacting with the family's crisis-meeting resources; (B) defining or giving meaning to the event; (C) resulting in a level or degree of crisis (X). If B and C are adequate, the level of stress and crisis will be minimal. If they are inadequate, the level of stress and crisis will be high. Since the original model was proposed, other writers have expanded it to include a double ABCX model, recommending the incorporation of new dimensions (such as the interrelating levels of various systems), and recognizing the sociohistorical context.

Abuse and **violence** are common events within families and among intimates. Violence, although frequent in most societies, is not an inevitable consequence of family life. Violence does not occur in societies in which family life is characterized by cooperation, commitment, sharing, and equality.

In the Unites States, the very prevalence of violence offers a persuasive counter-argument to the myth of the family as nonviolent. Other myths related to family violence include the suggestion that abusers are aliens and victims are innocents; that abuse is confined to poor minority families; that alcohol and drugs are the real causes of family violence; that all children who are abused grow up to be abusers; and that abused women like to be hit.

Physical punishment of children in the United States, as in most nations, is central to the socialization process. Physical punishment is widely believed to be an effective form of discipline. However, there is reason to be concerned that physical punishment produces a "spillover effect" in society, engendering violence in other social spheres.

To deal with **child abuse**, it is necessary to look beyond physical punishment. Severe violence against children is found in all social classes, but is more frequently found in poverty settings. Factors such as poverty and unemployment appear to be stressor events that tend to influence family functioning, as exhibited in greater

114

abuse of children. Most child abuse occurs behind closed doors and never comes to the attention of the public. Recent investigations have fostered an increasing awareness of this as an important issue. These investigations report a decrease in the incidence of child abuse.

Child **sexual abuse** appears to be widespread. One national survey found 27 percent of women and 16 percent of men reporting having been sexually abused. The males were more likely to have been abused by strangers than females. Non-biologically-related caretakers were found to be over-represented. The consequences of child sexual abuse appear to be severe and long-lasting.

There is disagreement as to whether child abuse and domestic violence have been reduced over time. Changes in family structure and in social values may have produced an actual decline in family violence (although it may not have been as substantial as initially believed). On the other hand, reported reductions in family violence may be due to changes in research techniques, or may be due to population shifts.

Children are not only the recipients of violence, but are perpetrators as well. Cases of parental abuse by children are typically under-reported.

Wife or **female partner abuse**, like child abuse, is not always viewed as inappropriate, particularly in contexts of male authority and dominance. Many wives do not or cannot leave their violent husband due to economic dependency or lack of alternatives. Some are able to utilize shelters. Sexual abuse and rape by a spouse or by an intimate partner is a common form of violence inflicted upon women. Many states now have provisions for the prosecution of marital rapes. **Husband abuse** is granted far less attention than the abuse of children and wives, but physical violence seems to be an aspect of marriage that approaches equality between the spouses. **Sibling abuse** is the most frequent form of violence within families. **Elderly abuse** frequently affects aging parents, particularly the mother. Other forms of **violence among intimates** include that of adolescents in the dating-courtship process, and that of adolescents toward parents.

Investigations into treating and/or preventing violence in families indicate that helping battered wives learn to negotiate an end to the violence, education in conflict resolution techniques, and the use of community resources are all useful. The elimination of cultural norms that accept violence as a means of conflict resolution can help in the prevention of family violence.

LECTURE AND DISCUSSION QUESTIONS

1. **What can be done about domestic violence?**
   <u>Answer guidelines</u>: One new area of prevention and treatment is among teenagers, who are increasingly urged to understand and avoid partner

abuse. Many high schools have education programs to prevent physical abuse and date rape. On most college campuses, there are rather intensive ongoing efforts to educate young people about date rape, in particular. Apparently, there is a real need for such programs. Studies show the rates of physical and sexual abuse among young people is very high, ranging from 30-37 percent reporting some form of abuse, and this abuse is rarely a one-time event.

Another interesting type of program that is apparently meeting with some success is the work being done with teenage mothers around the country. Such young mothers are being taught basic child development information, so that they may recognize--and learn to be patient with--normal child behavior such as temper tantrums, high levels of physical activity, etc. Thus, the young parents become are less likely to hold the kind of unrealistic expectations for their child's behavior that can lead to abuse. There is typically a component, in such programs, of help by nurses or volunteers so that the young mothers bond closely with their children early on, thus ameliorating future violence. The latter is particularly needed by teen parents who have been neglected themselves, and by those who've received inappropriate corporal punishment.

Another category of abuser is harder to address; that perpetrated by men. Men perpetrate most abuse. Due to the remnants of patriarchal norms in our society, there is deeply rooted tendency to allow and/or justify some violence and abuse on the part of men. Many police departments are putting increasing emphasis on training officers and staff to respond systematically to occurrences of domestic violence, but many others are lagging behind and failing to protect victims adequately. All police departments face difficult stumbling blocks in protecting victims from retaliation. Restraining orders are somewhat useless unless they are enforced. Even so, restraining orders are notoriously ineffective when an enraged abuser truly wants to harm the victim again. Shelters are extremely important in keeping women and children safe from violent husbands and fathers, but a woman must be prepared to take control of her own life in order for the shelter experience to have a lasting impact.

2. **Eshleman notes that marital rape is seldom viewed by either of the marital partners as rape, and, in fact, the wife often blames herself for the incident. Why is this kind of family violence so widely tolerated?** Answer guidelines: It has only been within the last two decades that rape has even been "possible," in the legal sense, within marriage.

Our culture features particular social relationships that are quite relevant to rape. The first is the phenomenon of inequality between the sexes. The second is the tradition of men perceiving women as sexual property. The norms of interaction between the sexes compel women to attempt to

116

manage situations to prevent sexual aggression. Men, on the other hand, are not expected to exercise much self-control. These very strong traditions influence the behavior of individual men in their relationships with their wives.

In some marital rape situations, consensual sex may be an alternative, but husbands are seeking to humiliate and subjugate their wives. What they have in common with stranger-rape is the objective of bolstering their own feelings of power, superiority, and masculinity through abusive behavior. As for the raped wife, she also has characteristics in common with the woman who is raped by a stranger: She may be physically and emotionally traumatized, and she may experience an effort to shift the blame for the attack from the rapist to her, the victim.

For the benefit of students who have not previously thought of rape as a power-related, it may be necessary to review the basic research findings on this topic.

3.   **What are the social costs of the extensive pattern of spouse and partner abuse occurring in our society?**
Answer guidelines: We tend to think of spouse abuse as a highly "private matter," affecting only the spouses and (perhaps) their children. However, this domestic violence *does* spillover into the public sphere. Police officers are typically quite apprehensive about intervening in domestic disputes. It is not surprising that they should be: A sizeable number of police officers are injured or killed each year while trying to cope with domestic violence incidents. It has also been established that spouse abuse results in absenteeism on the job, resulting in an economic loss equivalent to several *billion* dollars each year. Even the provision of medical services and "safe house" shelters to victims are often paid at public expense.

Ironically, one of the correlates of family violence is the social isolation of the violent families. It has been estimated that the average wife who presses charges against her husband has *already* been beaten more than 35 times! Thus, the "spill-over" effect seen and felt by society at large is only the "tip of the iceberg" experienced by families affected by violent behavior.

CLASSROOM ACTIVITIES AND PROJECTS

1.   By now, students should be very familiar with the theoretical approaches to family studies used by Eshleman throughout the text. See how skilled they are at applying those theories to the issue of family violence. This may require some real thought and effort on their parts, so take the time necessary for them to "work through" their responses. Remind students at the outset that each theory is simply a tool. In the area of family violence,

as other areas of family sociology, it is probably unwise to rely upon only one type of theory.

Here are a couple of examples of the sort of basic ideas that should emerge in the discussion: *Conflict theory* holds that people with power "make the rules," and are often able to impose their wills on those who have less power and/or resources. Typically, then, women and children are more likely to be victimized by physical violence or sexual exploitation than are adult men. Further, the institutions of society—legal, religious, family—support the existing normative structures, thus providing little support to prevent violence against those whom are low in power, resources, and status. *Exchange theory* might be used to emphasize that those who use violence within a family enjoy the "reward" of being in control, as well as the release of anger and frustration. Rewards for victims are a little harder to identify or understand. Some women might endure violent relationships because of the benefit of economic support.

2.   Family violence is a "hot" topic today. Brenda D. Phillips offers a unique approach to teaching about family violence in her article, "Teaching About Family Violence to An At-Risk Population: Insights from Sociological and Feminist Perspectives," which appeared in the July, 1988 issue of *Teaching Sociology* (Vol. 16, No. 3: 289-293). Phillips points out that many students who take sociology courses have themselves been victimized by various forms of family violence, and the article provides guidelines for discussing the subject with students.

3.   There are a number of professionals who confront the consequences of domestic violence in a very direct way: emergency room nurses and physicians, police officers, and counselors at spouse abuse shelters. Invite one or more of them into the class to discuss their experiences and to answer students' questions about the problem.

FILM AND VIDEO RESOURCES

Preventing Elder Abuse
This program shows how to recognize and prevent elder abuse. It recognizes that because of their increased dependence, older people are at risk for neglect and other forms of abuse.
Aspen Films, 27 min., color

When Romance Turns to Rape
This video examines the premise that three-fourths of all rapes are committed by acquaintances, and most occur during dates. The video describes what women can do to protect themselves.
Britannica Educational Group, 20 min., color

Someone You Know

This video about date and aquaintance rape is designed to stimulate discussion, based on the presentation of two very realistic situations. A man and a woman both present their reactions to each situation. This encourages the viewers to explore their own values and ideas about how to prevent violent sex acts.

AGC Educational Media, 30 min., color

Battered Women: Violence Behind Closed Doors

Real life victims and aggressors offer vivid insights into the wife-battering syndrome. Children are shown to be future participants in the "cycle of violence."

Coronet/MTI, 24 min., color

The Trouble With Evan

This video focus on the experience of a child who exhibited signs of abuse as early as age four. Cameras were permitted into Evan's home, revealing months of emotional abuse and family conflict.

Filmmakers Library, 90 min., color

Family Matters

This documentary crosscuts the workplaces, neighborhoods, schools, and social networks of American families, examining the stressors on modern families.

Cornell University Audio-Visual Resource Center, 29 min., color

Two Million Women: Domestic Violence

Of all the women murdered in American society, over half of them are killed by a husband or boyfriend. Each year, at least two million women will be beaten by the men they love. This film explores the phenomenon of domestic violence, and suggests strategies for doing something about it.

Coronet/MTI/Dystar Television, Inc., 29 min., color

Child Abuse: Cradle of Violence

This documentary provides a frank discussion of the disturbing topic of child abuse through a series of interviews with former child abusers. The presentation also discusses the value of self-help groups and community services to help parents cope.

Coronet/MTI/ Bonanza Films, 20 min., color

Crying in the Dark: Misdiagnosed Child Abuse

The flip side of unreported child abuse is falsely charged child abuse. This award-winning documentary tells the story of anguished families whose tranquility was shattered and whose very existence was placed into question--the children were removed to community shelters and the parents

cast under a cloud of suspicion and revulsion--because of a controversial diagnostic technique used by overzealous medical personnel.
Films for the Humanities and Sciences, 55 min., color

The Unquiet Death of Eli Creekmore

This film reconstructs a brutal child abuse case that ended in death, despite various reports of the abuse by teachers, relatives, and a doctor.
Filmmakers Library, 55 min., color

Four Men Speak Out on Surviving Child Sexual Abuse

Four male survivors tell their own stories, addressing the long-term effects of abuse. Topics covered include trust, "telling," homophobia, and healing. A discussion guide accompanies the videotape.
Campbell Education Foundation, distributed by Varied Directions

Child Abuse: A Perspective on Parent Aides

This video features a lively discussion among six parent aides from the Onondaga County Child Abuse Coordination Program. The discussion highlights the role of parent aides as the warm, nurturing persons who give parents the friendship and role modeling they lacked as children.
Cornell University Audio-visual Resource Center, 28 min., color

Child Abuse: A Perspective on Being A Parent

This video features a series of excerpts from interviews with six abusive parents. The parents' stories indicate what led to their abuse of their children--primarily isolation, the absence of having been loved as children, and economic stress.
Cornell University Audio-visual Resource Center, 28 min., color

Childhood Physical Abuse

This program covers the range of problems in the area of physical abuse of children: the kinds of adults likely to abuse their children, the telltale signs of such abuse, the effects on the children, the ways in which abuse should be dealt with, what happens to the children when the law steps in, the distinction between discipline and abuse, and how the physical abuse of children can be prevented.
Films for the Humanities and Sciences, 26 min., color

Abused Wives

The wife of a former chief enforcement officer of the Securities and Exchange Commission tells of a marriage marked by a constant pattern of abuse, in this Phil Donahue program especially adapted for the classroom.
Films for the Humanities and Sciences, 28 min., color

A House Divided: Elderly Abuse

This film explores the phenomenon of elder abuse through four portraits, ranging from neglect to physical attack. The emotional complexity of family relationships, and the isolation and helplessness of victims are explored. **Filmmakers Library, 35 min.**

Please Don't Hit Me, Mom!

This moving drama addresses the difficult subject of child abuse. Focusing on the reasons behind child abuse, it presents the abusive parent not as a hideous criminal, but as a troubled person who needs help. It also gives concrete information on what to do about suspected child abuse. **Public Media, Inc., 46 min., color**

Children and Domestic Violence

Part of the "Broken Wings" series, this video examines how to protect children from domestic violence--from the "build up," to the "blow up," to the "honeymoon"--and how children who are abused (or who witness abuse) derive emotional scars from this destructive cycle. **Menninger Clinic, 15 min.**

Men and Domestic Violence

Part of the "Broken Wings" series, this video tells the story of one man-- George--who is trying to change his lifelong pattern of behavior. Viewers learn that power and control are at the roots of domestic violence, and undoing violent beliefs is the key to ending domestic violence. **Menninger Clinic, 19 min.**

More Than Word: Domestic Violence

This video takes a close look at the issue of domestic violence, at the attitudes that perpetuate it, and at means of preventing it. **Baxley Media Group, 77 min., color**

Behind Closed Doors

An in-depth examination of domestic violence from a very personal perspective, this video focuses on David, an abuser, and Margaret, a victim, as each discusses his difficult childhood, his low self-esteem, his feelings of shame, and his determination to break the patterns of violence that have governed his life. **Filmmakers Library, 46 min., color**

Generations of Violence

This compelling video documents the legacy of family violence that is passed from one generation to another. We meet both the perpetrators and victims of domestic violence, and hear their personal experiences. **Filmmakers Library, 55 min.**

Incest

What are the rights and responsibilities of incest victims long after the event? How do victims overcome years of denial and guilt to confront their victimizers and accept the facts of their victimization? Phil Donahue is joined by experts in the field to discuss this topic and related issues.
Films for the Humanities and Sciences, 28 min., color

Incest: The Family Secret

Incest is a terrifying crime that occurs in all kinds of families. It is a widespread problem that is kept hidden. Most commonly, it takes the form of sexual abuse inflicted by the father on a nonconsenting daughter while she is still a child.
Filmmakers Library, 57 min.

Incest: The Family Secret

Women tell of early experiences that traumatized their later years. Some women protect their identity; others share their secret openly in a self-help group. We learn the behavior patterns that emerge in adolescence, when these girls often become runaways, drug addicts, and prostitutes. The program also explores the role of the mother in an incestuous family. Some mothers are unaware of what is happening, but others comply out of fear or dependency.
Filmmakers Library, 57 min.

CHAPTER 16

DIVORCE AND REMARRIAGE

CASE EXAMPLE
> Questions to consider
> Introduction to the chapter

DESERTION AND MARITAL SEPARATION

ANNULMENT

DIVORCE AROUND THE WORLD

DIVORCE IN THE UNITED STATES
> Divorce rates
> Trends in divorce
> Variations ion divorce
> Legal and social grounds for divorce
> Consequences of divorce for adults
> Children of divorced parents

REMARRIAGE AND STEPFAMILIES
> People who remarry
> Marriage among the remarried
> Remarried couples with stepchildren: reconstituted families

SUMMARY

OBJECTIVES

Based upon their reading and careful consideration of Chapter 16, students should:

1. Be able to distinguish between desertion, marital separation (including legal and informal separations), annulment, and divorce;

2. be familiar with divorce in other countries as well as in the United States;

3. be familiar with the three different ways that divorce rates are calculated, as well as the advantages and limitations of each method;

4. be familiar with the major trends in divorce rates in the United States, including variations by geographic, demographic, and social characteristics;

5.	understand the differences between legal grounds for divorce, no-fault divorce, and social grounds for divorce;

6.	understand the consequences of divorce for adults;

7.	understand the effects of divorce on children, as reflected in existing research findings; and,

8.	be familiar with what is known about remarriage, including rates of remarriage and the prospects for success, and the implications of stepchildren in such situations.

OVERVIEW

All societies have some mechanism to cope with marital discord or to terminate marital relationships. In some countries, **divorce** is not permitted, but other types of relationships may legally co-exist with marriage. In the United States, divorce is the most common means of ending a marital relationship, but desertion, marital separation (legal and informal), and annulments exist as well. In both the United States and other countries, divorce has increasingly been viewed as an escape valve, a way out of the marriage itself.

Rates of divorce are typically calculated in one of three ways: per 1,000 persons in the total population; per 1,000 women age 15 and over; or the ratio of divorces to the number of marriages in a given year. Regardless of method, the trend has been upward, with a leveling-off in recent years. Divorce rates vary widely in accordance with geographic, demographic, and social characteristics. Rates also vary considerably by state, as well as by particular areas within states.

The **legal grounds for divorce** vary from state to state. All states have now moved from the traditional adversarial system of divorce to **no-fault** statutes. **Social grounds for divorce** often differ substantially from legal grounds. **Divorce mediation** is an increasingly popular technique for conflict resolution. Mediation may diminish the bitterness and divisiveness that frequently accompany divorce.

The **consequences of divorce** for adults are complex. Typically, women are the economic losers in divorce. Children are a primary concern to those interested in the impact of divorce. Existing research does support the idea that unhappy marriages should be maintained for the sake of the children. However, research shows that children of divorced parents experience considerable stress and as a consequence of divorce.

Most persons who end one marriage eventually **remarry**. Men are more likely to remarry than women, divorcees are more likely to remarry than widows are, and younger persons are more likely to remarry than older people. The complexities of remarriage are compounded by the presence of children. The stepparenting experience is most difficult for the stepmother, but it may be more positive when the stepchildren live-in. Many structural variations of remarriage have the potential to create **boundary ambiguity**; the uncertainty of family members as to who is part of the family, and who performs certain roles within the family. **Simple stepfamilies** include children from just one parent. When both parents bring children into the new family arrangement, it is called a **complex stepfamily**.

LECTURE AND DISCUSSION QUESTIONS

1. ***Why* are men more likely to remarry, and remarry more quickly, than women are?**
    Answer guidelines: During the 1980s, there was a joke (which began as a research finding) that quickly became a cliché. It was said that a middle-aged divorced woman was "more likely to be attacked by terrorists than to remarry." Although this was hyperbole, it was based upon a difficult fact. Women *do* have a harder time finding a new husband after divorce. Men remarry more often and more quickly, than women. Part of the reason for this is that men generally have a larger pool of eligible mates to choose from than women do, since there are normally more "marriageable" females than males in any population. This is partly due to the social phenomena of men "marrying down" in social status and economically, while women "marry up."

    Some of the other reasons for the greater availability of marriageable mates for men are demographic. Males have a higher average death rate all along the continuum of life, which means, in practical terms, there are always more females than males. When there has been a "baby boom" (such as the baby boom of the 1950s and 1960s) that generation will experience a pronounced excess of females in relation to males in the population available to marry, since women tend to marry men a few years older (thus, women who are at the "top" or "vanguard" of their age cohort will experience a sharp shortage of men, both when they are ready to marry, and later, when they are ready to remarry). It is socially permissible for men to marry women several years younger, but this is frowned upon for women. Another reason men have an easier time dating and remarrying is the fact that men so rarely have custody of their children.

2. **Have liberalized divorce laws, the "no fault" divorce laws in particular, led to an increase in the incidence of divorce?**
    Answer guidelines: The intent of the first "no fault" legislation was to reduce the widespread acrimony and deceit of divorce proceedings, but it also made divorce much easier to obtain. It is not clear whether the removal of formerly tough divorce laws--which had presumably exerted some constraints on marital dissolution by making divorce difficult and unpleasant--actually helped push up divorce rates.

It is clear that the adoption of no-fault laws across the country did indeed coincide with a dramatic increase in the U.S. divorce rate in the 1970s. A series of early studies conducted in the 1970s suggested that no-fault divorce laws had little, if anything, to do with the increase in divorce in most states. The researchers generally concluded that the increase in divorce would have occurred even without no-fault. However, more recently it has been suggested that the liberalization of divorce laws *did* accelerate the upsurge in the incidence of divorce (see Paul Glick, "Fifty Years of Family Demography: A Record of Social Change." *Journal of Marriage and the Family* 50 (1988):868).

Whatever the actual role of the no-fault legislation, it is important to realize that debate over the causes of divorce have been going on for more than a century, and that the divorce rate began to accelerate around the turn of the Century. By the 1920s, one in six marriages were ending in divorce. This increase was not due to any liberalization in the divorce laws. In fact, early in the 20th Century divorce laws were made *more restrictive* across the country. Still, despite those attempts to restrict divorce, an increasing number of people were dissolving marriages that did not measure up to rising standards for personal fulfillment.

3. **What are the probable *reasons* for the pattern of so-called "serial monogamy" which has emerged so strongly within our marriage system?**
   Answer guidelines: First, it is essential to understand that *no* society has achieved perfect monogamy. Even in societies that prohibit divorce, there are elements of flexibility, which permit people (most often *men*) to leave or circumvent unhappy marriages. These mechanisms of flexibility include abandonment, adultery, and extramarital cohabitation. Our own society is particularly flexible--some insist "permissive"--in marriage norms.

   In the United States, as elsewhere, demographic factors have contributed to the remarriage phenomenon. Average life expectancy has increased dramatically. At the turn of the Century, the majority of the population did not live much beyond their '40s, and thus could not expect to "change partners" throughout the life course. Now, people expect to live through their mid-70s, and to enjoy good health throughout late middle age and even old age. Given these improvements, "serial monogamy" is a much more realistic prospect.

   Finally, a broad complex of sociocultural phenomena which reflect modernization and individual "liberation" combine to enhance the possibility of multiple partners throughout our lifetimes, including: (1) strong values of individualism; (2) an emphasis upon personal growth throughout life; (3) the expectation of intimacy as an entitlement; (4) sexual liberation and the expectation of sexual satisfaction as a personal "right" within relationships; and, (5) the movement of women into the workforce (making them economically more self-sufficient, and allowing both women and men to leave unhappy marriages and eventually enter into new relationships).

CLASSROOM ACTIVITIES AND PROJECTS

1. Ask students to consider what the outcome of divorce and remarriage will be for the current generations *in their old age.* One fact to consider is that the family available for comfort and support in old age will be quite different for "baby boomers" and those who follow than it is for the current generation of senior citizens.

    This will be partly dictated by the demographics of the situation. Senior citizens today have two or three children, on the average, Baby boomers and those who follow will have fewer children and grandchildren. Thus, more of them will have to rely more upon stepchildren—and nonrelatives—rather than biological children, as they become elderly and incapacitated. Another type of relationship that will probably change is that of older siblings. Research has shown that siblings typically draw closer as they age, and provide considerable support and companionship for each other in old age. The future generations of old people will have fewer natural siblings whose company they may rely upon and enjoy.

    Ask students what they think this will mean, in practical terms. Will people rely upon stepsiblings more than they do currently? Will people rely more on fictive kin? Will new social arrangements develop to provide support for old people in the future—not just for those who have fewer siblings, cousins and "bood relatives," generally, but also those who are never able to remarry after divorce?

2. Students are likely to react with impatience to the different ways of computing rates of divorce: "Why can't there be just *one* way of calculating the divorce rate?" An amusing way generating understanding of the need for several different forms of divorce rates is as follows: The crude divorce rate is a limited statistic because literal interpretation of it would parallel calculating the incidence of diaper rash among every 1000 people in the population...Older people don't get diaper rash--just as lots of people in the population aren't in a position to get divorced.

3. It might be a good idea to familiarize students with the divorce laws and procedures in your state. If you are not very familiar with them, it is probably worth inviting an attorney or advanced law student who works on divorce cases to make a presentation, allowing plenty of time for student questions.

FILM AND VIDEO RESOURCES

Torn Between Two Fathers

This film explores the right of children to have a voice in where they will live in custody disputes.

SVE & Churchill Media, 45 min., color

Disappearance of the Father

The filmmakers cite figures indicating that America is increasingly becoming a fatherless nation, and describe the social factors contributing to this phenomenon. The focus is on the reasons non-custodial fathers gradually drop out of their children's lives, and the detrimental effects on the children and society as a whole. The role of the stepfather is also examined.

Concept Media, Inc., 25 min., color

Stepparenting

The authors of the book, *Stepparenting* discuss the inevitable problems of this delicate form of parenting. Couples share their experiences, frustrations, and rewards.

Video 11, 28 min., color

Children of Divorce

This specially adapted Phil Donahue program examines the legacy of divorce on children. Research results from a series of studies are now making clear that children almost never totally recover from the pain, confusion, guilt, and displacement of divorce. The consequences of divorce follow children into adulthood.

Films for the Humanities and Sciences, 28 min. color

Do Children Also Divorce?

Vignettes show various responses of children in divorcing families.

Filmmakers Library, 30 min.

An American Stepfamily

This program examines the problems of conflicting loyalties and rivalries in stepfamilies. Trends that will result in more stepfamilies than traditional families by the year 2000 are examined.

Films for the Humanities and Sciences, 26 min., color

Me and Dad's New Wife

This film depicts a twelve-year-old girl whose parents are divorced. She discovers on her first day of junior high school that her mathematics teacher is her father's new wife. The problems involved in relationships between children and stepparents are illustrated. The film is based on the book, *A Smart Kid Like You*, by Stella Pevsner.

Daniel Wilson Productions, 33 min., color

Joint Custody: A New Kind of Family

Co-parenting is an increasingly popular custody choice. This film explores the rewards and difficulties of this post-divorce variation, and elicits reactions from legal professionals.
New Day Films, 85 min., color

Stepdancing: Portrait of a Remarried Family

This documentary chronicles a nuclear family dissolved by divorce and reformed into two new families. The problems associated with divorce and remarriage are explored. In the program, parents, stepparents, and children speak out about experiences in their "new families."
University of Minnesota Films and Videos, 27 min., color

Divorce

Part of the "ACA Historical Videotape" series, this video focuses on individual emotional issues. Vignettes are used to examine problems of personal identity and the stigma of divorce. Fears of establishing new relationships are dealt with, as well as the intertwined issues of relating to the ex-spouse and children after divorce.
Elliot Enterprises, 40 min. in two parts, guidebook included

When Families Divorce

Even though divorce has become commonplace, a family split can have serious effects on children. In this video, seven children of divorce tell parents how they can cope with divorce, remarriage, and stepfamilies. **PBS Video, 60 min. in two parts**

Divorced and Sorry

Hosted by Phil Donohue, this program is devoted to the stories of some divorced persons who regret having ended their marriages, and to an examination of those marital difficulties that should not have been magnified into grounds for divorce.
Films for the Humanities and Sciences, 28 min., color

Divorced Couples Face Off

In this specially adapted Phil Donohue program, several ex-spouses face off in a candid exposition of both sides of the story, and discuss the difficulties both ex-husbands and ex-wives have encountered since divorce.
Films for the Humanities and Sciences, 28 min., color

The Changing Family

Why is American marriage so fragile, the divorce rate so high? The answers lie in social conditions, processes of social change, varied expectations, and the search for personal happiness.
RMI Media Productions, Inc., 30 min.

CHAPTER 17

FAMILY SOCIAL POLICY

CASE EXAMPLE
Questions to consider
Introduction to the chapter

MEANING AND USE OF FAMILY POLICY

RESEARCH ON FAMILY POLICY
Research to establish family policy
Research on family evaluation
Research to analyze family impact
Overview of research

ISSUES SURROUNDING FAMILY POLICY
Goals and objectives of family policy
Levels of policy control
Public versus private positions
Preventative or ameliorative policy
Biological or relationship policy
Micro- versus macrolevel policy

FUTURE OF THE FAMILY SYSTEM

SUMMARY

OBJECTIVES

Based upon their reading and careful consideration of Chapter 17, students should:

1.   Be able to define family policy and social policy, and be familiar with the general types of family programs outlined in the text;

2.   be familiar with the major types of family policy research;

3.   understand the distinctions between conventional and progressive positions on family policy issues;

4.   be familiar with the debates over whether the family is a public or private institution, whether family policy should be directed toward all families or just "problem" families, whether family policy should be directed at families or at individuals, whether policy should focus on biological and birth ties or social

relationships and intimate attachments, whether family policy should operate at a micro- or macrolevel, and whether family policy should be set and regulated at the federal or local level; and,

5.   be familiar with the four generalizations Eshleman makes in relation to the future of the family system.

OVERVIEW

Family policy, as defined by Phyllis Moen and Alvin Schorr, is a widely agreed upon set of objectives for families, which the state and other major social institutions try to realize through deliberately structured programs and policies. A continuing difficulty in family policy is determining who and what constitutes a "family."

Family policy research raises anew the research issue of focusing on what *is*, as opposed to what *should* be. The three major types of family policy research are family evaluation research, family impact analysis, and research for family policy.

Policy issues involve many conflicting points of view, including the extent to which policies should maintain the status quo or serve as forces of change, the extent to which policies should be established or controlled at whichever level of government, the extent to which families and intimate relationships are public or private institutions, the extent to which policies should be directed toward all close relationships or toward families with problems, the extent to which policies should be directed at family group systems or at individuals, the extent to which policy should focus on biological and birth ties, or social relationships and intimate relationships, and the extent to which policies should operate primarily at either a micro- or macro-level.

Social policies will affect the future directions of the family and its members. The family is changing, and will continue to change. These changes are not good or bad, per se. The future of the family cannot be understood independently from other institutions and systems. The family of the future will not be a uniform entity. Any type of social projection into the future must be made cautiously.

LECTURE AND DISCUSSION QUESTIONS

1.   **Eshleman describes the advantages and disadvantages of establishing family policy at the national level. What about the advantages and disadvantages of *states*' control in many areas of family policy?**
Answer guidelines: The strongest argument for states' control over family practices is probably that it allows for enforcement of regional cultural standards of behavior. As Eshleman's example comparing the family laws of Nevada, Minnesota, and South Carolina illustrates, there are regional

differences that are meaningful to at least the most politically dominant segments of the population. The obvious disadvantage, in this regard, is that some proportion of the populace of any region will differ in cultural values in relation to the laws that regulate very important aspects of their family's lives. This is due, in part, to the overall mobility of our population, and in part due to long-standing religious and cultural differences between various segments of the population.

A different type of problem is that the variations between states in important areas of family law have created a patchwork of legal standards and rules that make it difficult--or impossible--for ordinary people to cope with some kinds of family problems across state lines. Although there has been some convergence in state laws on family issues, big differences still exist in such areas as marital relations, adoption, divorce, and third party rights of access to children. For example, adoption cases in which one of the parties crosses state lines may result in an unexpected and unfair change of the "rules of the game" for the other party who remains in the original jurisdiction. In many divorce cases, parents, siblings, stepparents, grandparents, and others lose access to the children they love because state laws lack uniformity (thus, their rights may not be enforceable in another state).

2. **To what extent should we expect to see an expansion of "children's rights" in the near future?**
   Answer guidelines: This is difficult to predict. On one hand, there have been a few legal precedents that *seem* to mark a shift in our perspective on the rights of children. In a few celebrated cases, children have been allowed to legally "divorce" their parents or parent, mostly on the basis that the parents were neglectful or abusive. These are deceptive cases, however, since there had already been a long tradition of parents loosing parental rights when they were truly unfit. What is "new" may be the language suggesting a revolution in children's power. In actuality, though, the child's right to "pursue happiness" independently remains a mostly a myth. Parent's rights to determine all custodial matters pertaining to their children are largely regarded as inviolable in the law, in the absence of abuse or serious neglect. Most children do not have the knowledge or resources to go to court on their own behalf.

   On the other hand, sometimes a shift in the language we use to describe reality, or the occurrence of "extreme cases," really do portend a real shift in social policy. Perhaps isolated cases described as illustrating "children's rights" will change our collective perception of reality, leading to more undeniable "children's rights."

3. **To what extent does the "crisis in the family" result from external stressors and influences on it, as opposed to the choices of individuals?**

<u>Answer guidelines:</u> This is perhaps the most difficult question to answer about the current state of our family institution. The traditional perspective rests largely on the outlook that the difficulties of families result from the moral breakdown of society, which is expressed through the "bad choices" of individuals--Individual partners end marriages. Individual women choose to work outside their homes. Individuals choose to engage in premarital sex, and, subsequently, may make further choices that weaken the institution of marriage. Men may choose not to commit to family life, while women may choose either abortion or to remain unwed and "keep" and raise their babies alone--The primary concern of this outlook is how individuals may be influenced to make choices that are viewed as better for the family system of our entire society. According to this perspective, if individuals could be convinced or compelled to make "more moral choices," then "the family" could return to its more healthy former state.

The alternative perspective holds that individual choices are not the only factors that have weakened the family, and, in fact, the range of options available to most families includes disadvantages that *cannot be overcome on an individual basis*. These adverse conditions include structural, social, and demographic factors.   In the economic sector, families face displacement of breadwinners due to deindustrialization, the decline of labor unions, and the increase of poorly paid service jobs. In the political sector, families encounter attacks on single parents and a paucity of legislative and judicial efforts on behalf of families. In the demographic sector, families are affected by imbalances in the sex ratio (reducing the numbers of "marriageable" mates to some segments of the population), the "graying of America" (exacerbating the old age dependency ratio), and increases in the number of minority families (families that are more likely than nonminority families to be poor).

CLASSROOM ACTIVITIES AND PROJECTS

1.   In the midst of the welfare reforms that swept the country at the close of the Century, there began a serious debate about what might actually be done, when, after welfare reform, some parents *still might not be able to support their children*. Ask students to discuss the solution seriously advanced by some politicians: putting the children in orphanages. Encourage the students to think deeply about the social meaning of this "solution." For the first time in roughly a century, are we actually considering taking children away from parents who love them, and placing them in orphanages where they'll be "better off"—simply because their parents are unable to earn enough money to support them? This type of thinking, if it was ever implemented, could affect large numbers of families, since millions of families currently live in poverty, or hover near poverty. Ask students if they think this is a reasonable or desirable solution.

2.   Ask students to consider how the tenor of the times influences the public outlook on the family. An atmosphere of considerable economic dislocation and "downsizing" currently frames the idea of "the family in crisis". Just as "the family" of the 1950s and '60s was defined, in part, by the tremendous optimism of that period, the "stagflation" of the 1970s, the recession of the 1980s, and the reduced expectations of the 1990s clearly affected family life. Students might be asked to consider the extent to which nostalgia for the "golden age" of the family has been reinforced by the replacement of good industrial jobs with poor-paying service jobs, the high cost of housing, the crisis in public education, and the necessity of "dual" family incomes for an adequate standard of living. Based on current trends, ask students what they predict for the future of the family, and what policies might hurt or help.

3.   Students sometimes find it difficult to understand how the family can possibly survive as an institution when such a variety family forms are appearing (especially when some of these forms are radical departures from the "traditional" family). In order to assist your students, ask them to think about how many different forms of friendship exist. Some friendships endure over long distances with little face-to-face contact; others thrive only if the participants are constant companions; still others are beset with frequent conflict or even violence. Some of these friendships last, while others do not. Some remain vital while others are passive-congenial. Yet, the institution of friendship, so to speak, prevails and has not lost its viability. This exercise may help students see that it is unreasonable to have different expectations for the family than for other institutions in society--Why should we expect the family to remain the same while everything else changes? Another approach might be to ask students to consider which aspects of family change are inevitable (even desirable), and which might *actually* pose serious threats to the stability of society.

FILM AND VIDEO RESOURCES

Workfare, Welfare: What's Fair?
    Most people agree that the current welfare system is ineffective. Conservatives claim that welfare exacerbates poverty, while liberals say that welfare grants are so small that people in poverty can't find their way out. This program focuses on "workfare" programs, their prospects and problems.
    Films for the Humanities and Sciences, 26 min., color

Love Makes a Family
    The concept of family, redefined to encompass lesbian and gay parents, is explored in this informative and heartening video. A look at the various ways

that lesbians and gay people become parents, this video dispels myths, as it promotes understanding and respect for alternative family structures.
Fanlight Productions, 16 min., color

Family Limits

This video is of a made-for-television investigation of current family issues.
Don Bosco Multimedia, 28 min., color

Family Law

This video is designed for the layperson who desires knowledge of the legal principles upon which family law is based, as well as how the system that administers family law operates.
RMI Media Productions, 30. min., preview booklet available

TEST BANK

to accompany

J. Ross Eshleman

THE FAMILY

9th edition

Allyn and Bacon

Test bank prepared by

J. Ross Eshleman
Wayne State University

CHAPTER 1

True/False Questions

F
p. 003
1. The text describes <u>the family</u> as one with one female legally married to one male

T
p. 003
2. The definition of family proposed by Jan Trost includes any system of dyads or set of dyads including those who cohabit, siblings, friends, or even pets.

F
p. 004
3. Sociology is labeled in the text as the most comprehensive of all disciplines in dealing with families and therefore has a "corner" on the market.

T
p. 007
4. A sociology of the family does not have a principal interest in the motivations, drives, or personalities of individuals.

F
p. 007
5. Sociology, social psychology, and sociology are identical in that each focuses on individuals and their personal life experiences.

T
p. 007
6. A basic or concrete approach to family study seeks knowledge for its own sake without much concern about how it will be applied.

F
p. 008
7. As it currently exists under an authoritarian political regime, the Chinese family is a relatively uniform entity.

T
p. 009
8. Sweden has been described as having one of the highest literacy rates and lowest infant mortality rates in the world.

T
p. 009
9. While the text does not focus on personalities, it states that perhaps the most important use of family sociology exists at a personal level.

F
p. 010
10. Family theories are either right or wrong and when proven wrong should be discarded.

F
p. 011
11. A conceptual framework is simply another name for a theory.

T
p. 012
12. Hypotheses and propositions are identical with the exception that hypotheses carry clear implications for measuring the stated relations.

T
p. 016
13. Latent functions of the family are neither intended nor recognized.

F
p. 016
14. Differing family structures (such as a single parent versus two parents) have been found to have minimal effects on children in things like school performance or emotional problems.

T
p. 017
15. The text suggests that changing the family structure may be a more effective way to decrease problematic conditions than focusing on the people with the problem.

F
p. 018

16. Within a social conflict frame of reference, social conflict is generally disruptive and should be avoided whenever possible.

T
p. 019

17. According to conflict theory, the family serves to support the capitalistic system by exploiting homemakers and mothers.

F
p. 019

18. Conflict theorists maintain that equality and the maintaining of order is essential for successful marriages and families.

F
p. 020

19. A symbolic interaction perspective shares with radical behaviorism an emphasis on the importance of meanings, definitions of situations, and other internalized processes in understanding behavior.

F
p. 021

20. Roles, according to an interactionist perspective, refer to the rules or set of expectations that are associated with a given status.

T
p. 023

21. Social exchange theory assumes that having social credit through giving is preferable to being socially indebted through receiving.

T
p. 024

22. Social exchange theory would suggest that if resources or exchange criteria are unequal or unbalanced, one person is at a distinct disadvantage and the other has power over the relationship.

T
p. 025

23. The family life cycle is a major conceptual tool in the developmental approach.

F
p. 026

24. Family scholars tend to agree that all families go through seven clearly defined stages of development.

F
p. 027

25. Feminist theories see the family as the key, if not the only, institution where women can realistically expect to achieve full equality with men and the ending of differential gender roles.

F
p. 028

26. Feminists today focus blame for all male/female inequalities on economic systems.

T
p. 030

27. Hermeneutics refers to the art or theory of interpretation.

F
p. 031

28. A critical social science approach suggests that we should be "critical" of all science and theories that are not rooted in objectivity and empirical evidence.

Multiple-Choice Questions

D
p. 002

1. The text suggests that the family is
   a. a social institution.
   b. a social system.
   c. a socially constructed phenomenon with widely varying norms, values, and behaviors.
   d. all of the first three.

C
p. 003

2. The author argues that marriages and families <u>not</u> be viewed as
   a. any close, primary, sexually bonded relationship.
   b. any dyadic unit, including same sex partners, unmarried parents, or siblings
   c. dyadic units that fit traditional notions of what families should be.
   d. a social system or social institution.

C
p. 004

3. According to the text's discussion of disciplines involved in family study
   a. sociology reveals more about marriages and families than any other discipline.
   b. older social science theories are just as viable today as they were at their inception.
   c. the study of the family is highly interdisciplinary.
   d. all of the above three are true.

C
p. 005

4. Which of the following topics would most likely be studied by family sociologists.
   a. housing, nutrition, and child development.
   b. venereal disease, maternal care, and health practices.
   c. family systems, interpersonal roles, and family change.
   d. the personalities of family members.

A
p. 006

5. A sociology of the family is most likely to focus on
   a. human groups and systems.
   b. assistance to children and the elderly.
   c. human growth and development.
   d. all of the first three about equally.

D
p. 007

6. Which of the following is the least likely goal of a family sociologist.
   a. question the obvious.
   b. seek patterns and regularities in family life.
   c. assess individual behavior in the context of the larger society.
   d. determine which theory is correct in explaining families.

B
p. 008

7. Mainland China has
   a. about one-third of the world's population.
   b. seen it's fertility rate drop more than 50 percent in the last half century.
   c. a life expectancy of under 50 years.
   d. a highly uniform, monolithic family system.

C
p. 009

8. The text suggests that few societies in the world parallel Sweden in
   a. its high marriage rate.
   b. its inequality between the sexes.
   c. its movement of women into the paid labor force.
   d. both a and c above.

A
p. 010

9. According to the text, concepts
   a. are miniature systems of meaning.
   b. predict and state relationships.
   c. are exclusive in their meaning.
   d. can explain relationships.

B
p. 011

10. When concepts take on two or more degrees or values, they are referred to as
    a. variables.
    b. conceptual frameworks.
    c. hypotheses.
    d. theories.

A
p. 011

11. Mary and John were having marital problems and decided to end their marriage. Which of the following choices is most likely to be the dependent variable?
    a. divorce
    b. lack of communication
    c. failure to do things together
    d. all of the above three are dependent variables

B
p. 012

12. The statement "the frequency of intercourse declines with age and/or the length of the marriage" would be considered a
    a. falsehood.
    b. theory.
    c. proposition.
    d. hypothesis.

C
p. 012

13. When a proposition is formulated for empirical testing, it is considered a
    a. variable.
    b. conceptual framework.
    c. hypothesis.
    d. theory.

D
p. 013

14. A theory can best be defined as
    a. a miniature system of meaning that allows a phenomenon to be viewed in a certain fashion by all observers.
    b. a set of interrelated concepts for viewing and classifying marriage and family behavior.
    c. a statement about the relationship between two or more concepts.
    d. a logically and systematically interrelated series of propositions.

B
p. 014

15. The way in which social units are arranged, the interrelationship of the parts, and the pattern of organization, are all part of a families
   a. hermeneutics.
   b. social structure.
   c. developmental processes.
   d. social stratification system.

D
p. 015

16. Within a structural-functional frame of reference, functions were said to include
   a. what families do.
   b. what consequences or results occur.
   c. what is best for families to maximize success or happiness.
   d. both a and b of the above three.

A
p. 015

17. Parsons and Bales suggested that the basic and irreducible family functions are two. These include
   a. primary socialization of children and stabilization of adults.
   b. reproduction and child rearing.
   c. legitimate sexual outlets and nurturant socialization.
   d. economic interdependence and social acceptability.

A
p. 017

18. Macrofunctionalists would most likely be concerned with the analysis of
   a. large-scale systems and institutions.
   b. individual families.
   c. group dynamics.
   d. both b and c above.

C
p. 018

19. According to conflict theory, conflict
   a. is a threat to society and marital stability.
   b. can be avoided through clearly separated groups of "haves" and "have nots".
   c. is an assumed and expected part of all systems and interactions.
   d. occurs most commonly between parents and their teenage children.

C
p. 018

20. The classical case for conflict theory stems from
   a. George Herbert Mead.
   b. Charles Darwin.
   c. Karl Marx.
   d. Talcott Parsons.

A
p. 019

21. According to a social conflict perspective, the family
   a. promotes and maintains inequality based on ascription rather than achievement.
   b. serves as a haven from a hostile world.
   c. is a key system in eliminating racial and ethnic conflict.
   d. does all of the above three.

B
p. 020

22. The use of participant observation, life history accounts, and personal documents such as diaries is most consistent with
   a. quantitative analysis.
   b. a phenomenological approach.
   c. a social conflict model.
   d. Skinnerian behaviorism.

C
p. 021

23. As used by a symbolic interactionist, the concept role refers to
   a. behavioral expectations wrapped up in a set of rules.
   b. behaviors attached to a given status.
   c. behaviors developed in relationship interaction.
   d. all of the above three.

C
p. 023

24. Social exchange theory rests on the assumption(s) that
   a. exchanges must be equal for marriages to survive.
   b. most gratification's of humans are derived from sexual and intimate relationships.
   c. new relationships are entered into because they are expected to be rewarding.
   d. all of the above three are true.

D
p. 024

25. Peter Blau's theory of exchange, in contrast to that of George Homans, maintains that
   a. humans react to stimuli based on external reinforcements.
   b. actual behavior is the focus of rewards and punishments.
   c. distributive justice is the key to satisfying exchanges.
   d. social exchanges are creative and subjective processes.

C
p. 025

26. The major conceptual tools for the time analysis involved in the developmental frame of reference is the
   a. developmental tasks and social maturity.
   b. manifest and latent functions.
   c. family life cycle and life course.
   d. fair exchange and distributive justice.

A
p. 027

27. A basic assumption(s) of a feminist frame of reference is that
   a. the personal is political.
   b. women are superior to men.
   c. women need to have a single vision of reality to be successful in the current system.
   d. all of the above three are basic assumptions.

A
p. 030

28. Which of the following is not perceived by Sprey as an alternative to current mainstream family theorizing.
   a. macro orientations.
   b. hermeneutics.
   c. critical social science.
   d. feminist theorizing.

Fill-in Questions

1. A _____ approach to family study would focus on social groups, social systems, and social institutions.

2. _____ is the study of how an individual influences other individuals or groups and how others influence the individual.

3. When a proposition is formulated for empirical testing, it is considered a _____.

4. A set of logically interrelated propositions that <u>explain</u> a process or set of phenomena is a _____.

5. _____ functions are both intended and recognized.

6. The person who provided the classic case for social conflict theory was _____.

7. _____ theory assumes that as we receive benefits from others, we are under an obligation to reciprocate by offering benefits in return.

8. The major concept used by a developmental approach in dealing with family change and differences over time is the _____.

9. A _____ frame of reference focused on women as different from men, less privileged than men, and oppressed by men.

10. _____ refers to the act or theory of interpretation that takes us beyond the methods of science.

Fill-in answers	Page Reference
1. sociological	2
2. Social psychology	7
3. hypothesis	12
4. theory	13
5. Manifest	15
6. Karl Marx	18
7. Exchange	23
8. family life cycle or life course	25
9. feminist	27
10. Hermeneutics	30

Short Answer/Essay Questions

1. Define <u>family</u>. Who is included or excluded? On what basis? How is a family group different from the institution we call the family?

2. What is meant by a sociobiological or biosocial approach to family study? Give examples.

3. How does a sociology of the family differ from a social psychological or psychological approach to the family?

4. The text lists a number of uses of family sociology. State two of them and indicate how they are useful.

5. Differentiate: a) concepts from variables; b) propositions from hypotheses; and c) theories from conceptual frameworks.

6. What is meant by the statement "family conditions can be improved by supporting certain types of structural arrangements rather than focusing on the individuals who suffer the consequences"? Explain. Give examples.

7. Contrast a functionalist family perspective with a conflict family perspective. Describe at least three different assumptions of the two approaches to understanding families.

8. In what way(s) is a symbolic interactionist perspective at odds with Skinnerian radical behaviorism?

9. Illustrate how exchange theory is applicable to understanding (a) mate selection, (b) husband-wife relationships, and (c) sexual relationships.

10. Develop a family life cycle model. How many stages does it have? How are the stages determined? What difficulties/problems exist with your scheme?

11. Discuss the basic assumptions of feminist though that are presented on page 27. Are there areas of social life in which women are not oppressed? Is the personal always political? Must wome have a double view of reality to be successful?

12. Define and discuss hermeneutics, critical social science, and feminist theorizing as alternatives to mainstream family theorizing.

CHAPTER 2

True/False Questions

F
p. 037

1. Institutionalized behavior within the family system refers to any behavior that occurs in families.

F
p. 038

2. Societies (including Sweden) in which traditional family patterns are not strong demonstrate a high level of negative outcomes for children.

T
p. 039

3. In sociological analysis, the basic units of a marital or family system are interrelated statuses rather than persons.

F
p. 039

4. Family groups differ from family systems primarily in terms of their size and importance.

T
p. 040

5. The text presents the argument that without primary group relationships such as exists in families, survival itself would be doubtful

T
p. 042

6. Black males and black females are more likely to be single (never married) than white males and white females.

T
p. 042

7. Over the past few decades, the percentage of those who have never married has risen sharply.

F
p. 044

8. Married/nonmarried differences in happiness appear to have increased over the past two decades.

T
p. 044

9. Mortality data indicate that married people in Japan can expect to live about 15 years longer than their single counterparts.

T
p. 044

10. Throughout the world, married men and women tend to live longer and experience better health than the never-married, widowed, or divorced.

T
p. 044

11. In the United States, being single and female is asociated with a higher level of education, higher median income, and higher level of achievement.

T
p. 045

12. Throughout the world, monogamy is the only form of marriage that is universally recognized and is the predominant form even within societies where other forms exist.

F
p. 045

13. Polygyny refers to several or many husbands.

F
p. 046

14. Among religious groups in the United States, only the United Methodist and Episcopal churches permit clergy to conduct same-sex marriages.

T
p. 047

15. In Nigeria, more stable marriages exist with two wives than in marriages with more than two wives.

F
p. 048

16. Women in polygynous marriages tend to have a higher rate of pregnancy than do women in monogamous marriages.

F
p.048

17. Data from Nigeria suggest that co-wives in polygynous marriage, (1) do not get along very well, and (2) resent their husbands taking on an additional wife.

T
p. 049

18. Jealously among plural wives seems to be more frequent than jealously among co-husbands.

F
pl 050

19. Polyandry seems to be most prevalent in those few societies that practivce male infanticide.

T
p. 052

20. All conjugal families are nuclear families but not all nuclear families are conjugal families.

F
p. 053

21. Today, many family scholars agree that the family in the United States is basically an isolated nuclear unit.

F
p. 055

22. The joint family is so termed because of the bonding that results between families upon the marriage of a child from each kinship grouping.

T
p. 058

23. Narrative accounts of incest perpetrators revealed that almost all of them defined incest as love and care and their behavior as considerate and fair.

T
p. 061

24. The Middletown study suggests, as do most other kinship studies, that women are more active than men in maintaining kinship ties.

T
p. 062

25. The study of Middletown provided little evidence of any weakening of kin ties in American society in the past fifty years.

A

p. 037

1. According to the discussion in the text
   a. institutionalized behavior is patterned and predictable.
   b. extramarital intercourse would be one example of institutionalized behavior.
   c. institutionalized behavior is any behavior that occurs within an institution.
   d. all of the above three are true.

A

p. 039

2. The basic units of a marital or family system are
   a. statuses.
   b. persons.
   c. interpersonal relationships
   d. intimate networks.

C

p. 039

3. In contrast to systems, family and marital groups are composed of
   a. norms.
   b. beliefs.
   c. people.
   d. abstractions.

B

p. 040

4. In contrast to a primary group, the characteristic most likely to exist in a secondary group is
   a. face-to-face contact.
   b. goal orientation.
   c. smallness of size.
   d. all are characteristics of secondary groups.

D

p. 042

5. Over the past several decades, the percentage of those who have never married has
   a. decreased for all age groups but the elderly.
   b. increased for the younger age groups (under 30) but decreased for those above age 30.
   c. increased for women but not for men.
   d. increased for men and women of all age groups.

C

p. 044

6. Single females, compared to married ones, are more likely to
   a. have a lower educational level.
   b. have a lower median income.
   c. be more nontraditional on sex roles.
   d. have or be all of the above.

7. Marriage seems to
   a. impede the career advancement of females.
   b. decrease the life expectancy of males and females.
   c. decrease the level of happiness of males but not of females.
   d. have little effect on anything when compared to single people.

8. Monogamy means
   a. more than one husband or wife is impossible.
   b. one husband is married to one wife at any one time.
   c. there can be only one husband married to more than one wife
      or only one wife married to more than one husband.
   d. all of the above in different cultures.

9. A sex ratio of 75 would tell us
   a. that three-fourths of all people have sex.
   b. that there are 25 more females for every 75 males.
   c. that it is a good situation for females to be in if they want to
      find an available mate.
   d. nothing since you can't have a ratio with one number.

10. A study by Welch and Glick of polygyny in fifteen African
    countries, found
    a. that most (more than half) of the men in these countries had
       two or more wives.
    b. that most polygnists had three wives rather than two, four or more.
    c. that a high sex drive was the determining factor in the number of
       wives a husband had.
    d. none of the above were found.

11. Which of the following can not include more than one wife.
    a. polygamy
    b. polygyny
    c. polyandry
    d. group marriage

12. Polyandry
    a. is more likely to be fraternal than polygyny is likely to be sororal.
    b. is only about half as common as polygyny.
    c. tends to lead to a greater fragmentation of land holdings than
       does polygyny.
    d. tends to exist most frequently where male infanticide is practiced.

D
p.051

13. The Oneida community
    a. began in California as a result of the gold rush.
    b. was an experimental polyandrous group.
    c. believed in marital chastity thus failed to survive.
    d. believed in a spiritual equality for all persons: materially, socially, and sexually.

B
p. 052

14. According to the text, the conjugal family
    a. is identical to the nuclear family.
    b. most include a husband and a wife.
    c. is exemplified by a single parent and child.
    d. is exemplified by a brother and sister.

C
p. 052

15. The most precise term for a family consisting of yourself, your spouse, and your children would be a
    a. consanguine family.
    b. family of orientation.
    c. family of procreation.
    d. nuclear family.

C
p. 053

16. Families in the United States today are perhaps most accurately described as
    a. isolated nuclear families.
    b. modified consanguinal families.
    c. modified extended families.
    d. joint kin networks.

D
p. 054

17. Which statement is false about families in Sweden. Families have
    a. a low rate of marriage.
    b. a small household size.
    c. a high rate of cohabitation.
    d. a low rate of family dissolution.

A
p. 055

18. The rural Irish family best illustrates and serves as an example of a _____ type of family structure.
    a. stem
    b. joint
    c. modified extended
    d. matrilineal

A
p. 055

19. A major difference between joint families and stem families is that joint families
    a. share a common treasury.
    b. pass on all property to the eldest son.
    c. provide a home and economic support for the father as he grows old.
    d. consist of the eldest son and his sisters' families.

C
p. 056

20. The tsu in traditional China referred to
    a. the wives of Chairman Mao.
    b. a plague that killed millions of children in the 1920s.
    c. a clan including all persons with a common surname descending from a common ancestor.
    d. the belief that sons are subordinate to fathers and daughters are subordinate to mothers.

B
p. 058

21. Interviews with more than 900 adult women in San Francisco, revealed that if a stepfather was the principal figure in the women's childhood years, incestuous abuse occurred with about
    a.   2 percent of the women.
    b. 17 percent of the women.
    c. 36 percent of the women.
    d. 54 percent of the women.

B
p. 059

22. Of the following, which one was not listed in the text as a basic function of extended kin.
    a. property holding and inheritance.
    b. nurturant socialization of children.
    c. housing and the maintenance of residential propinquity.
    d. affection, emotional ties, and primary relationships.

C
p. 060

23. Patterns of descent take on a special importance to many conflict theorists because
    a. intergenerational conflict is the key source of change.
    b. matrilineal systems give preferential treatment to females.
    c. social inequality is perpetuated through successive generations.
    d. many females assume their husbands name.

151

D
p. 061

24. The study of Middletown revealed that
    a. keeping in touch with relatives was more a duty than a pleasure.
    b. men appeared to be the primary "kinkeepers" in maintaining
kin contacts.
    c. kin ties weakened considerably over the past fifty years.
    d. residence patterns showed a surprising degree of local
       concentration.

C
p. 062

25. Pauline Boss and Jan Greenberg indicate that not knowing who
    is in and out of the family system is a key source of stress.
    They term this
    a. kinship ambivalence.
    b. network confusion.
    c. family boundary ambiguity.
    d. family kinship dysfunction.

Fill-in Questions

1. A family _____ consists of interrelated statuses such as husbands, wives, and children.

2. The family as a _____ group serves as the basic socializing agent and the basic instrument of social control.

3. A second spouse, not existing simultaneously with the first (such as a remarriage), is often referred to as _____.

4. The number of males per 100 females is known as a _____.

5. Polygamy was described as having various forms. When one male has several wives, all of whom are sisters, this is known as _____.

6. The _____ community of New York State practiced groups marriage.

7. A _____ family must include a husband and a wife.

8. The nuclear family in which you were born and reared (consisting of self, siblings, and parents) is termed a _____.

9. Families that extend beyond the nuclear family are _____.

10. Perhaps the most widely accepted norm among kinship relationships around the world is a taboo on _____.

11. Except for name, the system of descent most prevalent in the United States is primarily _____.

12. The residence pattern in which the newlywed couple establish a residence separate from either set of parents is known as _____.

Fill-in answers	Page Reference	Fill-in answers	Page Reference
1. system	39	7. conjugal	52
2. primary	40	8. family of orientation	52
3. sequential or serial monogamy	45	9. extended	55
4. sex ratio	46	10. incest	57
5. sororal polygyny	47	11. bilateral or bilineal	60
6. Oneida	51	12. neolocal	61

Short Answer/Essay Questions

1. Differentiate institutionalized behaviors in families from behaviors that are noninstitutionalized. Give examples.

2. Differentiate a family group from a family system. Illustrate.

3. What is the relationship between marital status and (a) suicide, (b) happiness, and (c) health. Explain.

4. In addition to monogamy, around the world the number of partners or spouses in a marriage takes a variety of forms. List three. Then select any one, give an example, and explain it's occurrence.

5. Jealousy among co-wives seems to be more frequent than jealousy among co-husbands. What reasons exist to explain this?

6. What are the arguments for or against families in the United States being isolated nuclear units.

7. What is meant by an extended family. Describe two specific varieties or types of extended family forms.

8. Most societies place a taboo in incest. What is incest? Who is the most frequent victim? Compare behaviors of fathers versus stepfathers. Explain why differences exist between the two.

9. Feminist theorists focus primarily on sexual (female/male) inequalities in lineage inheritance patterns. What is the significance of lineage systems and inheritance patterns to conflict theorists?

10. What are the basic functions of kinship groupings? What does research indicate about the fulfillment of these in the United States?

CHAPTER 3

True/False Questions

T
p. 070

1. The mass media, particularly television, has been shown to feature far more males than females and more young people than elderly persons.

T
p. 071

2. An increasing body of evidence suggests a general converging of values and behaviors among major religious-ethnic groups in the United States.

F
p. 071

3. Differences between particular religious groups such as Protestants or Catholics are more pronounced than differences between churchgoers and non-churchgoers.

T
p. 072

4. Adult offspring raised in households with high marriage happiness and both biological parents were found to have higher religiosity than those raised with negative parental relationships or in stepfamilies.

T
p. 072

5. Evidence suggests the "Families that pray together, stay together."

F
p. 073

6. The state and/or federal government only provides support to families; it does not regulate them.

F
p. 074

7. The hidden curriculum in education refers to integrating topics such as safe sex and contraceptive education into courses such as biology, literature, and sociology.

F
o. 075

8. According to Marxian conflict theorists, the family system is the key to understanding all inequality within society.

T
p. 077

9. Evidence tends to suggest that women in all cultures, even if employed, do most of the housework.

T
p. 077

10. The gender gap in housework is higher among married persons than among the never-married, divorced, or widowed.

T
p. 078

11. Wives' perceptions of the fairness of the division of household labor was found to be a better predictor of marital conflict than was the actual extent of inequality.

F
p. 080

12. Feminists and conflict theorists view housework as one of the few areas that approach gender equality, particularly when the female is employed outside the home.

F
p. 081

13. Numerous studies over the past two decades lend support to the hypothesis that women with jobs outside the home are generally happier and more satisfied with their lives than full-time homemakers.

F
p. 082

14. National surveys of female homemakers show that the majority (actually more than 75 percent) have negative or at least ambivalent opinions of housework.

T
p. 082

15. More than half of all women in the paid labor force are married (in contrast to being single, widowed, or divorced).

F
p. 083

16. While there has been a dramatic increase in the labor force participation of women, very little change has occurred in the percentage of employment of mothers with preschool-age children.

T
p. 085

17. Generally, an inverse relationship exists between the husband's level of income and the likelihood the wife will be employed.

T
p. 086

18. In Sweden, women who supervise day care are paid on roughly the same wage scale as men in industrialized employment.

T
p. 086

19. A direct relationship exists between women's economic attainment and an unmarried status.

F
p. 087

20. There seems to be little impact of pregnancy and first birth on female employment in that about 90 percent of employed women return to their full-time jobs within a year or two after birth.

T
p. 089

21. A female employment factor that affects marriage negatively, is that of holding a job not traditionally occupied by women.

T
p. 089

22. Regarding female employment, data from the United States and other countries suggest that the greater the number of hours worked as well as wage increases, increase the probability of marital instability and divorce.

T
p. 091

23. A review of twenty-seven studies covering thirty years, concluded that a wife's employment status alone has little or no effect on marital adjustment.

F
p. 092

24. Studies seem to indicate that financial difficulties surrounding the employment of husbands tends to increase marital communication and marital adjustment.

T
p. 093

25. Amish family organization is centered around the husband and his word is regarded as final.

F
p. 093

26. Women are more likely then men to gain status and identify through their work and employment.

F
p. 094

27. Evidence suggests a major trend toward full-time male homemakers.

T
p. 095

28. Women in professional positions are far more likely than comparable men to be single, married with no children, or divorced.

F
p. 097

29. Women have been found to respond <u>less</u> positively than men to a dual-earner arrangement.

T
p. 098

30. Couples in commuter marriages were found to be more dissatisfied with family life and companionship from their partner than couples not in commuter marriages.

Multiple-Choice Questions

A
p. 069

1. A macro-level analysis that link family systems with other systems
   a. are frequently ignored in family studies.
   b. are complex and more difficult to study than micro-level analysis.
   c. rarely are useful or of practical significance.
   d. simply do not exist.

D
p. 069

2. The most widely used form of media on a day-to-day basis appears to be
   a. the internet.
   b. the radio.
   c. the newspaper.
   d. television.

A
p. 071

3. A pathbreaking study by Lenski in the 1950s found that
   a. Catholics were less likely than Jews or Protestants to see personal autonomy as a key value in preparing children for life.
   b. Catholics were more mobile than Protestants and Catholics.
   c. Catholic, Protestant, and Jewish families all produced about the same number of children.
   d. all of the above three were found to be true.

D
p. 071

4. Compared to churchgoers, non-churchgoers are more likely to
   a. be conservative on issues related to sexuality.
   b. be married.
   c. stress traditional gender roles.
   d. have fewer children.

A
p. 073

5. Which of the following is not a government program that provides support for families.
   a. AARP
   b. AFDC
   c. OASDI
   d. All of the above are government programs.

C
p. 074

6. The "hidden curriculum" in education refers to
   a. not informing parents as to what their children are doing in school.
   b. contraceptive and sex education built into classes such as literature.
   c. teaching obedience to rules, respect for authority, and moral responsibility
   d. courses created, but not publicized, for slow learners or special children.

B
p. 075

7. The system viewed by Marxian conflict theories as the key to understanding inequality is the
   a. family system.
   b. economic system.
   c. educational and religious systems about equally.
   d. political system.

C
p. 076

8. The status of female homemaker or housewife
   a. has high economic value.
   b. has traditionally been categorized as a low status position.
   c. has no set qualifications.
   d. is highly researched today (when compared with women in paid employment).

B
p. 077

9. Which statement is true about gender and housework.
   a. husbands of employed wives do almost as much housework as do their wives.
   b. divorced and widowed men do substantially more housework than their married male counterparts.
   c. employed women and full-time homemakers spend about the same amount of time doing housework.
   d. all but (a) above are true.

D
p. 080

10. In both the United States and Australia, the chore/task that most approached equality between men and women was in
    a. working in the yard.
    b. grocery shopping.
    c. washing dishes.
    d. disciplining/punishing children.

A
p. 080

11. According to family sociologist Jessie Bernard, when wives are compared with husbands
    a. "his" marriage is considerably better than "hers"
    b. wives report less marital dissatisfaction and have generally happier marriages.
    c. doing housework revitalizes both wives and husbands.
    d. very few differences exist in marriage happiness or household tasks.

B
p. 082

12. The women who least likely favor housework seem to be
    a. traditional wives and mothers.
    b. college-educated, younger wives.
    c. full-time employed mothers on welfare.
    d. lower educated, middle-age wives.

C
p. 082

13. In 1997, the percentage of all females age 16 and over in the paid labor force was closest to
    a. 30 percent.
    b. 45 percent.
    c. 60 percent.
    d. 75 percent.

D
p. 083

14. The most dramatic increase over the past 30 years in the paid employment of mothers occurred among
    a. divorced women with the youngest child age 6-17.
    b. divorces women with the youngest child under age 6.
    c. married women with the youngest child age 6-17.
    d. married women with the youngest child under age 6.

D
p. 084

15. Mothers contributing all of more to the total family income are more likely than other employed women to
    a. remain employed.
    b. exit from employment more slowly.
    c. return to employment more quickly after childbirth.
    d. all of the above three.

C
p. 085

16. Results from North Carolina suggest that the best predictor of a wife's employment was
    a. the financial amount the job paid.
    b. motherhood.
    c. husband's emotional support.
    d. a college education.

C
p. 085

17. A woman's entry into the paid work force is related to
    a. a full-time employed husband.
    b. a husband with high income.
    c. the absence of a husband.
    d. all of the above are related to women entering the paid work force.

A
p. 086

18. According to the text's discussion of wife-mother employment
    a. singleness may be less a "marriage reject" for many employed single women than one of "rejecting marriage."
    b. an inverse relationship exists between the economic attainment of a woman and an unmarried status.
    c. the higher the woman's income the more likely she is married.
    d. none of the above three are true.

B
p. 087

19. The discussion in the text on employed women and children revealed that
    a. maternal employment has been shown to have nothing but a detrimental impact on dependent children.
    b. both sons and daughters of mothers with high status jobs do better in school and are more likely to enter college than those mothers not employed.
    c. pregnancy and first birth has little impact on female employment.
    d. daughters of working mothers have more traditional gender role concepts.

D
p.088

20. The one area that children of mothers employed full time seemed to do more poorly on than mothers not employed was
    a. behavior problems.
    b. insecurity.
    c. sociability.
    d. compliance.

B
p. 089

21. Female employment seems to affect a marriage
    a. positively as the number of hours worked increases.
    b. negatively if a wife holds a job not traditionally occupied by women.
    c. negatively simply by being employed.
    d. in none of the above ways.

160

C
p. 093

22. The discussion in the text on employed husbands and fathers indicates that
   a. for men in American society, marriage (more than work) typically defines their worth, their success or failure, and their major source of identity.
   b. job insecurity tends to improve marital communication and adjustment.
   c. in the gender role socialization process, more emphasis is placed on getting ahead in a job for men in comparison to women.
   d. for men, unemployment has little effect on personal functioning.

A
p. 095

23. Data on dual-careers seems to suggest
   a. problems related to stress, role strain and work overload.
   b. women in the professions are far more likely than comparable men to be married and with children.
   c. professional women represent a significant proportion of those employed in the elite professions.
   d. all of the above are true.

D
p. 095

24. Data on latchkey children suggest that
   a. the numbers are far greater than popularly believed (perhaps as many as 6 or 7 million).
   b. most are such for more than two hours each day.
   c. they are the children of low-income, single parents who cannot afford stable child care arrangements.
   d. none of the above three are true.

B
p. 098

25. Couples in commuter marriages, compared to single-residence dual career couples
   a. were less satisfied with their life work.
   b. reported less overload and a less stressful life-style.
   c. had less appreciation for spouse and family life.
   d. all of the above are true for couples in commuter marriages.

Fill-in Questions

1. The mass media serves as a powerful force in reinforcing _____ , widely held beliefs (often false) about the character and behavior of all members of a group.

2. A government program that provides medical care for the elderly is known as _____ .

3. The _____ curriculum in schools refers to teaching civic responsibility, obedience to rules, punctuality, and respect for authority.

4. Marxian conflict theories tend to view the _____ system as the key to understanding all inequality.

5. Jessie Bernard argues that when wives are compared with husbands, _____ marriage is considerably better than _____ marriage.

6. The sharpest increase in the labor force participation rates of mothers by marital status are _____ women with children ages _____ .

7. The country in the Western world with the highest percentage of women in the paid labor force and the lowest percentage of full-time homemakers is _____ .

8. The work overload situation brought about by dual-careers and family work is referred to by Fox and Nichols as the _____ .

9. "Self-care" children who come home after school to an empty house until a working parent gets home are known as _____ children.

10. _____ marriages are those in which the husband and wife live separately and work in different cities but maintain visiting and other patterns of communication.

Fill-in answers	Page Reference
1. stereotypes	70
2. medicare	73
3. hidden	74
4. economic	75
5. his/her	80
6. married/6 and under	83
7. Sweden	86
8. time crunch	95
9. latchkey	95
10. Commuter	98

Short Answer/Essay Questions

1. In what ways does the mass media influence families? What stereotypes tend to be portrayed?

2. List any three findings on the linkage that exists between the family system and the religious system. How would you explain their existence?

3. How does the amount of time spent in doing housework differ (a) between men and women, and (b) between employed women and full-time homemakers?

4. Jessie Bernard wrote that "in truth, being a housewife makes women sick." What does research suggest about the "truth" or accuracy of that quote?

5. Contrast changes in the labor force participation rates of (a) married and divorced women, and (b) those with children under age six and those between the ages of six to seventeen.

6. Discuss the effects, if any, of maternal employment on children.

7. Discuss the effects, if any, of maternal employment on a marriage.

8. What are the most common problems that existing literature suggests about dual-career marriages? Select one from your list and discuss how it is handled.

9. How do husbands and wives differ in their reactions to commuter marriages?

10. What does research suggest about the quality of life of commuting couples compared to single-residence dual-career couples?

CHAPTER 4

True/False Questions

F
p.. 104
1. In the United State, quite literally, people are free to marry anyone they choose.

F
p. 105
2. Exogamy and heterogamy are identical in that each focuses on marriages between persons that are in any way different.

T
p. 195
3. An operational definition is one in which variables are defined according to the way they will be measured.

T
p. 106
4. The mixed marriage rate for individuals may be equal to but will never be greater than the mixed marriage rate for marriages.

T
p. 107
5. Generally, the smaller the group, the greater the probability of intermarriage.

T
p. 107
6. Research supports the idea that intermarriage is more likely to occur when people reside in heterogeneous communities.

F
p. 109
7. Over the past several decades, the general trend around the world in age at marriage appears to be slightly lower or to remain constant.

F
p. 110
8. Since 1900, there has been a gradual but steady increase in the median age at first marriage for both men and women in the United States.

T
p. 111
9. The difference in the age at marriage increases as the age at first marriage for the male increases.

T
p, 111
10. Evidence suggests that women married to younger men tend to live longer than expected while women married to older men tend to die sooner than expected.

F
p. 112
11. There is widespread agreement among researchers that age homogamous marriages are much more stable than marriages among couples from age-dissimilar categories.

F
p. 113
12. A marriage squeeze resulting in a restricted field of eligibles for black males is one explanation for a lower rate of marriage for blacks than for whites.

T
p. 114

13. No state in the United States has a legal age at marriage for females that is older than that for males.

F
p. 115

14. An increase in divorce rates in the United States over the past thirty years can be explained by the changes in median age at marriage.

T
p. 117

15. Educational endogamy has been found to be more important than social-class origins in partner selection.

F
p. 117

16. Hypogamy is more prevalent than hpergamy.

T
p. 119

17. The mating gradient results in an excess number of unmarried women at the higher classes and unmarried men at the lower classes.

F
p. 119

18. Evidence suggests that religion has become a more significant factor than education in mate selection.

T
p. 120

19. Protestants tend to not only marry other Protestants but tend to marry those who share the same denominational affiliations.

F
p. 121

20. Research tends to support the idea that interfaith marriages have a secularizing effect on children, that is, children who are weakly religious.

T
p. 122

21. There is no evidence to support the idea of a pure race or the idea that racial mixtures result in biologically inferior offspring.

F
p. 122

22. A Gallop Poll in the early 1990s revealed that a substantial majority of respondents (72 percent) said they approve of marriage between Blacks and whites.

F
p. 123

23. Most interracial marriages in the United States occur between blacks and whites.

T
p. 125

24. Black males tend to marry white females more frequently than white males marry black females.

T
p. 127

25. Offspring of cross-racial/cross-ethnic marriages have not been found to have lower self-esteem or feel more alienated than their single heritage peers.

Multiple-Choice Questions

A
p. 104

1. The tendency for people to marry someone similar to themselves more often than could be due to chance is referred to as
   a. assortive mating.
   b. Russian roulette.
   c. mesalliance.
   d. hypergamy.

B
p. 105

2. The incest taboo is an example of
   a. assortive mating.
   b. an exogamous norm.
   c. the mating gradient.
   d. hypogamy.

C
p. 105

3. Operational definitions are those in which
   a. variables operate effectively in accomplishing their intended purpose.
   b. variables are defined clearly, precisely, and without double meanings.
   c. variables are defined according to the way they are measured.
   d. the definition does not vary across class or culture.

B
p. 107

4. In terms of group size, the larger the group relative to other groups
   a. the greater the sex ratio.
   b. the lower its intermarriage rate
   c. the less the marriage squeeze.
   d. all of the above three factors take place.

D
p. 110

5. As of 1997, the median age at first marriage in the United States was
   a. 20.2 for males, 18.0 for females.
   b. 22.2 for males, 20.0 for females.
   c. 25.2 for males, 23.0 for females.
   d. 27.2 for males, 25.0 for females.

C
p. 111

6. Which of the following is generally not an explanation as to why males tend to marry younger females.
   a. the excess of males through the early twenties.
   b. the mating gradient.
   c. the increase in the employment of women.
   d. the males slower physiological maturity.

D
p. 113

7. The marriage squeeze describes
   a. an obscene gesture if performed in public.
   b. the combined consequences of hypogamy and hypergamy.
   c. a recommended expression of affection for newlyweds.
   d. an imbalance between the number of males and females in the prime marriage ages.

C
p. 113

8. The imbalance between the number of males and females in the prime marriage ages is known as
   a. the mating gradient.
   b. the sex ratio.
   c. the marriage squeeze.
   d. hypergamy.

A
p. 114

9. In the United States, the legal control of age at marriage and divorce lies with the
   a. individual states.
   b. federal government.
   c. local community.
   d. the Supreme Court.

D
p. 116

10. The norm segregation theory of mate selection combines norm similarity with
    a. physical attraction.
    b. social class.
    c. race.
    d. geographical proximity.

B
p. 117

11. Educational endogamy has been found to
    a. occur about as often as would be expected simply by chance.
    b. have increased between the 1930s and the present.
    c. to be of less importance than social class origins.
    d. only exist for those who have not completed high school.

B
p. 117

12. Mesalliance refers to marriage
    a. to the wrong person.
    b. with a person in a lower social position.
    c. between an older person and a much younger one.
    d. between incompatible men and women.

D
p. 117

13. From an exchange theory perspective, the social advantages of hypergamy seem to exist primarily for the
a. high status man.
b. low status man.
c. high status woman.
d. low status woman.

D
p. 119

14. The mating gradient suggests that
a. norm segregation theory explains mesalliance.
b. women seek out lower status men and men seek out higher status women.
c. intermarriage is more frequent than intramarriage.
d. none of the above apply to the mating gradient.

A
p. 119

15. The mating gradient works to prevent marriage for many
a. highest status women and lowest status men.
b. highest status men and lowest status women.
c. middle status men and middle status women.
d. promiscuous men and unattractive women.

C
p. 119

16. National data suggest that religious endogamy in the United States is lowest for
a. Jews.
b. Protestants.
c. Catholics.
d. the religiously devout irrespective of religion.

B
p. 120

17. In regard to religious endogamy, Glenn believes that marriage has become
a. an increasingly sacred institution.
b. very largely as secular institution.
c. more religiously endogamous.
c. irrelevant.

A
p. 120

18. Interfaith marriages are most frequent among
a. those religiously less devout.
b. Protestants.
c. Catholics.
d. Jews.

A
p. 121

19. According to the discussion in the text on interracial marriage
a. these restrictions remain the most inflexible of all the partner selection boundaries.
b. these marriages are not accepted socially anywhere in the world.
c. most countries permit them legally but only under stringent age and class conditions.
d. they are illegal in more than half of the states in the United States.

168

D
p. 122

20. Removal of the legal prohibition against interracial marriage in the United States came in
    a. 1776 with the signing of the Declaration of Independence.
    b. 1863 with the freeing of slaves.
    c. 1954 in the Brown vs. Board of Education decision.
    d. 1967 with a Supreme Court decision that declared a Virginia law unconstitutional.

B
p. 122

21. Based on a Gallop Poll in the early 1990s, which statement is true about the approval of interracial marriage?
    a. whites were more likely to approve than blacks.
    b. males were more likely to approve than females.
    c. those over age 50 were more likely to approve than those under age 30.
    d. the less educated were more likely to approve than the higher educated.

C
p. 123

22. Black-white intermarriages in the United States
    a. have been decreasing over the past decade.
    b. are considerably more common than other types of interracial marriages.
    c. most frequently involve a black husband and white wife.
    d. all of the above are true.

A
p. 123

23. Which statement is true about black-white intermarriage in the United States.
    a. the fewest interracial marriages occur in the south.
    b. the majority occur between a white male and a black female.
    c. the increase in black-white intermarriage over the past 25 years had been less than the increase of all marriages.
    d. none of the above are true.

C
p. 127

24. Compared to their single-heritage peers, children of cross-racial/cross-ethnic marriages have been found to
    a. have lower self esteem.
    b. feel more alienated.
    c. have better relations with single-heritage groups than single-heritage groups have with one another.
    d. both (a) and (b) above are true.

B
p. 127

25. The trend in interracial marriage over the past several decades is
    a. downward.
    b. upward.
    c. about the same with little change up or down.
    d. very unstable with increases in some decades and decreases in others.

Fill-in Questions

1. The tendency for people to choose those like themselves more often than could be due to chance is known as _____.

2. The marriage of persons who are outside of specifically defined social groups is an _____ one.

3. In research, _____ definitions are used to define variables according to the way they are measured.

4. The number of males per 100 females is the _____.

5. Throughout the 1990s in the United States, the median age at marriage for males has been about _____ years older than for females.

6. The _____ describes the effects of an imbalance between the number of males and females available for marriage.

7. Jane married Joe who lived in her neighborhood. This is an example of residential _____ .

8. One explanation for residential propinquity has been the _____ theory that suggests people of similar expectations, values, and social categories reside in homogamous clusters.

9. The pattern of mesalliance where a female marries into a higher social stratum is known as _____ .

10. The tendency for women to seek out similar or higher status men and for men to seek out similar or lower status women is called the _____.

Fill-in answers	Page Reference
1. assortive mating	105
2. exogamous	105
3. operational	105
4. sex ratio	107
5. two	110
6. marriage squeeze	112
7. propinquity	115
8. norm segregation	116
9. hypergamy	117
10. mating gradient	119

Short Answer/Essay Questions

1. Are you free to marry anyone you choose? Discuss restriction that societies place on the selection of an intimate partner.

2. What factors foster intermarriage? Indicate the conditions which would increase the likelihood that your children would marry exogamously.

3. In the last three decades in the United States, the median age at marriage for both males and females has increased by about four years. Why? How is this increase explained?

4. It appears that women married to younger men tend to live longer than expected while women married to older men tend to die sooner than expected. Why? Explain.

5. What is the marriage squeeze? Show how this effects males and females differently as birth rates rise or fall?

6. It is known that hypergamy is more prevalent than hypogamy. What does this mean? Why does it exist?

7. Define the mating gradient. Give examples. How does this affect the marriage chances of certain men and women?

8. Describe the probability of interfaith marriage by religious affiliation and intensity of belief. What does research suggest about the consequences of interfaith marriages on (a) the marriage, and (b) the children of that marriage?

9. What makes a marriage interracial? It is based on biological differences, skin color, ethnic heritage, or some other factors? Explain.

10. How do black-white marriages differ by sex? How can these differences be explained?

CHAPTER 5

True/False Questions

F
p. 133   1. The love between a couple about to be married appears to be one of the few factors found in all societies to be important in partner selection.

T
p. 133   2. The text suggests that in Japan today, about 25 to 30 percent of all marriages are arranged.

F
p. 134   3. According to the insert on arranged marriage in China, today more than two-thirds of marriages partners in China are arranged by parents or a third party.

T
p. 134   4. Research suggests that there are virtually no societies where individuals have total free choice of mate.

T
p 135   5. Love is socially constructed therefore it takes on different meanings and importance according to the social context.

F
p. 136   6. Recent research suggests that instinct is far more important than traditionally thought in bringing two people together for marriage or intimate relationship.

F
p. 137   7. Evidence appears to suggest that in partner selection, boys seek out someone like their mothers and girls seek out someone like their fathers.

F
p. 138   8. There is a general consensus among researchers that people tend to marry those whose needs complement their own.

F
p. 138   9. One of the most fruitful approaches to the study of mate selection has been to analyze the personality traits of each spouse.

F
p. 139   10. Value theory tends to support the idea that opposites attract.

F
p. 140   11. With role theory, the focus of attention is on behaviors and attitudes that are characteristic of the person, irrespective of the situation.

T
p. 142   12. Exchange theorists argue that if one person does all the giving and the other does not reciprocate, the relationship is likely to terminate.

T
p. 143   13. Murstein's sequential theory of mate selection described dyadic pairing as a three stage process involving (1) stimulus, (2) values, and (3) roles.

T
p. 145

14. The male-female game of partner selection has been described as one in which the goal of the male was sexual intimacy while the goal of the female was commitment.

T
p. 146

15. Dating has been described as a United States invention that emerged after World War I among college students and other young adults.

T
p. 147

16. Studies suggest that scripts for dating today maintain the traditional dominant/subordinate relationship between the sexes.

T
p. 148

17. The Principle of Least Interest suggests that the person most interested in a relationship is in a position to be dominated or even exploited.

F
p. 148

18. Bundling was a practice in the New England Colonies and among the Amish to provide sexual privacy and compatibility for engaged couples.

T
p. 149

19. Pinning was a form of steady dating that existed over the past few decades among various fraternity/sorority members on college campuses.

T
p. 149

20. Some form of engagement has existed in almost every society in the world.

F
p. 151

21. Census data reveals that the majority (over 50 percent) of nonmarital cohabitors are young people under the age of 25.

T
p. 151

22. In most western nations, cohabitation is increasing while first marriage and remarriage rates are declining.

T
p. 153

23. Jan Trost notes that in Sweden couples who see themselves as a married couple but keep separate housing arrangements is increasing in incidence and may soon be regarded as a social institution.

F
p. 155

24. Couples who cohabited before marriage reported higher quality marriages than married couples who did not cohabit premaritally.

T
p. 156

25. Over the past 20 years, both the number and proportion of unmarried heterosexual cohabitors age 65 and over has declined.

Multiple-Choice Questions

A

p. 133

1. Of the following, which would be the most important factor in the selection of mates in societies with arranged marriages?
   a. the dowry or size of the bride's price.
   b. the compatibility of the couple getting married.
   c. the ability of the daughter to produce children, particularly male children.
   d. all are equally important.

C

p. 133

2. In regard to mate or partner selection in Japan, the text suggests that
   a. arranged marriage was common in the past but few (about 5 percent) exist today.
   b. in existing arranged marriages, the couple does not meet until their wedding day.
   c. a " marriage drought" exists making it very difficult to find desirable partners.
   d. all of the above are true.

B

p. 134

3. According to the discussion in the text of arranged marriage,
   a. families that arrange marriages are generally unemployed or poor.
   b. most cultures exert some type of pressure on who marries whom, that is, total free choice is practically nonexistent.
   c. as traditional cultures are exposed to Western cultures, the arrangement of marriages becomes more entrenched in the normative system of those cultures.
   d. all of the above are true.

C

p. 135

4. The text says that love is
   a. a many splendored thing.
   b. universal in partner selection.
   c. socially determined.
   d. all of the above three.

D

p. 136

5. Instinct as a factor in partner selection appears to be
   a. one of the few important universal criteria, that is, is found everywhere.
   b. supported by recent research as one of the most important factors.
   c. basic in men but less important in women.
   d. nonexistent not only in mate selection but in humans generally.

C

p, 137

6. The Freudian idea that a female wants to marry a male much like her father is called.
   a. penis envy.
   b. castration anxiety.
   c. the electra complex.
   d. the oedipus complex.

B
p. 137

7. Jack Sprat could eat no fat, his wife could eat no lean, could be described as an example of marital
   a. propinquity.
   b. complementarity.
   c. neurosis.
   d. mesalliance.

A
p. 138

8. The theory of complementary needs has been
   a. found to have little empirical support.
   b. proven to exist in all societies.
   c. shown to be most important where marriages are arranged.
   d. developed by Eshleman, the author of the text.

D
p. 138

9. A value theory of mate selection suggests that
   a. when persons share similar value orientations, interpersonal attraction is reduced.
   b. opposites attract.
   c. the interaction of persons with similar values is boring and nonrewarding.
   d. interpersonal attraction is facilitated when persons share similar value orientations.

A
p. 141

10. According to the discussion of role theory found in the text
    a. this explanation appears to be conceptually more justifiable as an explanation of mate selection than the individualistic theories.
    b. roles and personality needs are one and the same thing.
    c. role consensus or agreement is unrelated to marital satisfaction.
    d. the role itself is as important as the consensus of the partners in regard to the role.

C
p. 142

11. An exchange theory of mate selection would assume
    a. people tend to overlook costs when they are in love.
    b. individuals with similar values and roles will make the best partners.
    c. the behavior of socialized persons is purposive and goal oriented.
    d. all of the above three statements are true.

B
p. 143

12. Murstein sees dyadic pairing as a three stage sequence involving
    a. attraction, love, and sex.
    b. stimulus, values, and roles.
    c. instincts, interactions, and intimacy.
    d. complementary needs, interpersonal development, and exclusivity. that is, commitment.

D
p. 146
13. The partner selection process in the United States has been compared
   in the text to a
   a. boxing match where each gets hit, fakes moves, and hits back.
   b. race which has a beginning, a process, and an end.
   c. school where each is taught new ideas and behaviors.
   d. game which has rules, goals, and strategies.

A
p. 146
14. The social norm described for the female in the dating game was to move
   the relationship toward
   a. commitment.
   b. equality.
   c. sexual intimacy.
   d. cohabitation.

B
p. 146
15. An analysis of published advertisements about what females and males were
   looking for in dating partners, revealed that females sought
   a. older mature men and marriage.
   b. financial security and longer-term relationships.
   c. physical appearance and sexual partners.
   e. companionship, loyalty, and integrity.

C
p. 148
16. The purpose of bundling in the Amish courtship system was to
   a. determine sexual compatibility.
   b. determine fertility.
   c. provide privacy for young people.
   d. test will power and ego strength.

B
p. 149
17. In colonial days, the announcement of intent to marry was made public by
   a. the male and female wearing a big E (signifying engagement)
   b. the posting of banns.
   c. a party put on in the town square by the females parents.
   d. the female wearing a vale that covered her face.

C
p. 149
18. During the Colonial period in America, the function of banns was to
   a. get young people together in a public place.
   b. set the young couple up in housekeeping.
   c. publicly announce the intent to marry.
   d. serve as a bride-price or dowry.

A
p. 151
19. According to the discussion in the test of nonmarital heterosexual cohabitation
   a. in 1997, there were about 4.1 unmarried couple households in the United
      States.
   b. this lifestyle is primarily the domain of young people and college students.
   c. this behavior is quite unique to the United States.
   d. all of the above three are true.

B
p. 151

20. According to census data, the greatest number of nonmarital cohabitors are
    a. under age 25.
    b. age 25 to 34.
    c. age 35 to 63.
    d. over age 65.

A
p. 151

21. In most western nations, the rate of
    a. unmarried cohabitation is increasing while rates of first marriage and remarriage are declining.
    b. unmarried cohabitation is increasing but so are rates of first marriage and remarriage.
    c. unmarried cohabitation is increasing but rates of first marriage and remarriage remain about the same.
    d. unmarried cohabitation is decreasing while rates of first marriage and remarriage are increasing.

B
p. 153

22. Jan Trost notes that in Sweden, what he labels LAT, is increasing in incidence among couples. LAT refers to
    a. leaving and telling.
    b. living apart together.
    c. lying about taxes.
    d. letting anything transpire.

D
p. 154

23. Studies reveal that cohabiting couples
    a. are more traditional in gender-role behavior than married couples their age.
    b. have intercourse nearly as frequently than married couples.
    c. report higher quality marriages after cohabiting.
    d. are nearly twice as likely as daters to be physically abusive.

A
p. 311

24. The relationship between cohabitation and marital stability appears to be that
    a. couples who cohabit before marriage have higher marital dissolution rates.
    b. couples who cohabit before marriage report higher quality marriages.
    c. cohabitation is an effective training ground for marriage.
    d. both (b) and (c) are true.

D
p. 313

25. The legal case of Marvin versus Marvin was significant in changing cohabitation laws because it
    a. guaranteed meretricious spouses one-half of the property acquired during the cohabiting relationship.
    b. emphasized the need for a written contract between cohabitants.
    c. reaffirmed common law practices of legally recognizing a relationship as marriage after seven years.
    d. set a precedent by defining the value of a woman's services for purposes of property settlement.

Fill-in Questions

1. A/an _____ theory claims that partner selection is innate and unlearned. It also closely linked to a genetic similarity explanation.

2. The _____ complex is the Freudian idea that women will select a man with the characteristics of her father.

3. Robert Winch developed the theory of _____ that suggests we select partners not on homogamous factors but on characteristics of opposites or at least differences.

4. An _____ theory of mate selection examines the transactions, bargaining, and attempts to maximize gains and minimize costs.

5. _____ theory was the idea of Murstein who saw mate selection as going through a three-stage sequence involving a mutual stimulus, similar values, and consensus of roles.

6. The _____ suggests that the person least interested in continuing a relationship is in a position to dominate the other.

7. An Amish courtship practice where males and females shared a bed with a board separating them was known as _____.

8. In colonial days, the announcement to marry was accomplished by _____.

9. Unmarried couples who share a household is known as nonmarital _____ or consensual unions.

10. Jan Trost nots that married-like couples in Sweden are increasingly keeping separate housing units. This phenomenon he terms LAT which means _____.

Fill-in answers	Page Reference
1. instinct	136
2. electra	137
3. complementary needs	137
4. exchange	141
5. SVR (stimulus - value - role)	143
6. principle of least interest	147
7. bundling	148
8. posting of banns	149
9. cohabitation	150
10. living apart together	153

Short Answer/Essay Questions

1. Using a world wide perspective, contrast the variables or conditions important in the selection of a mate depending on whether it arranged or based on "free choice". Why are they different?

2. What is meant by the social construction of love. Explain.

3. Explain what is meant by individualistic explanations of partner selection. What are they? Why do they appear to have little empirical support?

4. Explain the theory of complementary needs. Does research evidence support it? Why or why not?

5. List and describe three sociocultural explanations of partner selection. How does each differ from individual explanations?

6. Explain Willard Waller's "Principle of least interest". What does it mean? To whom does it apply?

7. Bundling was described in an insert as a mate selection process. What is bundling? Where has it occurred? What functions did/does it perform?

8. How prevalent is nonmarital cohabitation? What changes are occurring?

9. How do cohabiting couples differ from noncohabitors? To what extent is cohabitation a "trial" marriage?

10. Discuss the issue of cohabitation and the law. Do/should couples who live together have the same legal rights as married couples in terms of benefits, property rights, or separation settlements? Why or why not?

CHAPTER 6

True/False Questions

T
p. 163

1. Ira Reiss suggests that the basic reason for the universal importance of human sexuality is that it encompasses the elements of physical pleasure and self-disclosure.

T
p. 163

2. There are no societies that do not regulate and control the sexual behavior of its members.

F
p. 163

3. In the United States, the Judeo-Christian doctrine embodies a hedonistic orientation toward sex.

T
p. 165

4. Research by Masters and Johnson suggested that, in general, women tend to respond faster, more intensely, and longer to sexual stimulation then men.

T
p. 165

5. Researchers such as Kinsey as well as Masters and Johnson suggest that the anatomic structures most essential to sexual response and orgasm are nearly identical in the human male and female.

F
p. 166

6. Social network theory remins us that sexual behavior involves a dyad who decide between them what they will or will not do.

F
p. 168

7. Sexual scripting is designated at the moment of birth or when one is identified as male or female.

F
p. 170

8. In a study of sexual scripting at an Australian University, female students who had gone topless on the beach had lower self-esteem and lower body image than those who had not gone topless.

T
p. 171

9. The text contends that apart from fantasies that exceed possibilities, beliefs are likely to be more conservative than actual behaviors but that more permissive behaviors tend to change the beliefs.

F
p. 172

10. Findings support the hypothesis that individuals brought up in sexually conservative homes have less premarital heterosexual involvement than those from more liberal home environments.

T
p. 173

11. Data from China suggests that teenage sexual attitudes are quite conservative but much more permissive toward respecting others who have engaged in premarital sex.

F
p. 173

12. Both strict and lenient parental disciplinary patterns were found to result in lower levels of sexual permissiveness with the highest permissiveness among adolescents with moderately strict parents.

T
p. 175

13. The decision to engage in sexual activity is seldom influenced by school based clinics or sex education programs.

F
p. 176

14. The author argues for and research supports the idea that teaching students to "just say no" is an extremely effective method of preventing intercourse and pregnancy.

T
p. 176

15. Data from college students revealed that men reported experiencing more pleasure and less guilt from their first sexual intercourse experience than did women

F
p. 177

16. From a global perspective, the key question for females is whether premarital intercourse will be permitted not whether unmarried motherhood will be allowed.

T
p. 179

17. While there has been a steady decline in negative attitudes toward premarital sex since the 1970s and 1980s, a greater percentage of both males and females now consider promiscuity immoral or sinful.

F
p. 179

18. The text suggests that the so-called "sexual revolution" in the United States has encompassed premarital, extramarital, and homosexual relations.

F
p. 180

19. High-risk sexual behavior refers to frequent sexual relationships with your partner using only the rhythm method of contraception.

F
p. 183

20. Research suggests that sexually transmitted diseases, particularly AIDS, have been influential in pushing college students toward sexual abstention.

T
p. 183

21. African-Americans and Hispanic-Americans account for reported cases of AIDS far in excess of their proportion in the United States population.

F
p. 184

22. The third year of marriage is clearly the time of most frequent marital coitus.

T
p. 185

23. Cohabiting relationships were said to be "sexy relationships" since they report intercourse frequency at a higher level than sexually active marrieds or singles.

F
p. 185

24. Research results from couples between the ages of 60 and 80 reveal that the majority had little interest in sexual activity.

T   25. Catholic women under age 45 are as likely to use contraceptive practices as
p. 188   non-Catholic women.

F   26. The greater the degree of role segregation that exists between husband and
p. 188   wife, the more gratifying the interpersonal sexual relationship.

F   27. Studies suggest that sexual adjustment is the keystone to marital adjustment.
p. 189

F   28. Evidence supports a trend toward a convergence of attitudes and behavior
p. 190   between men and women regarding extramarital sex.

T   29. In Japan, men have considerable sexual freedom while women face harsh
p. 190   restrictions in sexual activities.

T   30. Married women who belonged to no religious group were found to be twice as
p. 191   likely to be less sexually exclusive as those who belonged to a religious group.

Multiple-Choice Questions

A   1. In a sociological analysis of human sexuality, Ira Reiss
p. 163   a. defines sexuality as erotic and genital responses produced by the cultural
          scripts of a society.
              b. demonstrates that some societies have very few regulations on human
                 sexual expression.
              c. suggests that certain sexual behaviors such as extramarital intercourse are
                 taboo in nearly all known societies.
              d. does all of the above three.

B   2. Kinsey, as well as Master's and Johnson, would likely agree that
p. 165   a. male/female differences in sexual behavior are primarily based on biological
                 or genetic factors.
              b. men and women are basically homogamous in the physiologic responses to
                 sexual stimuli.
              c. biological components can be ignored in studying and understanding sexual
                 responses and behaviors.
              d. males respond faster and more intensely to sexual stimulation than do
                 females.

C   3. The process by which persons learn and internalize their sexual self-concepts,
p. 167   values, attitudes, and behaviors, is termed
              a. genderization.   c. sexualization
              b. anatomic socialization.   d. symbolic interaction theory

D
p. 168

4. William Simon and John Gagnon conceptualize the outcome or product of sexualization in terms of
   a. sex roles.
   b. gender roles.
   c. cultural scripts.
   d. sexual scripts.

A
p. 168

5. According to Simon and Gagnon, the process of sexualization or the formulation of sexual scripts does <u>not</u> include
   a. training in human anatomy and reproductive functions.
   b. cultural scenarios.
   c. interpersonal context-specific behavior.
   d. intrapsychic processes.

B
p. 168

6. The instructional guides that exist at the level of collective life are termed
   a. interpersonal scripts.
   b. cultural scenarios.
   c. intrapsychic scripting.
   d. internal dialogue.

C
p. 171

7. Female students in Australia who had gone topless at a beach
   a. agreed that their behavior was sexual and exhibitionist.
   b. tended to view toplessness as appropriate on or around the beach area.
   c. had a higher self-esteem than those who had not gone topless.
   d. felt that the community and most of their peers disapproved of their behavior.

A
p. 171

8. People tend to be most conservative in
   a. what they believe to be proper sexual behavior.
   b. their personal sexual behavior.
   c. what they perceive members of the same sex to be doing.
   d. what they fantasize.

C
p. 171

9. Factors that preceded or took place prior to a given sexual activity are termed
   a. precursors of sexual behavior.
   b. preludes to sexual behavior.
   c. antecedents of sexual behavior.
   d. initiation rituals.

D
p. 172

10. Studies suggest that teenagers sexual and contraceptive behavior is strongly influenced by
    a. parental attitudes toward premarital sex and contraception.
    b. parent-child communication about sex and contraception.
    c. both a and b above.
    d. neither a or b above.

11. The relationship between parental disciplinary practices and sexual permissiveness of adolescents seems to suggest higher levels of adolescent permissiveness from
    a. both strict and lenient parents.
    b. moderately strict parents.
    c. only lenient parents.
    d. all of the above, that is, no relationship appears to exist.

12. Studies of adolescents suggest that sexual involvement is directly related to
    a. peer influences.
    b. parent-child communication.
    c. parental attitudes toward premarital sex.
    d. all of the above.

13. Studies of the impact of formal sex education programs on premarital sexual behavior indicate that they are directly related to
    a. greater use of contraceptives.
    b. a greater incidence of premarital sexual activity.
    c. more permissive attitudes toward premarital sex.
    d. a higher incidence of teenage pregnancy.

14. Premarital sexual intercourse is likely to increase
    a. as sex education increases.
    b. as an ability to separate intercourse from pregnancy increases.
    c. as parent-child sexual communication increases.
    d. under all of the above conditions.

15. Data from U.S. college students showed that whether the behavior was heavy petting, sexual intercourse, or oral-genital sex, the percentage that agreed that all three behaviors were acceptable during engagement was about
    a. one-fourth or 25 percent.
    b. one-half or 50 percent.
    c. three-fourths or 75 percent.
    d. nearly everyone, that is more than 95 percent.

16. According to the insert on sexual behavior in Sweden, research suggests that
    a. about 70 percent of both males and females believe it is acceptable for 15-year-old girls or boys to have sex with a steady friend.
    b. teen pregnancy is rare (less than 2 percent compared to about 11 percent in the U.S)
    c. nearly all respondents disapproved of a cohabiting person having intercourse with anyone other than their partner.
    d. all of the above three are true.

D
p. 179
17. The one sexual area where there may be a return to the 1970s is in regard to
    a. behaviors such as heavy petting rather than intercourse.
    b. negative attitudes toward premarital intercourse.
    c. positive attitudes toward masturbation and oral-genital sex.
    d. negative attitudes toward promiscuity.

B
p. 180
18. The Center for Disease Control reports that as of 1997, the number of reported AIDS cases in the United States was about
    a.   64,000.
    b.   640,000.
    c. 1,640,000.
    d. over 2.5 million.

D
p. 181
19. A study in Australia revealed that a primary reason for young people in the United States and around the world engaging in high risk sexual behaviors, such as the non-use of condoms, is because they
    a. deny the existence of an AIDS risk.
    b. think the partner should be responsible.
    c. are fatalistic, that is, life is full of risks and AIDS is simple another example.
    d. do all of the above. All three were primary reasons.

D
p. 182
20. Compared to low risk-takers, high risk-taking adolescents were found to have
    a. lower GPA's.
    b. more frequent alcohol consumption.
    c. a greater history of sexual and physical abuse.
    d. all of the above three.

C
p. 183
21. Groups that have reported cases of AIDS far in excess of their proportion in the United States population include
    a. African-Americans.
    b. Hispanic-Americans.
    c. both African- and Hispanic-Americans.
    d. neither African- and Hispanic-Americans.

A
p. 184
22. In regard to marital sexual activity, the Kinsey studies revealed that
    a. early in marriage, many husbands wanted coitus more than their wives but in the later years of marriage, many wives wanted coitus more than their husbands.
    b. the third year of marriage is clearly the time of most frequent marital coitus.
    c. declining coital frequency with age implies that sex becomes less important in marriage as time passes.
    d. for all couples, the frequency of sex increases with the length of time together.

B
p. 185

23. Most studies agree that in the United States, the frequency of marital coitus
    a. increases with age and length of time married.
    b. decreases with age and length of time married.
    c. shows tremendous variability with age and time with increases among those
       with higher income levels and decreases among those with lower income
    levels.
    d. no one knows how frequently coitus occurs in marriage at any age so all
       may be true.

C
p. 185

24. The frequency of sexual intercourse appears to be highest for
    a. those married more than ten years.
    b. those in their first year of marriage.
    c. cohabitors.
    d. the unmarried but in committed relationships.

D
p. 187

25. Research suggests that female coital frequency in marriage
    a. decreases with the amount of education of the wife.
    b. is negatively related to the effectiveness of contraception.
    c. increases with length of time married.
    d. is highest among career motivated women in paid employment.

B
p. 188

26. Compared to the working and lower classes, people from the middle and
    upper classes
    a. are less likely to engage in oral/genital contact.
    b. are more likely to enjoy their first sexual experiences.
    c. are less likely to react positively to masturbation.
    d. are not likely to do any of the above. All three are false.

D
p. 189

27. Regarding the relationship between sexual adjustment and martial
    adjustment, it appears that
    a. no one knows the relationship between the two.
    b. there is no relationship between the two.
    c. a good sex life will maintain an otherwise poor relationship.
    d. sexually inactive marriages are less happy than those that are sexually
       active.

A
p. 190

28. Lynn Atwater argues that several myths contribute to an unrealistic faith in
    sexual exclusivity in the United States. Among them is
    a. one person can and will supply all of anothers needs.
    b. marriage eliminates most sexual dysfunctions.
    c. sexual exclusivity in unnatural.
    d. there is only one right sexual partner for each of us.

C
p. 191

29. Of all the factors <u>Kinsey</u> examined, the factor more than any other that affected the incidence of extramarital coitus, particularly for females, was
   a. sexual deprivation.
   b. their sexual script.
   c. religious devoutness.
   d. sexual satisfaction in marriage.

B
p. 191

30. The most common justifications for extramarital relationships for women were
   a. sexual dimensions.
   b. emotional dimensions.
   c. extrinsic dimensions.
   d. none of the above were justifications for extramarital relationships for women.

Fill-in Questions

1. _____ theories of sexual behavior assume that without social restraints, everyone would engage in socially undesirable (deviant) sexual activity.

2. _____ or sexual socialization, is the process by which persons learn and internalize their sexual self-concepts, values, attitudes, and behavior.

3. The who, what, when, where, and why, that is the outcome of sexualization, has been termed _____.

4. Prevalence is the frequency of a sexual experience whereas _____ refers to the occurrence or nonoccurrence of a sexual experience.

5. Data suggest the so-called "sexual revolution" was real but has been restricted to _____ relations.

6. Sex with multiple partners with no use of protection against sexually transmitted diseases or unwanted pregnancies is referred to as _____ sexual behavior.

7. As of 1997, _____ Americans accounted for about forty-five percent of all reported cases of AIDS in the United States.

8. Human sexuality was brought into the public arena with the publication of the _____ studies in 1948 and 1953.

9. More than any other factor that Kinsey examined, _____ affected the active incidence of extramarital coitus, particularly for women.

10. Justifications for extramarital relationships included three dimensions: sexual dimensions, extrinsic dimensions, and _____ dimensions, the most common justification for women

Fill-in answers	Page Reference
1. Social control	164
2. Sexualization	167
3. sexual scripts	168
4. incidence	177
5. premarital heterosexual	179
6. high-risk	180
7. African	183
8. Kinsey	183
9. religious devoutness	191
10. emotional	191

Short Answer/Essay Questions

1. List various ways in which human sexuality is socially regulated?

2. How do biological theories differ from sociological theories of sexual behavior? Discuss the significance of biological factors and social factors in understanding female/male differences in sexual behavior.

3. What are the major ideas of and contributions made by social network theory and choice theory in our understanding of human sexuality.

4. Simon and Gagnon argue that sexual scripting must occur at three distinct levels. What are they? Describe each.

5. What does research indicate about the relationship between the sexual behavior of adolescents and (a) parent-child communication, and (b) parental discipline? Explain how each finding might be explained?

6. Many people believe that sex education should be taught in and belongs in the home. What are the arguments for and against this idea? What does research suggest about such an approach to sex education?

7. Describe changes in premarital intercourse for both males and females prior to 1980 and since 1980. How can these changes be explained?

8. List three examples of high-risk sexual behavior. Why do people engage in these types of behaviors?

9. Data suggest a probable increase in the frequency of both marital and nonmarital sexual activity over the past fifty years. If this is so, how might it be explained?

10. What does research suggest about intercourse and sexual activity (a) by age generally, and (b) for those over age 60?

11. What is the relationship between sexual adjustment and marital adjustment?

12. Justifications for extramarital sexual relationships were found to relate to three specific dimensions. What were they? Give examples of each.

CHAPTER 7

True/False Questions

F
p. 200
1. Studies indicate that the unmarried are generally happier and less stressed than the married.

T
p. 200
2. Compared to singles, married people are more likely to drink moderately, avoid risk-taking behavior and lead more scheduled life-styles.

T
p. 201
3. Public opinion polls show that more married men are satisfied with their marriages than are women.

F
p. 201
4. Noral Glenn and others present evidence that the institution of marriage in terms of stability and quality is as strong as ever.

T
p. 202
5. High sex ratios are positively associated with the proportion of women who marry and inversely associated with women's average age at marriage.

T
p. 202
6. Marriage rates are highest for white males and lowest for black females.

T
p. 204
7. Today, Sweden has the lowest marriage rate in the industrialized world.

F
p. 204
8. The 1996 marriage rate of 8.9 marriages per 1,000 population was the lowest rate ever recorded in the United States.

T
p. 205
9. Over half of all marriages take place on a Saturday.

T
p. 206
10. Authority refers to power that is prescribed and legitimate within a social/cultural setting.

F
p. 207
11. Power is inherent within certain persons.

F
p. 207
12. Wives have more power in marriages with extended family structures than in those with nuclear family structures.

T
p. 210
13. Karen Pyke contends that the employment of women is not considered a resource in some marriages and hence does not have a positive effect on marital power.

190

T
p. 211
14. Increases in egalitarianism were found to be associated with declines in reports of problems, disagreements, and divorce proneness in marriage.

T
p. 212
15. Evidence suggests that personal happiness and higher level of marital satisfaction occurs among spouses who perceive equity in their relationship.

T
p. 212
16. Steil concludes that a wife's dominance in decision making, while rare, is associated with a low level of satisfaction for both persons.

T
p. 213
17. Social attachments have been found to be stronger predictors of well-being than marital status.

T
p. 215
18. Findings consistently indicate that couples with high rates of self-disclosure experience greater marital satisfaction.

T
p. 216
19. Alan Booth and others, using longitudinal data from a large sample of married persons, found little support for the idea that an increase in religious activity lead to improved marital relations.

T
p. 217
20. From a relativistic point of view, a marital relationship is successful if it is preferable to any other alternative.

T
p. 218
21. Richard Udry suggests that the dimension of marital alternatives is a better predictor of marital disruption than are measures of satisfaction.

F
p. 218
22. Research suggests that the absence of marital conflict is a key positive factor in assessing the quality of the marriage.

F
p. 219
23. Economic distress such as income loss in the major depression or more recently in studies of economic hardship in agriculture were found to draw couples closer together.

T
p. 220
24. In comparing two generations of marriage cohorts in 1980 and 1992, Rogers and Amato found the younger cohort to report higher levels of marital conflict and marital problems than the older cohort.

F
p. 221
25. Studies that have attempted to show how marital quality changes over the life course suggest that quality declines rapidly in the first year or two but among marriages that survive, tends to increase sharply after the third year.

T
p. 221
26. Marital satisfaction appears to be higher in the later stages of the life cycle because of a relaxation of sex roles, the time a couple has together, and a greater sense of belonging.

27. Studies have consistently demonstrated that the presence of children in the family increases the marital happiness of the parents.

28. That parents want and have children is based on solid evidence that the psychological rewards of having children outweigh the costs or penalties, particularly in terms of their marriage.

Multiple-Choice Questions

1. By sex, marriage is
   a. a burdensome trap for men.
   b. a blessed state for women.
   c. no different for men and women.
   d. none of the above.

2. Women, when compared to men
   a. are more satisfied with their marriages.
   b. receive greater mental health benefits from marriage.
   c. provide emotional and other support in marriage.
   d. are, receive, and provide all of the first three.

3. Norvall Glenn reported a change in the relationship between being married and marital happiness. This change occurred primarily through an
   a. increase in happiness of never married males and a decrease in happiness of married females.
   b. increase in happiness of never married females and a decrease in happiness of married males.
   c. decrease in happiness of never married males and an increase in happiness of married females.
   d. decrease in happiness of never married females and an increase in happiness of married males.

4. An investigation of 111 countries showed that high sex ratios are positively associated with
   a. a woman's average age at marriage.
   b. the proportion of women who marry.
   c. male infanticide.
   d. polygyny.

5. Marriage rates are highest in the United States for
   a. black females.
   b. black males.
   c. white males.
   d. Hispanic males.

D
p. 204

6. Today, marriage rates in Sweden
    a. are increasingly reaching the highest level since the 1960s.
    b. are nearly identical to those in the United States.
    c. are unknown as cohabitation has replaced marriage.
    d. are the lowest in the industrialized world.

C
p. 204

7. Marriage rates appear to go down
    a. at the outset of a major war.
    b. in the immediate postwar years.
    c. under periods of economic recession and depression.
    d. under all of the above three conditions.

D
p. 204

8. Marriage rates over the past 20 to 30 years in the United States have tended to
    a. remain about the same.
    b. fluctuate wildly with no pattern or consistency.
    c. approach the highest level in about 30 years.
    d. approach the lowest level in about 30 years.

A
p. 204

9. The seasonal low for marriage in the United States tends to occur in
    a. January, February, and March.
    b. April, May, and June.
    c. July, August, and September.
    d. October, November, and December.

B
p. 205

10. Marriages are more likely to occur
    a. in August than any other month.
    b. on Saturdays than any other day.
    c. in Pennsylvania than any other state.
    d. in all of the above three. That is, all are true.

A
p. 206

11. The lowest marriage rates appear to be in states like
    a. West Virginia and Pennsylvania.
    b. Nevada and Hawaii.
    c. Tennessee and South Carolina.
    d. Michigan and Wisconsin.

C
p. 206

12. Power involves the crucial dimensions of
    a. male dominance and female submissiveness.
    b. wealth and property.
    c. authority and influence.
    d. caste and class.

C
p. 207

13. Mary Rogers makes several points about power. Which statement is true?
   a. power in inherent in a person.
   b. power is the exercise or acting out of the ability to influence others.
   c. power is linked to specific social systems and the positions occupied within that system.
   d. power involves all of the above three, that is, (a), (b), and (c) are true.

D
p. 207

14. Wives will have more power in societies
   a. where the marriages are based in nuclear rather than extended family structures.
   b. with matrilateral rather than patrilateral customs of residence and descent.
   c. with neither nuclear or matrilateral forms of organization.
   d. with both nuclear or matrilateral forms of organization.

A
p. 208

15. In their research involving conjugal power and decision making, Blood and Wolfe determined the area to be predominantly the wife's province was
   a. food expenditures.
   b. where to go on vacation.
   c. what doctor to have when someone is sick.
   d. what car to buy.

B
p. 208

16. Blood and Wolfe concluded that power in a marriage seems to be primarily related to
   a. religious intensity.
   b. resource availability.
   c. love and/or sex.
   d. strength.

C
p. 209

17. Hyman Rodman refined the resource theory of conjugal power relationships by adding an emphasis on
   a. hormonal differences between men and women.
   b. physical strength advantages favoring men.
   c. the cultural context in which decision making take place.
   d. in-born personality differences reflected in greater male aggression.

A
p. 210

18. In studying conjugal power, Mark Rank found that
   a. increments in wives' resources correlate positively with wives' influence, thus supporting the theory of resources argument.
   b. there is very little credibility for the theory of resources argument.
   c. increments in husbands' resources correlates positively with husbands' influence, thus supporting the greater resources leading to greater influence and power argument.
   d. as husbands and wives gain resources, men become less economically dependent upon their spouses.

A
p. 211

19. The highest levels of marital satisfaction appear to be when
    a. an egalitarian ethic exists.
    b. both husbands and wives hold traditional views regarding role performance.
    c. women recognize they hold most power in a relationship.
    d. husbands and wives both believe they are contributing more than the other to the relationship.

D
p. 213

20. The effect of the marriage laws of 1950 and 1980 in China was to
    a. eliminate many cases of polygamy.
    b. shift marriages from arranged to free choice.
    c. delay the age at marriage for young people.
    d. do all of the above three.

B
p. 214

21. The concept that generally refers to the achievement of one or more goals, such as permanence, companionship, and fulfilling the expectations of the community, is
    a. marital happiness.
    b. marital success.
    c. marital bliss.
    d. marital adjustment.

D
p. 216

22. Various components of Spanier's dyadic adjustment scale were described. The one not included was
    a. dyadic satisfaction.
    b. dyadic cohesion.
    c. dyadic consensus.
    d. dyadic complementarity.

B
p. 218

23. According to Udry, a better predictor of marital adjustment than measures of satisfaction is
    a. sexual adjustment.
    b. marital alternatives.
    c. conjugal power.
    d. whether or not divorce has occurred.

C
p. 219

24. Scanzoni, in writing about marital conflict, argues that
    a. equilibrium or stability is a necessary ideal.
    b. conflict is by nature, bad and unhealthy within marriage.
    c. conflict brings issues considered unjust into the open, thus is a positive force.
    d. both (a) and (b) are true.

D
p. 221

25. Studies suggest that marital/family satisfaction over the life course tends to
    a. change very little as it depends on each marriage.
    b. increase gradually with time as love grows.
    c. decrease gradually with time as routineness and familiarity set in.
    d. decrease continually through the childrearing years and then increase in the launching, middle and later years.

D
p. 221

26. The effect of children on the marital happiness of parents is
    a. highly inconsistent, with no clear effects emerging.
    b. to increase their happiness.
    c. to decrease their happiness in the launching years as they depart from the parental home.
    d. to decrease their happiness generally.

Fill-in Questions

1. A marriage _____ hypothesis suggests that marriage provides a buffer against physical and emotional pathology.

2. The country with the lowest marriage rate in the industrialized world and one of the highest mean ages at first marriage is _____ .

3. By day of the week, more marriages take place on _____ than any other day.

4. _____ is the ability of husband and wives to influence each other and affect their behavior.

5. The theory of _____ contends that those who have the attributes or possessions will have more power.

6. Spanier developed a _____ scale that focused on marital satisfaction, cohesion, consensus and affectional expression.

7. Udry suggests that the dimension of marital _____ appears to be a better predictor of marital disruption than are measures of satisfaction, adjustment, or marital quality.

8. Scanzoni, who argues that marital _____ is a positive force, suggests the need to get rid of the notion that equilibrium or stability is a necessary idea for all marriages.

9. Marital quality over the life course tends to follow the shape of a _____ trend.

10. Glenn argues that differences in marital success between midterm and long-term marriages are largely _____ differences of people within a specific time period.

Fill-in answers	Page Reference
1. protection	200
2. Sweden	204
3. Saturday	205
4. Conjugal power	206
5. resources	209
6. dyadic adjustment	216
7. alternatives	218
8. conflict	218
9. curvilinear or U-shaped	221
10. cohort	223

Short Answer/Essay Questions

1. What does research suggest about differences in happiness and differences in mortality between the unmarried and the married? Between men and women? Explain.

2. What types of factors tend to explain variations in marriage rates (a) over time, (b) between blacks and whites, and (c) from one state to another.

3. Define conjugal power. How can anyone get it?

4. Rodman, Rank, Pyke, and others modified and refined the resource theory of conjugal power. How did they modify it? Illustrate and give examples.

5. Discuss the relationship between equity in decision-making/family work and marital or relationship satisfaction. Is a feminist ideology of full equality compatible with marriage? Explain.

6. What did Jessie Bernard include as the three major dimensions of marital quality or adjustment? Explain each.

7. What is meant by the statement that "marital alternatives appears to be a better predictor of marital disruption than are measures of satisfaction?

8. Scanzoni has a chapter titled "Marital conflict as a positive force." How is that possible? Explain.

9. What appears to be the change in marital quality over the life course? How might these changes be explained?

10. Some precautionary notes are presented in regard to research that supports a curvilinear or U-shaped curve in marital adjustment over the life course. What are they? What is meant by a cohort effect?

CHAPTER 8

True/False Questions

T p. 229	1. According to the U.S. census, in addition to black and white, "other races" include American Indian, Eskimos, Filipinos, and others.
F p. 230	2. The census considers families and households to be identical if households consist of more than one person.
T p. 230	3. The average size of households in the United States has decreased quite consistently over the past 100 years.
T p. 231	4. The percentage of nonfamily households has increased quite dramatically (by about 300 percent) over the past 50 years
F p. 232	5. As 0f 1997, more than 25 percent of both women and men age 25-44 were divorced.
F p. 233	6. As of 1996, the median family income in the United States was about $26,000.
F p. 235	7. An ideal type refers to a type or form of family that is better, more desirable, and a preferred form.
T p. 235	8. Ideal types are hypothetical constructs of polar extremes.
F p. 237	9. The text takes the position that the family in the United States is not merely changing but is declining.
T p. 239	10. It is suggested that the most basic family issue presented in the first chapter centers around the meaning given to marriage and the family.
T p. 239	11. Both the sacred and the social meaning of marriage represent traditional norms but differ primarily in the source of authority.
T p. 240	12. Orderly replacement includes children being socialized basically to be duplicates of their parents.
F p. 240	13. Universal permanent availability refers to everyone always having sufficient money or resources to exist above a level of poverty.

T
p. 243

14. Families have not only lost functions but gained some as well.

T
p. 244

15. A 1997 Gallup poll revealed that men were perceived as more likely to dominate their wives than was true in a 1949 Gallup poll.

F
p. 245

16. Androgyny refers to a society with extremes of gender-role differentiation.

F
p. 246

17. Today in Sweden, fathers have assumed equal responsibility to mothers in the socialization and care of their children.

F
p. 247

18. The text suggests that the United States has one of the few completely open class systems.

T
p. 247

19. Traditionally, around the world, the predominant method of partner selection has been for arranged marriage rather than free choice of spouse.

T
p. 249

20. From a nontraditional perspective of love, if an individual is to grow and develop, one person cannot fulfill all intimacy needs of the partner.

T
p. 249

21. The traditional sacred view of marriage prior to the turn of the century held that even within marriage, sexual relations for the purpose of pleasure was taboo.

F
p. 251

22. The rhythm method of fertility control is totally inconsistent with nontraditional means of family size limitation.

T
p. 252

23. A social meaning of marriage and fertility control suggests that any means is legitimate that is effective, nonharmful, and agreeable to both spouses.

F
p. 253

24. A celestial marriage among Mormons is one in which a marriage cannot be dissolved until "death do us part."

F
p. 253

25. Legal grounds for divorce are determined by the federal government.

F
p. 254

26. Divorce rates reached levels in the 1980s unsurpassed only by those of the depression years of the 1930s.

T
p. 254

27. Norval Glenn claims that when people have the option or are encouraged to end unsatisfactory relationships, existing marriages become so insecure that rational people will not invest a great deal of time, energy, or money in such unions.

T
p. 254

28. Prior to the Civil War, remarriage was a right only of the innocent party.

Multiple-Choice Questions

B
p. 229

1. As of 2000, the total resident population of the United States was estimated to be about
   a. 200 million.
   b. 275 million.
   c. 350 million.
   d. 425 million.

D
p. 229

2. The term family, as used in census reporting, refers to
   a. anyone who occupies a separate housing unit.
   b. two or more people residing together who fulfill the functions of a family
   c. more than one generation of persons related by blood, marriage, or adoption.
   d. two or more persons related by blood, marriage, or adoption and sharing a household.

B
p. 230

3. According to census data, the average size of all families in the United States as of 1997 was closest to
   a. 2.69.   c. 3.69
   b. 3.19.   d. 4/19

A
p. 232

4. Men are more likely than women to be
   a. married or single.
   b. widowed or divorced.
   c. married or divorced.
   d. single or widowed.

C
p. 233

5. Census data indicates that as of 1997, about _____ percent of both males and females over age 55 married at some point in their lives.
   a. 85   c. 95
   b. 90   d. 99

B
p. 233

6. As of 1997, the percentage of men and women who were divorced in the maximum age category for divorce (ages 35-64), was closest to
   a. 4 percent of men, 7.5 percent of women.
   b. 14 percent of men, 17.5 percent of women.
   c. 24 percent of men, 27.5 percent of women.
   d. 34 percent of men, 37.5 percent of women.

D
p. 234
7. Which statement is true about changes in U.S. familis since 1980.
   a. fewer people are single.
   b. births to unmarried women have decreased slightly.
   c. the number of interracial marriages as remained about the same.
   d. none of the first three are true.

A
p.235
8. Ideal types represent
   a. the extremes or polar opposites of a continuum.
   b. an average or central tendency.
   c. an approved form or characteristic.
   d. all of the above three.

D
p. 235
9. An example of an ideal type would include
   a. fiftieth wedding anniversaries.
   b. a commitment to love until death do us part.
   c. sexually-bonded primary relationships.
   d. patriarchy - matriarchy.

A
p. 236
10. The concept ideal type was developed by
    a. Max Weber.
    b. Kari Marx.
    c. Charles Cooley.
    d. Talcott Parsons.

B
p. 236
11. Family change in China was greatly influenced by Friedrich Engels
    who advocated
    a. the elimination of abortion.
    b. male-female equality.
    c. polygamy.
    d. all of the above three.

B
p. 237
12. According to the text, issues in families exist because
    a. social problems are unavoidable.
    b. traditional and nontraditional sets of norms and values exist simultaneously.
    c. someone in a position of power says they exist.
    d. adequate funding is not available to resolve them.

C
p. 239
13. It is the authors belief that the most basic issue presented and the one
    which all others center around is
    a. masculine/feminine and male/female roles.
    b. social class and social mobility.
    c. the meaning and purpose of marriage and family.
    d. sexual and intimate relationships.

B
p. 239
14. A social meaning of marriage places the source of authority in
    a. some God or Supreme Being.
    b. the community, kin groups, or in what others think.
    c. each personal individual.
    d. all of the first three.

C
p. 239
15. An emergent norm concerning family organization suggests that
    a. marriage is sacred.
    b. divorce is a serious social problem.
    c. marriage becomes a personal rather than a kinship problem.
    d. all are emergent norms concerning family reorganization.

D
p. 240
16. The idea (Farber) that individuals are potentially marital partners to
    anyone at anytime was referred to as
    a. marriages made in heaven
    b. orderly replacement
    c. gender role equality
    d. none of the above three

C
p. 0240
17. Which one of the following is not a characteristic of universal
    permanent availability
    a. love rather than arranged marriages.
    b. a decline in premarital chastity or marital fidelity.
    c. power residing in the elderly or in a single source.
    d. pluralism.

B
p. 241
18. Since 1995, Wayne State University has provided employee benefits
    for same-sex domestic partners. To receive benefits, they must
    a. have lived together for two years or more.
    b. not be involved in any other domestic partnership or marriage.
    c. both be 25 years of age or older.
    d. do/have all of the above three things.

B
p. 242
19. In the 1930s William Ogburn argued that the dilemma of the modern
    family was
    a. the increasing divorce rate.   c. domestic violence and abuse.
    b. its loss of functions.   d. all of the above three.

A
p. 244
20. Compared to a 1949 Gallup poll, a 1997 poll has indicated that
    a. men are still perceived as considering a woman's looks over brains when
       considering marriage.
    b. full sexual equality has been achieved in housework.
    c. men are more likely than women to have a difficult life.
    d. both a and b were found to be true.

D
p. 245

21. Androgyny refers to a society that
    a. follows traditional norms.
    b. is based on biblical teachings.
    c. clearly differentiates the gender roles of men and women.
    d. none of the above.

A
p. 247

22. A classic representation of a closed mobility system where people remain in the position in which they were born is
    a. the caste system of ancient India.
    b. the urban ghettos of the United States.
    c. the communist system of China.
    d. none of the above represent closed mobility systems.

B
p. 248

23. The emergent norm concerning mate selection emphasizes
    a. nonmarital chastity.
    b. personal choice.
    c. same-sex partner selection.
    d. parents having the final say.

B
p. 249

24. The traditional <u>sacred</u> view of sexual relationships holds that
    a. sex is equally important to men and to women.
    b. a good wife "submits" to her husband as her duty.
    c. sex for purposes of pleasure is approved if confined to marriage.
    d. all of the above represent traditional sacred view.

A
p. 252

25. The most <u>nontraditional</u> norm pertaining to family size, family planning, and childbirth, suggests that
    a. family limitation is a personal choice.
    b. the primary responsibility for the prevention of a pregnancy lies with the women.
    c. the state should dictate what contraceptive methods are approved.
    d. people should adhere to religious teachings.

C
p. 254

26. The most likely reason for increasing divorce rates in the United States is due to
    a. changes in the law.
    b. supreme court decisions liberalizing alimony, custody, and property settlements.
    c. an increased social tolerance toward divorce.
    d. the decreasing church attendance of the U.S. population.

Fill-in Questions

1. According to the U.S. census, a _____ is a group of two or more persons related by birth, marriage, or adoption who reside together.

2. A _____ consists of all persons who occupy a housing unit.

3. As of the 1990s, census data suggest that about _____ percent of men and women over age 55 have been married at some point in their lives.

4. _____ are hypothetical constructs based on "pure" characteristics that represent polar extremes.

5. The text suggested that three basic meanings of marriage exist today. These include (1) personal or individualistic, (2) social, and _____ .

6. The concept _____ was used by Bernard Farber to illustrate behavior patterns and values that remain constant from one generation to the next.

7. _____ refers to a society that has an egalitarian emphasis and no gender role differentiation.

8. The classic example of a closed-system is that of the _____ system of ancient India.

9. The most traditional family norm, highly consistent with the sacred meaning of marriage, suggests the primary purpose of sex is for _____ .

10. _____ is a type of marital dissolution that, in effect, deems a marriage null and void.

Fill-in answers	Page Reference
1. family	229
2. household	230
3. 95	233
4. Ideal types	235
5. sacred	239
6. orderly replacement	240
7. Androgyny	245
8. caste	247
9. reproduction	250
10. Annulment	253

Short Answer/Essay Questions

1. How is the family defined by the U.S. census? How does a family differ from a household?

2. How does marital status differ by sex or gender and age? Explain.

3. What is an ideal-type construct? List a number of the functions it performs.

4. Describe the three meanings of marriage and family listed in the text. What differentiates one from the others?

5. Apply the traditional sacred norm, the traditional social norm, and the personal norm to an issue such as abortion. What impact does each perspective have on family life?

6. What is meant by universal permanent availability? Discuss some of its characteristics and the relevance it has for interpersonal relationships today.

7. An increasing number of companies/universities are recognizing same-sex domestic partners as eligible for benefits (review insert on p. 291). What are the pros and cons of such a policy? What criteria should the partners meet to be eligible?

8. Make a list of traditional family functions that have been "lost" by the family and assumed by another agency. What family functions have been "gained" by the family?

9. What is meant by social class? How is it determined? Differentiate an open-class society from a closed one.

10. The issue of partner selection was said to center around two questions. What were they? How do traditional and nontraditional norms differ on these two questions?

CHAPTER 9

True/False Questions

F
p. 260
1. Biological differences between persons and groups constitute racial categories and groups.

F
p. 261
2. As viewed by social scientists, a minority group is any that has fewer members than some other group in a society.

T
p. 262
3. Darker blacks have been found to be at a disadvantage and experience more discrimination than fairer-skinned blacks in the contemporary United States.

T
p. 263
4. Miscegenation refers to marriage and interbreeding between members of different races.

T
p. 263
5. For thousands of African Americans, emancipation brought with it freedom to die of starvation and illness.

T
p. 263
6. Following emancipation, the majority of African Americans remained on plantations as tenants of their former owners.

F
p. 264
7. Today, more than half of all African Americans live in the midwest and northeastern part of the United States.

F
p. 264
8. Southern African American immigrants to the north carried with them a "dysfunctional" family culture, especially when compared to northern born blacks.

F
p. 265
9. According to the Moynihan Report, the family was the institution that constituted the "one true source of strength and hope" in the black community.

F
p. 266
10. In any given year over the past several decades, the unemployment rate for black females was about equal to that of white females, but for black males was four times as high as that for white males.

T
p. 266
11. For the first time in the twentieth century, black women are participating in the labor force at lower rates than are white women.

F
p. 267
12. Largely as a result of "great society" and anti-poverty programs, the dollar gap between blacks and whites in the United States has narrowed (decreased) considerably over the past 20 years.

T   13. Broman has shown that black women are less likely to be satisfied with their
p. 268   marriages than white women.

T   14. The text suggests that strain in black marriages would be somewhat relieved
p. 269   if black men had better employment prospects and higher educational
attainment relative to black women.

F   15. Most studies tend to support the idea that when compared to whites, blacks
p. 271   have lower levels of self esteem and self-worth.

T   16. White males have higher rates of suicide than black males and white females
p. 271   have higher rates of suicide than black females.

F   17. The author of the text argues that the African American family is "falling
p. 272   apart" and basically incapable of adapting to the historical and contemporary
            conditions confronting it.

F   18. The number of female householders with no husband present is higher
p. 273   for blacks than for whites, hispanics, or asians.

T   19. The predominant pattern of black family life today is the matricentric female-
p. 273   headed one.

F   20. For African Americans or any other group, there is only a slight relationship
p. 274   between female-headed households and poverty.

T   21. A high sex ratio is associated with higher rates of marriage and lower rates of
p. 275   out-of-wedlock births.

F   22. African American unmarried women are much more likely to place their
p. 276   babies for adoption than are white women.

T   23. It appears that black leaders emerge from families in which both a husband
p. 277   and a wife are present.

F   24. Research suggests that affluent African Americans engage actively in black
p. 279   organizations.

T   25. Particularly at higher socioeconomic levels, when economic factors are held
p. 279   constant, black American families differ little from white American families.

Multiple-Choice Questions

C
p. 260

1. Racial groups are best classified according to
   a. biological and inherited physical traits.
   b. percentage of black ancestry.
   c. socially defined groups distinguished by inherited physical characteristics.
   d. cultural and ethnic differences.

B
p. 261

2. The key characteristic of minority groups to a social scientist is
   a. fewer numbers than exist in the larger groups of a society.
   b. subordination to the majority in power.
   c. not being white, Anglo-Saxon or Protestant (WASP).
   d. fewer exogamous marriages.

B
p. 261

3. As of 1997, there were about 34 million African Americans or about
   _____ percent of the U.S. population.
   a. 9.8
   b. 12.8
   c. 15.8
   d. 18.8

A
p. 262

4. The characteristic that appears to be most relevant in the transition of families from Africa to America is
   a. color.
   b. religion.
   c. social class.
   d. family size.

D
p. 263

5. The transition from slavery to emancipation, revealed that
   a. many male/female ties were severed.
   b. the transition was easiest for artisans, preachers, or house servants.
   c. most African Americans remained on plantations.
   d. all of the first three are true.

D
p. 264

6. The percentage of African Americans living in metropolitan areas in the early 1990s in the United States was about
   a. 41 percent.
   b. 55 percent.
   c. 71 percent.
   d. 86 percent.

C
p. 264

7. When compared with northern-born blacks, southern immigrants had
   a. fewer children living with two parents.
   b. less traditional family patterns.
   c. less unemployment, poverty, and welfare dependency.
   d. both a and b above.

B
p. 265

8. Some sociologists argue that the single most important variable to understanding African American families today is not race but
   a. place of residence.
   b. social class.
   c. religion.
   d. family structure.

A
p. 265

9. The classic <u>Moynihan Report</u> contended that among blacks
   a. the deterioration of the family was at the heart of problems in the community.
   b. the family was the one source of strength in a troubled community.
   c. problems in families would improve if the church and volunteer agencies would provide more needed services.
   d. gangs, drugs and sex were the major issues in the "tangle of pathology" that existed in communities.

B
p. 266

10. For many years the unemployment rate for both black males and females, when compared to the nation as a whole, was about
    a. the same or just slightly higher.
    b. double.
    c. three times.
    d. four times.

A
p. 268

11. As of 1996, the median income was highest for _____ families and lowest for _____ families.
    a. Asian; black and Hispanic
    b. Hispanic; white
    c. Hispanic; black
    d. white; black

C
p. 268

12. As of 1993, the percentage of blacks below the poverty level was about
    a. 9 percent.
    b. 19 percent.
    c. 29 percent.
    d. 50 percent.

A
p. 269

13. Over the past two decades, the percentage of African Americans who graduated from high school has
    a. increased considerably for both males and females.
    b. increased for females but decreased for males.
    c. decreased considerable for both males and females.
    d. shown only slight, if any, change.

D
p. 270

14. Generally, as economic conditions improve
   a. family disorganization decreases.
   b. conformity to the sexual mores of society increases.
   c. neither (a) or (b) occur.
   d. both (a) and (b) occur.

C
p. 271

15. Compared to white Americans, black Americans have been found to
   a. suffer from negative self-esteem and feelings of self-hate.
   b. have higher rates of depression and suicide.
   c. have positive self-esteem and lower rates of suicide.
   d. both a and b above are true.

A
p. 271

16. Suicide rates appear to be consistently highest for
   a. white males.
   b. black males.
   c. white females.
   d. black females.

C
p. 273

17. The greatest number of female-headed households with no husband present exists among
   a. African American families.
   b. Hispanic American families.
   c. white American families.
   d. Asian American families.

B
p. 273

18. For white, black, and Hispanic origin families, the average number of children under age 18 is highest for
   a. male householders.
   b. female householders.
   c. married couple householders.
   d. grandparent householders.

D
p. 275

19. According to Robert Staples, the most significant change in the African American family in the last thirty years is the
   a. increase in family income.
   b. increase in education among family members.
   c. increase in occupational prestige among males.
   d. proliferative growth of female-headed households.

D
p. 275
20. Regarding the sexual activity of black and white unmarried women
    a. white women initiate intercourse at an earlier age than black women.
    b. white women are less likely to marry than black women.
    c. white women are less likely to have an abortion than black women.
    d. the rates of nonmarital sexual activity of white and black women are
       converging

A
p. 275
21. Fewer marriages and more out-of-wedlock births among African Americans
    seem to be related to
    a. a shortage of black men.
    b. a higher socioeconomic status of black men.
    c. a higher educational status of black women.
    d. all of the above three.

B
p. 276
22. Which one of the following is true among unmarried women in the U.S.
    a. The number of babies born to unmarried women is higher for blacks
       than for whites.
    b. Twice as many African Americans as white Americans favored having
       unmarried mothers raise their babies themselves as opposed to adoption.
    c. Black women are much more likely to place their babies for adoption than
       white women (7 percent versus 3 percent)
    d. Both a and b above are true.

D
p. 277
23. According to the text, middle-class two-parent African American families
    are those
    a. in which the father plays a less dominant role.
    b. in which husbands tend to be less satisfied with life in their families.
    c. in which wives maintain dominance over family members.
    d. from which African-American leaders are most likely to emerge.

B
p. 278
24. Charles Willie described the patriarchal affluent family pattern as
    a. macho elitists.
    b. affluent conformists.
    c. wealthy dominators
    d. rich radicals.

D
p. 279
25. The most significant feature of affluent African American families in the United
    States seems to be the
    a. high rate of juvenile delinquency.
    b. tendency toward assimilation into mainstream African American society.
    c. extensive participation in the upper echelons of white society.
    e. a husband-dominant patriarchal power pattern.

Fill-in Questions

1. A _____ group is subordinate to a dominant group in terms of poser and prestige.

2. The largest racial/ethnic minority group in the United States is _____ .

3. With few exceptions, most Africans came to America under conditions of _____, a factor that made their mobility different from almost any other immigrant group.

4. Marriage and interbreeding between members of different races, especially blacks and whites in the United States, is known as _____ .

5. Some sociologists argue that the single most important factor in understanding the African American family today is not race, but _____ .

6. The "now-famous" _____ Report published about 25 years ago, concluded that the structure of family life in the African-American community constitutes a "tangle of pathology."

7. Generally, as _____ conditions improve, family disorganization decreases, family life becomes more stable, and aspirations for children become higher.

8. By race (black/white) and sex (male/female), suicide rates are highest for _____ and lowest for _____ .

9. Robert Staples indicates that the proliferative growth of _____ is probably the most significant change in the black family in the last thirty years.

10. The _____ family pattern is illustrated by what Charles Willie terms "affluent conformists."

Fill-in answers	Page Reference
1. minority	260
2. African American	261
3. slavery	262
4. miscegenation	263
5. social class	265
6. Moynihan	265
7. economic	270
8, white males - black females	271
9. Female-headed households	275
10. patriarchal	278

Short Answer/Essay Questions

1. What is the difference between a racial group, an ethnic group, and a minority group? Discuss the significance of each.

2. Three factors were cited as significant for African Americans in the transition from Africa to America. What were they? Describe each.

3. What differing patterns of African American family life emerged following emancipation from slavery. Explain.

4. Discuss sthe movement of African Americans from rural and southern areas. Where did they move to? Why? With what consequences?

5. What is the impact of economic conditions on African American family life? Discuss how employment, education, and income affect family stability, single parenthood, divorce, and the like.

6. What factors are suggested as explaining the positive self-concepts of African-Americans in spite of oppressive social and economic conditions?

7. Suicide rates are given as one index of depression and low self-esteem. How do they differ by race (black/white) and sex (male/female)? How can these differences be explained?

8. Three distinct patterns of African American family life have emerged from the social transitions described. What are they? Explain each.

9. What factors account for the increase in the percentage of African-American families that are headed be females?

10. It is often assumed that family stability and adequate socialization of children requires a two-parent married couple. Willie alerts us to overcome this ethnocentrism. What does he mean by this?

CHAPTER 10

True/False Questions

F
p. 285
1. The Hispanic American population includes one of every six people (16.7 percent) in the United States.

T
p. 285
2. The Mexican American population is larger than all other Hispanic American groups combined.

T
p. 285
3. The unemployment rate for Hispanic teenage males is about three times that of Hispanic adult males.

F
p. 286
4. The Mexican-American poverty rate is the highest among all Hispanic American groups.

T
p. 286
5. About two-thirds (64 percent) of all U.S. Latinos are native born.

T
p. 286
6. Only about one-third of Latinos were registered to vote in 1992 (compared to 64 percent of African Americans).

F
p. 288
7. Endogenous (as opposed to exogenous) causes of death explain the high rate of infant mortality for Puerto Ricans and Mexicans in contrast to Cubans and other Hispanic Americans.

T
p. 288
8. Nonmarital cohabitation or informal unions are higher among Puerto Rican American women than any other Hispanic American group.

T
p. 289
9. Puerto Rican women who engage in nonmarital cohabitation were found to be more similar to married women than single women in respect to childbearing behaviors and employment pursuits.

F
p. 290
10. Compadres are uncles and aunts of a newborn who agree to care for and raise the child should something happen to the parents.

F
p. 291
11. Studies suggest that husband dominance is not only prevalent among Mexican American men but is increasing in importance in the family.

T
p. 291
12. As of 1993, one-third of Mexican American families had five or more members.

T
p. 292

13. Cesar Chavez, a Chicano leader, formed the National Farm Workers Union and organized Mexican migrant farm workers.

F
p. 292

14. The Pacific Islanders can be considered to be an ethnic, racial, and minority group.

T
p. 294

15. Asian Americans are better educated and have a lower percentage in poverty than the U.S. population as a whole.

F
p. 296

16. "War brides" between Asian women (particularly Korean and Vietnamese) and American servicemen, make up more than half of all Asian American intermarriages.

F
p. 297

17. Asian children of intermarriages are more likely to have an American identity if their father, rather than their mother, is the Asian parent.

T
p. 297

18. The Asian American population more than doubled since 1980, making it the fastest growing minority population in the United States.

T
p. 298

19. Among Asian Americans, the lowest proportion of out-of-wedlock births existed among Korean women and the highest among Pacific Islanders.

T
p. 298

20. Asian American mothers born in the United States were about three times as likely to be unmarried as were mothers born elsewhere.

F
p. 299

21. Unlike Asian or Hispanic Americans who came from many nations, the Native American people are highly homogamous.

F
p. 301

22. In 1871, President Grant passed an education fund designed to assist American Indians in maintaining their native languages, preserve their religious ceremonies, and strengthen their family ties.

T
p. 301

23. Harjo notes that between 1969 and 1974, one-fourth to one-third of American Indian children were separated from their families and placed in non-Indian homes.

F
p. 303

24. Compared to most racial, ethnic, or minority groups, the role of the Native American grandparent in the lives of their grandchildren is one of restraint and distance.

T
p. 303

25. Eshbach, in studying Indian intermarriages, found that in some regions, more than three-fourths of married Indians were married to non-Indians.

Multiple-choice Questions

A
p. 284

1. An ethnic group is any group differentiated by
    a. a sense of identity based on a common national origin or cultural tradition.
    b. biological traits such as hair texture, skin color, or eye shape.
    c. ideologies that result from immigration and social mobility.
    d. similar patterns of prejudice and discrimination.

C
p. 285

2. As of 1997, Hispanic-Americans comprised about _____ percent of the total United States population.
    a. 5.5
    b. 8.1
    c. 10.7
    d. 13.3

D
p. 285

3. While the U.S. population increased by about 6.7 percent between 1990 and 1996, the Hispanic American population increased by about
    a. 14.5 percent.
    b. 18.5 percent.
    c. 33.5 percent.
    d. 26.5 percent.

B
p. 285

4. The largest Hispanic American group is
    a. Central and South American.
    b. Mexican.
    c. Cuban.
    d. Puerto Rican.

A
p. 286

5. The poverty rate among Hispanic American groups is highest for _____ and lowest for _____ .
    a. Puerto Rican; Cuban.
    b. Mexican; Central/South American.
    c. Central/South American; Puerto Rican.
    d. Cuban; Mexican.

C
p. 286

6. Three-fourths of all Latinos live in the following five states. They are
    a. Arizona, California, Florida, New Mexico, and Texas.
    b. California, New York, Massachusetts, Ohio, and Pennsylvania.
    c. California, Florida, Illinois, New York, and Texas.
    d. Arizona, California, Florida, New York, and Virginia.

B
p. 287

7. Two factors were said to account for 78 percent of the differences in child poverty between Puerto Ricans and whites. These two factors are
   a. language problems and lack of employment.
   b. employment patterns and female-headed households.
   c. single parenthood and inadequate welfare benefits.
   d. large family size and employment patterns.

D
p. 288

8. Exogenous mortality rates for Puerto Ricans and Mexicans are much higher than for Cuban and other Hispanics. These exogenous factors include
   a. the highest percentage of births to teenagers.
   b. the highest percentage of nonmetropolitan residents.
   c. the lowest onset of prenatal care.
   d. all of the above.

D
p. 288

9. Nonmarital cohabitation rates are highest among
   a. Mexican-Americans.
   b. Cuban-Americans.
   c. Central/South Americans.
   d. Puerto Rican-Americans.

A
p. 289

10. Mexican-American temporary workers who returned to Mexico when their services were no longer needed were referred to as
   a. braceros.
   b. illegal immigrants.
   c. compadres.
   d. wetbacks.

C
p. 290

11. A typical feature of Mexican American families is to put the needs of the family above personal or individual needs. This is termed
   a. family compadrism.
   b. family collectivism.
   c. familism.
   d. braceroism.

B
p. 290

12. Compadres, to Mexican-American families are
   a. braceros.
   b. godparents.
   c. uncles and aunts.
   d. any family member related by marriage rather than birth.

C
p. 291

13. In 1993, non-Hispanic families had an average of 3.08 persons. In contrast, Mexican-American families had an average of
   a. 2.87 persons.
   b. 3.48 persons.
   c. 4.01 persons.
   d. 5.14 persons.

D
p. 292

14. Cesar Chavez, a well-known Chicano leader, formed the
   a. American Association of University Professors (AAUP).
   b. National Council on Family Relations (NCFR).
   c. Future Farmers of America (FFA).
   d. National Farm Workers Association (NFWA).

B
p. 292

15. The largest Asian American group is
   a. Filipino.
   b. Chinese.
   c. Japanese
   d. Asian Indian

A
p. 293

16. Among Asian American groups, the youngest age at marriage and highest fertility rate occurs among the
   a. Hmong.
   b. Filipino.
   c. Korean.
   d. Vietnamese.

D
p. 294

17. The rate of female households with no husband present among Asian Americans, when compared with Hispanic Americans, is
   a. higher by about six percent.
   b. about the same.
   c. lower by about six percent.
   d. lower by about twelve percent.

B
p. 296

18. Asian Americans who reside in U.S. Chinatowns
   a. exhibit children's strict obedience to parental authority.
   b. display a wide range of social problems including poor health, a high rate of suicide, and poor working conditions.
   c. are almost exclusively of the Buddist religion.
   d. all of the first three are true.

D
p. 297

19. Nearly two-thirds of Japanese and Chinese births in the United States were to mothers who were
   a. teenagers.
   b. between the ages of 20 and 24.
   c. between the ages of 25 and 34.
   d. at least 35 years of age.

B
p. 298

20. In 1492, the Native American population was estimated to be about ten million. Today, it is closer to
   a. 0.9 million.
   b. 2.1 million.
   c. 4.6 million.
   d. 12.1 million.

C
p. 298

21. The percentage of Native Americans living in communities other than reservations, land trusts, or tribal designated statistical areas is about
   a. 6 percent.
   b. 26 percent.
   c. 46 percent.
   d. 66 percent.

A
p. 298

22. The largest American Indian population tribe or nation is the
   a. Cherokee.
   b. Navaho.
   c. Sioux.
   d. Hopi.

A
p. 299

23. The median age of the U.S population is about 34.6 years. For Native Americans it is closer to
   a. 27   c. 35
   b. 31   d. 39

C
p. 301

24. In the late 1800s, President Grant appropriated funds to churches to assist in American Indian education. What churches did was
   a. provide reading and writing training in their native language.
   b. integrate Indian dances and traditions with Christian teachings.
   c. send children to off-reservation boarding schools.
   d. both (a) and (b) above.

C
p. 303

25. In 1990, Eschbach studied regional differences in American Indian intermarriage. What he found was that
   a. very few intermarriages occurred anywhere.
   b. rates were particularly high in the southwest, North Carolina, Alaska and the Northern Plains.
   c. in six regions, 80 percent of married Indians under the age of 25 were married to non-Indians.
   d. both (b) and (c) were true.

220

Fill-in Questions

1. The _____ American population is the largest Hispanic group in the United States.

2. The _____ family has the highest rate of poverty among Hispanic American groups.

3. _____ Americans are also identified as Chicanos.

4. Mexican Americans who have come to the U.S. can be classified as three types: legal immigrants, _____ , and illegal aliens.

5. Where the needs of the family collectively supersedes individual needs is referred to as _____ and appears to be a highly typical feature of Mexican American families.

6. The ideal of manliness equated with authority and strength among Mexican American men is referred to as _____ .

7. Of all Asian American groups, the _____ have the youngest age of marriage and the highest fertility level of any immigrant group.

8. For Native Americans, _____ are properties associated with a particular tribe but located outside of reservation boundaries.

9. The largest Native American tribe or nation is the _____ comprising about 16 percent of the Native American population.

10. In 1871, President _____ delegated specific reservations to churches who stripped children of their native dances and languages by sending them to off-reservation boarding schools.

Fill-in answers	Page Reference
1. Mexican	285
2. Puerto Rican	286
3. Mexican	289
4. braceros or temporary workers	289
5. familism	290
6. machismo	290
7. Hmong	293
8. trust lands	298
9. Cherokee	298
10. Grant	301

Short Answer/Essay Questions

1. Five reasons were presented as to why most national policy discussions fail to address Latino poverty. List three and show how they are relevant.

2. Two factors were said to account for 78 percent of the difference between Puerto Ricans and whites in child poverty. What were those two factors. Explain.

3. What is meant by familism? Show how familism is related to remaining in school or to school performance.

4. Describe the concepts of compadres and machismo. What functions did each perform in relation to the traditional Mexican-American family?

5. Who are the "Pacific Islanders?" Explain. How are they different from Asian Americans?

6. Who are the Hmong? As immigrants to the United States, where is their homeland? What is unique about them, particularly in terms of age at marriage and fertility levels?

7. What is the difference between a reservation, a trust land, and a tribal designated statistical area?

8. Explain the high rates of death and the low life expectancies among Native Americans.

9. What is unique about the Native American experience as related to education and the family?

10. Explain the high rates of intermarriage among select Asian and Native American groups.

CHAPTER 11

True/False Questions

T
p. 310
1. Social Stratification refers to the ranking of people into positions of equality and inequality

T
p. 311
2. Functionalists view a stratified society as an inevitable and necessary feature of society that contributes to stability and order.

F
p. 311
3. Karl Marx believed that inequality is essential in a marriage in order to fulfill all tasks, many of which are not very rewarding.

F
p. 312
4. There is a high degree of consensus among researchers, that wives, even when employed, simply assume the class identification of their husbands.

F
p. 313
5. Social scientists agree that there are three distinct social classes in American society.

F
p. 313
6. In the western world, the age of men at marriage is lower as class position rises.

T
p. 314
7. Women in wealthy families are said to serve as gatekeepers for many of the institutions of the very rich.

F
p.314
8. Of all the social classes, gender equality is greatest among the wealthy or upper classes.

T
p. 317
9. In contrast to working-class women, middle-class women espouse the ideal of equality in their marriages.

T
p. 317
10. The Kohl hypothesis suggests that middle class parents are more likely than lower class parents to use psychological rather than physical approaches to discipline.

F
p. 318
11. While today social class differences are increasingly evident in China, traditional Chinese families, were for the most part, all of one class.

F
p. 319
12. Collins argues that most white collar working women are order-givers, not order-takers.

T
p. 320
13. Blue-collar employed women appear to experience more sexual harassment in the workplace than white-collar women but are less likely to report it.

T	14.	Members of the blue-collar family, more than any other, conform to the
p. 320		traditional roles of husband and wife.

T	15.	The poverty index is based solely on money income and does not reflect non-cash assistance such as food stamps or public housing.
p. 322		

T	16.	In a study of the gender poverty gap in eight industrialized countries, only Sweden revealed poverty rates of men to be higher than those of women.
p. 322		

T	17.	One study cited in the text suggests that changes in family structure accounted for nearly 50 percent of the increase in child poverty rates since 1980.
p. 325		

F	18.	Most (more than 75 percent) welfare recipients grew up in homes that received welfare.
p. 327		

F	19.	In the mid-1990s, the US House of Representatives "Contract with America" placed a strong emphasis on getting persons out of poverty.
p. 327		

T	20.	The "welfare trap" was said to be not one of dependency but one in which welfare pays better than low-wage jobs
p. 328		

T	21.	Evidence suggests that women on welfare have a rate of fertility below that of women in the general population.
p. 329		

F	22.	Fictive kin was the term given by Carol Stack to refer to welfare recipients who make up names of relatives to increase the amount of support they receive from the government.
p. 330		

T	23.	While the underclass is a multiracial/multiethnic phenomenon, the underclass p. is particularly prevalent among African American and Puerto Rican families.
331		

T	24.	As of 1996, about one-third of all families and more than half of Spanish-origin families with a female householder, no husband present, were below the poverty level.
p. 332		

T	25,	In 1997, the majority of white single mothers were divorced or married with a spouse absent while most black single mothers had never been married.
p. 334		

T	26.	Single mothers cohabiting with unrelated males where income is shared have been found to differ little from young married couples with children.
p. 335		

T	27.	A review of research on female-headed families concluded that the majority of these families, when not plagued by stigma or poverty, tend to have children as successful as those from two parent families.
p. 337		

28. Significant benefits have been found among children to living with the same-sex single parent as contrasted to living with the opposite-sex parent.

29. Vertical social mobility refers to movement up or down from one social class to another

30. A review of studies on upward social mobility suggested stressful emotional relationships, tension, and parent-child estrangement associated with actual mobility.

Multiple-choice Questions

1. Social class refers to an aggregate of individuals who occupy a similar position on scales of
   a. wealth, prestige, and power.
   b. authority, influence, and position.
   c. status, caste, and party.
   d. all the above about equally.

2. According to the conflict perspective on social stratification
   a. since social class differentiation's are inevitable, the "havens" must be sensitive to the needs of the "have-nots".
   b. social class differentiation's are essential for the performance of the varied tasks in society.
   c. stratification lead to alienation and exploitation.
   d. all societies need wealthy people to provide jobs and blue-collar workers to perform them.

3. According to the text, given the increasing number of women and wives in the paid labor force, research evidence today makes it clear that he class identification process
   a. is the same for men and women.
   b. needs to be gender specific.
   c. no longer is a relevant issue in American society.
   d. remains unaffected by women in the paid labor force.

4. Higher or upper strata persons are more likely to
   a. marry at younger ages.
   b. have more divorces.
   c. have more children.
   d. be granted less freedom in the choice of mates or marital partners.

A
p. 314

5. Wealthy or upper class families tend to be
   a. very gender segregated.
   b. the most studied of all social classes.
   c. extremely concerned with what they do rather than who they are.
   d. all of the above three.

B
p. 315

6. Most Americans indicate the class they belong to is the
   a. upper or wealthy class
   b. middle class.
   c. white-collar working class.
   d. blue-collar working class.

B
p. 316

7. A Querida, as exists in the Philippines, refers to a married man
   a. having several wives, not legally, but with the consent of the first wife.
   b. seeing, supporting, and possibly having children by a woman who is not his wife.
   c. being punished or shunned for not supporting his wife and children.
   d. who has many concubines and mistresses.

D
p. 316

8. From a Marxian perspective, the middle class is composed of
   a. working class people who depend on wages.
   b. people who have little control over their lives.
   c. female homemakers or housewives.
   d. the bourgeoisie.

C
p. 317

9. In disciplining children, studies tend to suggest that middle class parents, in contrast to blue-collar parents, tend to
   a. rely more heavily on physical punishment.
   b. more heavily supervise their children.
   c. use reason, verbal threats, or withdrawal of rewards.
   d. do both (b) and (c) above.

D
p. 319

10. Which of the following appears to be characteristic of blue-collar workers and families.
    a. Women are order takers not order givers.
    b. Jobs of workers generally require some sort of manual skill.
    c. Women experience more sexual harassment than white-collar women.
    d. all of the above are characteristics of blue-collar workers and families.

A
p. 320

11. When compared to other classes, in the blue-collar family
    a. the members conform to the traditional image of husband and wife roles.
    b. the role of children is one of contributing to family decision-making.
    c. the husband and wife share equally in the rearing and discipline of children.
    d. all three of the above are true.

B
p. 321

12. According to a classic investigation of blue-collar families by Mirra Komarovsky
   a. husbands and wives in Glenton displayed a blurring of gender roles.
   b. the majority of men and women saw the principal marital ties as sexual union, complementary tasks, and mutual devotion.
   c. the married men and women were very successful in sharing their hurts, worries, and dreams with each other.
   d. the couples believed that the function of marriage was to be friends.

D
p. 322

13. The poverty index, as developed by the Social Security Administration, is based on
   a. governmental benefits received.
   b. inflation rates.
   c. unemployment figures.
   d. money income alone.

C
p. 322

14. The poverty index takes into account
   a. marital status and number of children under age 18.
   b. age and the cost of health care.
   c. family size and the cost of food.
   d. all of the above factors.

B
p. 322

15. In 1997, the number of families in the United States below the poverty level was about
   a. 5 percent or about one in twenty.
   b. 10 percent or about one in ten.
   c. 16 percent or about one in six.
   d. 20 percent or about one in five.

A
p. 323

16. Which trend is not evident in the feminization of poverty.
   a. child support from absent husbands supplemented by social assistance.
   b. women living independently with custody of her dependent children.
   c. a decreasing marriage rate and high divorce rate.
   d. women earning less than their male counterparts in the labor market.

B
p. 324

17. As of 1997, the poverty rate was highest for
   a. black families.
   b. Hispanic families with a female householder.
   c. children under 18 years of age.
   d. persons age 65 years and older.

B
p. 327

18. Which statement is true about public assistance and poverty.
    a. 75 percent of families in poverty receive food stamps.
    b. 75 percent of welfare recipients did not grow up in homes that received welfare.
    c. The 1990's "Contract with American" was aimed at getting families out of poverty
    d. both a and b are true.

D
p. 329

19. Which statement is true based on research evidence?
    a. women on welfare tend to have more children to receive more benefits.
    b. women on welfare have a rate of fertility higher than women in the general population.
    c. both (a) and (b) are true.
    d. both (a) and (b) are false.

C
p. 330

20. The concept "fictive kin" refers to the
    a. upper class' preoccupation with genealogy and the tracing of lineage.
    b. increasing geographic separation of nuclear families from their immediate kin.
    c. exchange of goods and services between friends that resembles kinship.
    d. replacement of legal marriage by the increasing incidence of long term nonmarital cohabitation.

B
p. 330

21. Research suggests that the single most important event associated with the transition into and out of poverty for both black and white children were changes in
    a. salaries of the principle wage earner.
    b. the labor supply of secondary earners in the family.
    c. the unemployment rate.
    d. births of additional children.

C
p. 332

22. According to the text, the female-headed single-parent family
    a. originates in a fundamental lack of female initiative.
    b. is relatively uncommon among Hispanic-origin families.
    c. has more dependents and a high rate of mobility.
    d. is decreasing in numbers in the United States.

D
p. 332

23. Data from the 1997 U.S. census suggests that the number of children who were not living with two parents was close to
    a. one in nine or about 11 percent.
    b. one in five or about 19 percent.
    c. one in four or about 24 percent.
    d. one in three or about 32 percent.

24. In 1997, about _____percent of African American single mothers had never been married (not divorced, widowed, or married with a spouse absent).
    a. 61
    b. 51
    c. 41
    d. 31

25. Which statement is <u>not</u> true about mothers as single parents.
    a. children raised in mother-only families are more likely to be poor in adulthood than those who lived with both parents.
    b. children living with single mothers are more likely to become single parents themselves.
    c. major problems in mother-only families stem from poverty and stigma.
    d. cohabiting single mothers differ little from those mothers living alone.

26. Studies of fathers as single parents suggest they
    a. are less effective parents than single mothers.
    b. are glad to be fathers and have little trouble fulfilling either the instrumental or expressive roles.
    c. prefer that role over a two-parent situation.
    d. simply can not "mother" and should only be given custody under very special conditions.

27. Which statement about downward social mobility is true.
    a. very few people experience it in America as most children are doing better than their parents.
    b. the largest share of downward mobility come from the upper middle and upper classes.
    c. women separated or divorced face the highest risk of downward mobility.
    d. all three of the above statements are true.

28. Which statement is true about social mobility.
    a. downward mobility is as likely as upward mobility.
    b. close to 45 percent of all persons will move upward at least one social class level during their lifetime.
    c. more children will find themselves at the same level as their parents than at any other level.
    d. all of the above have research support and are true.

Fill-in Questions

1. _____ is the ranking of people into positions of equality and inequality.

2. _____ theorists view a stratified society, not as leading to stability and order, but to dissatisfaction, alienation, and exploitation.

3. The _____ (names of upper class families) is used to consolidate upper class repute and maintain "good breeding".

4. According to Marx, the middle class is composed of the bourgeoisie, while the working class comprises the _____ .

5. In disciplining children, _____ parents are most likely to rely on physical punishment.

6. The _____ is based on the Department of Agriculture's economy food plan and reflects different consumption requirements based on family size and composition.

7. Carol Stack, in dealing with strategies of survival among the poor in the black community, said that exchange patterns result in a _____ by which friends are turned into "family".

8. Within the poverty population and usually concentrated in urban ghettos, is a(n) _____ of families that are characterized by persistent poverty.

9. Upward or downward social mobility is referred to as _____ social mobility.

10. The likelihood of upward social mobility was described in the text as a function of three separate factors; the individual themselves, a frictional factor, and a(n) _____.

Fill-in answers	Page Reference
1. Social stratification	310
2. Conflict	311
3. social register	314
4. proletariat	316
5. blue collar / working class	317
6. poverty index	322
7. fictive kin	330
8. underclass	330
9. vertical	339
10. opportunity structure	339

Short Answer/Essay Questions

1. What is meant by social stratification? Compare and contrast the functionalist and conflict explanations of stratification.

2. What are some of the ways upper class families differ from those below them? Examine the importance of lineage, the different roles of women and men, and gender equality. What is the significance of the social register?

3. How do middle-class and working-class parents differ with regard to child-rearing practices? Explain.

4. How is poverty determined?

5. The text says that "it is clear that poverty is linked to family structure". What does that mean? Give examples.

5. Define, give examples of, and explain the "feminization of poverty."

7. Describe how families in poverty survive? How important are public assistance programs, work requirements, kin, or friends?

8. What is meant by the underclass? Who is in it? What factors are related to its' existence?

9. Define vertical and horizontal mobility. What three phenomena are influential in terms of social mobility?

10. What are some of the consequences of social mobility on family relationships, marriages and individual well-being?

CHAPTER 12

True/False Questions

T   1. Mothers, when asked about caregiving for preschool age children, gave
p. 349   priority to the maternal role over the worker role.

F   2. Data seems to suggest that fathers in the U.S., for the most part, are
p. 350   indifferent to and distant from their children.

T   3. Nurturant involved parenting behaviors reduce the risk of adolescent tobacco
p. 351   use and the association with peers who encourage tobacco use.

T   4. Data suggests that the strongest and most consistent determinant of
p. 351   satisfaction with parenting is the quality of the marriage.

T   5. A study of 600 couples in the early years of marriage revealed that for both
p. 352   husbands and wives, "being alone with my spouse" took precedence over
           child rearing.

F   6. David Demo documents that primarily as a result of expanding work and family
p. 353   roles, there has been a delimitation and decline in the parental role.

F   7. Children in the family, irrespective of age, provide a significant delay in and
p. 354   deterrent to divorce.

F   8. Evidence suggests that with the increased availability and reliability of
p. 355   contraceptives, most pregnancies and births (about 68 percent) are planned.

T   9. One national study found that about 85 percent of adolescents who had a child
p. 356   outside of marriage had no intention to do so.

T   10. Teenagers in the United States are far more likely to become pregnant than
p. 358   are comparable women in other developed countries.

F   11. Teenagers who placed their child for adopton suffered far more long term
p. 359   negative psychological consequences than those who raised their children.

T   12. The vast majority (over 90 percent) of teenage parents live with their husbands
p. 360   or other relatives.

T   13. More than two of three births (about 70 percent) to African American
p. 361   women were born outside of a marital context in 1996.

F
p. 363
14. Census data reveal that between 1970 and 1996, unwed mothers, on the average, have been getting younger.

F
p. 363
15. Unwed parenthood is more common among teenagers than any other group.

F
p. 364
16. Illegitimacy and births to unmarried women in Sweden is a significant social problem

T
p. 365
17. Adopted children born to unwed mothers do as well or better than children born to wed mothers.

F
p. 366
18. The "baby boomlet" of the late 1980s was attributed solely to births among older persons or couples who delayed childbearing.

F
p. 366
19. The post World War II baby boom was largely caused by an increase in the proportion of families who were having three or more children.

F
p. 368
20. The low fertility rate in Japan is attributed primarily to contraceptive availability, combined with education about them and lack of stigma against buying and using them.

T
p. 368
21. There is a positive relationship between a short spacing time between births and mortality among infants.

F
p. 368
22. Research suggests a biological instinct between being female and a natural desire for children.

F
p. 369
23. In the United States, two or three children is the ideal family size but in Japan it is one child followed by no children.

T
p. 371
24. Voluntary childlessness was found to have a positive effect on marital adjustment and family satisfaction.

T
p. 371
25. Involuntary childlessness was found to be a major negative life event that has deleterious effects on the subjective well-being of both women and men.

F
p. 372
26. Compared to children with siblings, only children were found to be less happy and score lower on adjustment measures.

T
p. 374
27. When parental background is controlled, only children do better than children from any other family size.

T
p. 376
28. National surveys have found no relationship between sibling number and sociability or being affiliative as an adult.

F
p. 376

29. Last born or youngest children tend to be the most sexually conservative and more traditionally oriented.

T
p. 379

30. Choosing the sex of the child would likely increase the proportion of male births by seven to ten percent.

Multiple-Choice Questions

A
p. 349

1. When parents were asked how their lives changed after their babies were born, the one consistent response was
   a. time.
   b. money.
   c. privacy for sexual relationships.
   d. a need for child care.

C
p. 350

2. Mothers, when asked about ideal caretakers for preschool-age children, gave priority to
   a. nursery schools and day-care centers.
   b. grandparents, particularly grandmothers.
   c. mothers themselves.
   d. fathers.

B
p. 351

3. Data suggest that
   a. Harsh parenting may be the most effective way to prevent adolescent tobacco use.
   b. Marital quality may be the strongest determinant of parenting satisfaction.
   c. Increased children's autonomy is making parenting less difficult around the world.
   d. all three of the above are true.

D
p. 352

4. In industrialized countries, cultural pressures to become parents appear to have
   a. increased as seen in rising birth rates.
   b. Increased as seen in an increase in earlier first pregnancies.
   c. decreased as seen in the emphasis on one-child families.
   d. decreased as seen in the increased ability to control conceptions and birth.

B
p.352

5. The idea that children are of value in providing security in old age or in case of divorce, widowhood, or financial difficulties, is referred to as a/an
   a. insurance protection theory.
   b. uncertainty reduction theory.
   c. survivor's benefit theory.
   d. economic conflict theory.

C
p. 353

6. It is known that most women leave their jobs with the birth of a child. The number that have been found to return to their employment within two years after the birth is about
   a. 20 percent.
   b. 40 percent.
   c. 60 percent.
   d. 80 percent.

A
p. 355

7. The majority of teenagers who become pregnant
   a. have an out-of-wedlock birth and keep the child.
   b. have an out-of-wedlock birth and give it up for adoption.
   c. marry before childbirth.
   d. obtain an abortion.

D
p. 355

8. Black unwed teenagers who become pregnant, are more likely than their white counterparts to
   a. place their child for adoption.
   b. marry the father.
   c. end the pregnancy through abortion.
   d. do none of the above three.

D
p. 359

9. Adolescents who relinquished (put up for adoption) their children, when compared with adolescents who kept and raised them, were more likely to
   a. become pregnant again sooner.
   b. have lower educational aspirations.
   c. suffer more negative consequences.
   d. delay marriage.

A
p. 361

10. Fathers least likely to live with their first child are
    a. black teenagers.
    b. Hispanic teenagers.
    c. disadvantaged white teenagers.
    d. nondisadvantaged white teenagers.

A
p. 361

11. As of 1996, of all births, the number that were born to unmarried women was
    a. 10 percent or about one in ten.
    b. 20 percent or about one in five.
    c. 32 percent or about one in three.
    d. 40 percent or about two in five.

B
p. 362

12. Birth rates among mothers who are not married is lowest among
    a. Native Americans.
    b. Chinese Americans.
    c. Hispanic Americans.
    d. non-Hispanic white Americans.

D
p. 363

13. The biggest percentage increase over the past twenty years in births to unmarried women was to
    a. the very young or those under age 15.
    b. teenagers age 15-19.
    c. those age 20-24.
    d. those over age 25.

A
p. 364

14. In Sweden, most concern appears to center around
    a. a low birth rate.
    b. illegitimacy.
    c. unplanned and unwanted pregnancies.
    d. the poverty of children.

B
p. 365

15. Evidence suggests that welfare programs
    a. have been a total failure in helping dependent children.
    b. have little impact on the decision for mothers to have more children.
    c. are a central motivational factor to have additional children.
    d. do all but (b) above. Both (a) and (c) are true.

A
p. 366

16. The birth rate in the United States
    a. increased slightly in the late 1980s resulting in a baby boomlet.
    b. increased steadily since the depression of the 1930s.
    c. decreased steadily since the baby boom following World War II.
    d. showed no pattern of increase or decrease in the past thirty years.

C
p. 366

17. The baby boom refers to
    a. the boom that occurs when an unwanted pregnancy is revealed.
    b. the increase in the number of births that accompanied the depression when men were without jobs and at home.
    c. the increase in the number of births that followed World War II.
    d. the increase in the number of births that has occurred each year due to the increased number of women existing to have them.

B
p. 369

18. Which statement is true.
    a. the one child family is the preferred one in Japan.
    b. the rate of childlessness in the U.S. has increased over the past few decades.
    c. about 18 percent of currently married women in the U.S. do not expect to have any children in their lifetime.
    d. all of the first three are true.

A
p. 369

19. When compared to couples with children, voluntary childless couples were found to
   a. have higher levels of marital satisfaction.
   b. experience lower levels of health.
   c. be of lower socioeconomic status.
   d. experience lower levels of health and be of lower socioeconomic status.

C
p. 371

20. In the United States, infertility is estimated to affect approximately
   a. 5 percent of all couples.
   b. 10 percent of all couples.
   c. 15 percent of all couples.
   d. 20 percent of all couples.

D
p. 372

21. National data that looked at adults who were the sole or only child and had no siblings, found that on eight dimensions of well-being
   a. all of the effects of having siblings were positive.
   b. six of the effects of having siblings were positive.
   c. six of the effects of having siblings were negative.
   d. all of the effects of having siblings were negative.

C
p. 373

22. The government in China instituted a one-child policy. It was announced that couples with two children should
   a. totally abstain from sexual intercourse.
   b. put up one of the children for adoption.
   c. have one partner sterilized.
   d. practice infanticide on any future births.

A
p. 373

23. Explanations for the higher than normal sex ratios in China include
   a. gender-specific abortion.
   b. the underreporting of male births.
   c. male infanticide.
   d. all of the above three.

C
p. 374

24. Blake's research findings on the only child suggest that
   a. only children tend to be spoiled, overly dependent and lonely.
   b. children with siblings were more satisfied with important aspects of their lives, notably jobs and health.
   c. only children do better than children from any other family size
   d. both a and b are true.

B
p. 375

25. Blake and Downey illustrate that increased family size effects each child negatively. Their explanation for this is called a
a. fertility failure hypothesis.
b. resource dilution hypothesis.
c. financial diminuation hypothesis.
d. demographic transition hypothesis.

B
p. 376

26. Research on the effects of birth order has revealed that first-born females tend to be
a. more sexually permissive.
b. more traditionally oriented.
c. more likely to engage in social activities,
d. less conservative on political and social issues.

A
p. 377

27. Middle borns, compared to first or last borns, were found to
a. have significantly lower levels of self-esteem.
b. be very similar to first borns.
c. be very similar to last borns.
d. have the positive benefits and characteristics of both the first and last born.

D
p. 379

28. Studies involving gender preference in the having of children suggest that
a. most couples in the world want two girls and two boys.
b. there is a preference for female children in much of Africa, Asia, and the Middle East.
c. choosing the sex of the child is illegal in most countries.
d. choosing the sex of children would decrease the proportion of female births.

Fill-in Questions

1. An _____ theory of parenthood suggests that in many developing countries children are of value in providing security and assistance in old age.

2. White and Booth suggest that although children do not prevent divorce, they may cause couples to approach the divorce decision more slowly. They refer to this as the _____ hypothesis.

3. Among industrialized countries, unmarried teenagers in _____ are most likely to become pregnant.

4. About _____ percent of all births are to unmarried women.

5. The _____ was a post World War II event that upset what had been a century long decline in the fertility rate in the United States.

6. Infertility seems to be a negative life event only for couples who are _____ childless.

7. In terms of family size, for most positive child adjustment, school performance, health, and life satisfaction, the _____ child family does best.

8. Studies of the "missing girls" of China tend to focus on three explanations: gender-specific abortion, an underreporting of births of girls, and _____ .

9. The _____ hypothesis of Judith Blake predicts, on average, the more children per family, the lower the quality of each child.

10. By birth order, _____ children have been found to have the lowest levels of self-esteem.

Fill-in answers	Page Reference
1. uncertainty reduction	352
2. braking	354
3. United States	358
4. 32	361
5. baby boom	366
6. involuntary	371
7. one - only	372
8. female infanticide	373
9. resource dilution	375
10. middle born	377

Short Answer/Essay Questions

1. What is the role and importance of fathers in "mothering"?

2. Discuss the accuracy of the statement that "children prevent divorce"?

3. What social consequences of parenthood have been documented in regard to (a) the employment patterns of women, and (b) marital stability.

4. The teenage pregnancy rate in the United States is much higher than in other developed countries. Why? So what, that is, why should this be of any concern?

5. Explain the increase in the percentage of births to unwed mothers. Does birth out of wedlock make a difference? How?

6. What do demographers mean when they talk about a "baby boom"? What caused it? What are some of the consequences of it?

7. What is the trend in regard to childless marriages? What categories of people are more likely to choose childlessness? What are some of the consequences in terms of being voluntary or involuntary?

8. China has adoped what is now referred to as the one-child policy. How was it enforced? What are some of the positive and negative effects of this policy?

9. Discuss research findings regarding the effects of large or small families. Include a discussion of the sole or only child and the dilution hypothesis.

10. List three differences among children by birth order. How can these differences be explained?

CHAPTER 13

True/False Questions

F
p. 387
1. Socialization, the process of developing the self and of learning the ways of a given society and culture, is basically completed by ages 5 to 7.

T
p. 387
2. Parents not only influence and shape the behavior or children, but children do the same to parents.

F
p. 388
3. The one and only essential precondition necessary to socialization to occur is to inherit a biological system that is "normal" and/or functions.

T
p. 388
4. The learning theory behaviorist framework assumes that the same concepts and principles that apply to lower animals apply to humans.

T
p. 389
5. Instrumental or operant conditioning places the focus on the response, whereas classical conditioning links a response to a known stimulus.

T
p. 390
6. Classic psychoanalytic theory stresses the importance of biological drives and unconscious processes.

F
p. 390
7. The earliest and most important stage of development according to the psychoanalytic frame of reference is the phallic stage.

T
p. 392
8. Traditionally, the socialization and education of kibbutz children were performed primarily by nurses and teachers rather than parents.

F
p. 393
9. Claims of Freudian psychoanalytic regarding the importance of specific infant training practices to adult adjustment have received wide empirical support.

F
p. 393
10. Erikson sees the social order as completely in conflict with his eight stages of development.

T
p. 394
11. Piaget, like Freud, believed that children pass through stages of development but unlike Freud, emphasized reasoning and consciousness..

F
p. 396
12. A symbolic interactionist frame of reference assumes that the same concepts and principles that apply to lower animals apply to humans.

T
p. 397
13. Sweden, one of the most egalitarian countries in the world, still assigns the primary responsibility for home and child care to women.

T
p. 397
14. According to a symbolic interaction perspective, the most fruitful approach to understanding the behavior of individuals is to analyze the society of which they are a part.

F
p. 397
15. According to the symbolic interaction perspective, the newborn infant is basically antisocial.

T
p. 399

16. Fathers with high self-esteem were less likely to report using a physical means of punishment.

F
p. 400

17. According to a symbolic interaction perspective, spanking is harmful, period: irrespective of the intensity, time, place, or context.

F
p. 401

18. Murray Straus suggests that the failure of more parents to use corporal punishment is a basic, if not the basic reason for the sex, drug, and delinquent behavior of adolescents.

T
p. 401

19. According to a symbolic interactionist, "mother" is a social concept and may include father or brother.

F
p. 404

20. The generalized other refers to labeling or stereotyping groups of people without regard to their personal qualities or characteristics.

F
p. 405

21. According to the text, the most important years of the socialization process are the preschool years, less important are the school years, with the socialization process basically concluded by adolescence.

T
p. 406

22. The way one defines or perceives oneself in terms of one's masculinity or femininity is referred to as gender identity.

F
p. 406

23. A study of more than 400 lesbian and bisexual women noted that by early adolescence, these women were clear about their homosexual or bisexual identity.

F
p. 407

24. In China, the yin stood for all things bright, strong, and active while the yang stood for all things dark, weak, and passive.

T
p. 407

25. In the traditional Chinese family, the oppression of women was evident in their need to obey her father before marriage, her husband after marriage, and her son after her husband's death.

T
p. 408

26. Research suggests that men and husbands believe in innate, inborn gender roles more than women and wives.

F
p. 409

27. Research has shown that chemical substances such as progesterone, testosterone, or estrogen determine and predict behavior.

F
p. 409

28. Studies of hermaphrodites present convincing evidence that ones biological sex proves to be a powerful determinant of current gender role behavior.

T
p. 410

29. The Khasi tribe in northeast India passes property and the family name from mother to daughter.

T
p. 412

30. In the socialization of males and females, empirical evidence suggests a continuation of gender-role stereotyping and gender segregation in spite of tremendous shifts in gender-role attitudes.

Multiple-Choice Questions

B
p. 387

1. It appears that the one function of the family that is universal is
   a. reproduction.
   b. nurturant socialization.
   c. social placement.
   d. economic need fulfillment.

A
p. 388

2. Classical conditioning
   a. links a response to a known stimulus.
   b. places the focus of attention on the response.
   c. has little to do with either stimulus or response.
   d. requires internalized meaning.

C
p. 389

3. Socialization, according to a learning/behaviorist frame of reference, assumes and requires
   a. language and reasoning.
   b. breastfeeding and toilet training.
   c. stimulus-response conditioning.
   d. all of the above.

D
p. 391

4. The psychoanalytic stage of development in which a parent's child rearing techniques sets the stage for adults who are motivated to create things that will please another person is
   a. oral.
   b. phallic.
   c. latent.
   d. anal.

C
p. 391

5. According to traditional Freudian psychoanalytic theory, the key to feminine psychology is
   a. the oral and anal stages of development.
   b. the oedipal complex.
   c. penis envy.
   d. castration anxiety.

D
p. 393

6. The theorist who views the social order as resulting from and in harmony with his eight stages was
   a. Freud.
   b. Piaget.
   c. Mead.
   d. Erickson.

B
p. 394

7. Child development frames of reference like those of Erikson and Piaget, tend to share with symbolic interaction theories an emphasis on
   a. eight clearly defined stages of development throughout the life course.
   b. language, reasoning, and social influences.
   c. overt behaviors and learning through conditioning.
   d. erotic impulses and unconscious processes.

D
p. 395

8. Which statement is true from the perspective of the symbolic interaction frame of reference.
   a. personality becomes fixed by age 5 or 6.
   b. the biological mother is the most important figure for children.
   c. physiological needs and drives explain most motivation.
   d. none of the above are true.

A
p. 396

9. Which one of the following is not a basic assumption of symbolic interaction theory?
   a. much of human behavior can be inferred from the study of animals.
   b. social behavior can be best understood through an analysis of the society in which people operate.
   c. at birth, the human infant is asocial.
   d. socialized human beings are actors as well as reactors and can take the role of other.

C
p. 399

10. The organization of internalized roles is the
    a. reference group.
    b. significant other.
    c. social self.
    d. generalized other.

B
p. 399

11. Personality, according to a symbolic interactionist, consists of
    a. the interplay between the id, ego, and superego.
    b. definitions of self and the predisposition to act and behave consistently.
    c. operant and classical conditioning.
    d. biological drives and innate processes.

B
p. 401

12. Persons who are important to us and with whom we psychologically identify are termed
    a. reference groups.
    b. significant others.
    c. generalized others.
    d. all of the above depending on the time and place.

C
p. 402

13. Significant others
    a. are the same as reference groups.
    b. always include the biological mother.
    c. are role models.
    d. are or include all of the above three.

A
p. 402

14. To most adolescents, the key group of reference is
    a. peers.
    b. parents.
    c. siblings.
    d. teachers.

A
p. 404

15. In Mead's theory of the development of the self, the generalized other becomes important during the stage known as
    a. game.
    b. preparatory.
    c. latency.
    d. play.

B
p. 404
16. According to Mead, the generalized other refers to
   a. perceptions we hold toward those whom we don't know intimately.
   b. responding to the expectations of several other people at the same time.
   c. reacting to a reference group in contrast to a specific person.
   d. the collection of all our significant others.

D
p. 406
17. The way one defines or perceives oneself in terms of being masculine or feminine is termed
   a. androgynous capacity.
   b. gender expectation.
   c. sexual identity.
   d. gender identity.

C
p. 407
18. In traditional Chinese cosmology, the world was composed of two complementary elements, the yin and the yang. The yin stood for things
   a. bright.
   b. unknown.
   c. weak and passive.
   d. masculine.

A
p. 408
19. In terms of value orientations, females were found to be more likely than males to
   a. express concerns and responsibility for others.
   b. accept materialism and competition.
   c. indicate that purpose and meaning in life are not overly important.
   d. do none of the above.

C
p. 408
20. The category of persons who are most likely to believe in innate, inborn, sex roles are
   a. anthropologists.
   b. women and wives.
   c. men and husbands.
   d. symbolic interactionists.

D
p. 409
21. Margaret Mead's classic study of three primitive tribes in New Guinea found that
   a. human behavior was totally unpredictable and illogical.
   b. men in all three tribes were the more aggressive and combative.
   c. both men and women in the Arapesh and the Mundugumor tribe were passive, gentle, and unaggressive.
   d. the typical gender roles found in Western cultures were reversed among the Tchambuli.

C
p. 409
22. Research by John Money, found that biological males, defined and reared as females
   a. preferred gun and truck toys over doll and cooking toys.
   b. fell in love with females.
   c. had an interest in mothering.
   d. did both a and b above.

D
p. 410

23. The Khasi tribe in northeastern India was
    a. pacifist.
    b. patrilocal.
    c. egalitarian.
    d. matrilineal.

A
p. 411

24. Studies today suggest that when men and women are employed within the same occupation
    a. traditional sex-typed behaviors continue.
    b. women are more concerned than men about income, job security, and promotion.
    c. men, more than women, prefer part-time employment.
    d. gender role expectations become similar and approach equality.

B
p. 412

25. Regarding gender role stereotyping and segregation in modern society, empirical evidence suggests
    a. a dramatic decrease in these phenomena.
    b. a continuation of these phenomena, despite tremendous shifts in gender role attitudes.
    c. socialization to gender roles no longer emphasizes a differentiation between males and females.
    d. gender role stereotyping is a myth perpetuated by feminists.

Fill-in Questions

1. _____ is the process of developing the self and of learning the ways of a given society and culture.

2. Two prerequisites of adequate socialization include_____ and _____.

3. Within a learning-behaviorist frame of reference, instrumental conditioning, or what Skinner calls _____conditioning, places the focus of attention on the response rather than any known stimuli.

4. According to Freud, the _____ stage is the period of growth during which the child is preoccupied with the genitals.

5. _____, a Swiss social psychologist, believed that there are four major stages of intellectual development: sensorimotor, preoperational, concrete operations, and formal operations.

6. According to a symbolic interactionist, the organization of internalized roles is the _____.

7. Those persons who are very important to us and with whom we psychologically identify are termed _____.

8. The _____ involves a process of responding to the expectations of several other people at the same time.

9. _____ roles are the expectations associated with being masculine or feminine.

10. A classic study of three primitive tribes in New Guinea by anthropologist _____ found great diversity in the attitudes, values, and behavior of both men and women.

Fill-in answers	Page Reference
1. Socialization	387
2. biological inheritance / ongoing society	388
3. operant	389
4. phallic	391
5. Piaget	394
6. social self	399
7. significant others	401
8. generalized other	404
9. Gender	406
10. Margaret Mead	409

Short Answer/Essay Questions

1. Define socialization and briefly discuss each of its preconditions.

2. Compare the similarities and contrast the differences between the learning, Freudian, and child development theorists in their explanations of socialization.

3. When symbolic interactionists claim the difference between humans and infrahumans or animals is not simple one of degree but one of kind, what do they mean? Explain.

4. List and briefly describe four basic assumptions of symbolic interaction theory.

5. What is personality according to a symbolic interactionist perspective? How does the self-fulfilling prophecy come into play from this perspective?

6. Describe the research concerning spanking. How does parental spanking vary by sex, age of children, marital status of parents, social class, and region of the country? Why does Murray Straus want to eliminate spanking and make it a public health agenda?

7. What is the generalized other? Why and how is it significant or important in our behavior?

8. Differentiate concepts such as sex, sex roles, gender, gender roles, and gender identity. Discuss the role of biological and/or social factors in each.

9. Differentiate behaviors that anthropologists and others indicate are commonly associated with being male or female. How are these patterned differences explained? Why is gender equality evasive even in countries like Sweden and contexts like the Kibbutz that emphasize egalitarianism.

10. Describe sex-typed behaviors and sex-role stereotypes. How have these changed over the past several decades, of if they haven't changed, why not?

CHAPTER 14

True/False Questions

T
p. 410

1. Postparental suggests that the children are now legally and socially adults.

T
p. 420

2. The period after the children leave home lasts longer than any other in the marital life cycle.

T
p. 420

3. Recent demographic indicators suggest that more young adults reside with their parents than they did a few years ago.

T
p. 421

4. Coresiding young adults report significantly lower affective relationships with their parents than nonresidential children.

F
p. 421

5. Parental characteristics such as health, marital status, and employment status are the most important predictors of parent-child coresidence in the middle years.

F
p. 423

6. There is considerable research documenting the existence of a universal mid-life crisis among men.

F
p. 423

7. Most research finds that the majority of families, farm or nonfarm, are affected negatively when their children leave home.

T
p. 423

8. A study of 700 women found that those in their early fifties rated their quality of life higher than did younger or older women.

T
p. 424

9. For women, the launching of the last child increased both labor market involvement and economic well-being while both divorce and widowhood decreased well-being.

F
p. 425

10. In contrast to the lower-class grandparent, the middle-class grandparent appears to be far more integrated into ongoing daily life.

F
p.426

11. Black-white racial differences in grandparenting were said to be based on economic or structural factors and not on cultural distinctiveness.

T
p. 427

12. All fifty states now statutorily provide an avenue by which grandparents can petition the courts for visitation with their grandchildren over a parent's objection

T
p. 428

13. Since 1900, although a higher percentage of people are living longer, there has been a relatively small increase (about five years) in the life expectancy of those who reach age 65.

F
p. 428

14. Life expectancy is the maximum biological age limit that anyone can expect to live.

T
p. 432

15. Marital satisfaction may be higher for the elderly than for those in the intermediate stages of the family life course.

F
p. 433

16. Among the elderly, dating was found to provide a means of self-disclosure for women while for men it provided increased prestige and status rewards.

T
p. 435

17. Sons are motivated to provide support to older parents more out of an expectation of financial reward than out of sentiment.

F
p. 435

18. According to the text, the belief that adult children abandon their elderly relatives or fail to meet their needs is basically true.

T
p. 436

19. Elderly Chinese and Japanese Americans are more likely to live with their children than are other Americans.

F
p. 438

20. The majority (about 53 percent) of people over age 85 are living in nursing homes or long-term care institutions.

T
p. 439

21. In spite of housing provided by the government, the vast majority (about 75 percent) of aged over age 60 in China live with their children.

T
p. 441

22. The percentage of elderly below the poverty level in 1997 was one-third to about one-half of what it was in 1970.

F
p. 444

23. Retirement has been shown to be less stressful for women than for men.

F
p. 445

24. A study in rural Iowa revealed that retired elderly tended to turn to formal support services rather than family members for assistance.

F
p. 446

25. Active euthanasia refers to the deliberate ending of a persons life by refusing to provide life support systems.

F
p. 447

26. Hospice refers to a hospital setting for the terminally ill where privacy is stressed and full medical support facilities are available.

T
p. 447

27. A study of 44,000 deaths in Sweden revealed that persons whether separated, divorced, cohabiting or remarred, had higher mortality risks than those who stayed married with the same spouse.

T
p. 448

28. Mortality is lower for married persons than unmarried ones and lower for those with children than those without children.

T
p. 450

29. In 1997, the ratio of unmarried males age 65 and over to unmarried females age 65 and over was 31.

F
p. 450

30. The text suggests that programs to assist mate selection and remarriage among widows would be an effective was to deal with the problems associated with older persons.

Multiple-Choice Questions

D
p. 419

1. According to the text, the middle years cover the ages
   a. 35 to 45.
   b. 35 to 55.
   c. 45 to 55.
   d. 45 to 65.

C
p. 419

2. In the middle years, as of 1997, the percentage of men and women married with a spouse present was about
   a. one-half of the men and one-half of the women.
   b. two-thirds of the men and one-half of the women.
   c. three-fourth of the men and two-thirds of the women.
   d. 90 percent of the men and 80 percent of the women.

B
p. 420

3. Today, both men and women tend to
   a. marry in their teens.
   b. have their last child in their early thirties.
   c. see their last child launched in their mid-to-late fifties.
   d. not lose their spouse until the early or mid-sixties.

A
p. 421

4. "Boomerang kids", those who leave home and return, were found to
   a. give and receive more support from their parents than nonresident children.
   b. have a more positive experience when they were younger and not employed.
   c. increase the marital satisfaction of the parents.
   d. be highly related to the health and employment status characteristics of the parents.

C
p. 422

5. The most important predictors of parent and child coresidence in the middle years are
   a. home ownership and financial stability.
   b. parent characteristics such as health or employment status.
   c. the child's needs and situation.
   d. all of the above about equally.

A
p. 423

6. Farrell and Rosenberg's study of men entering middle age revealed that a major factor determining the amount of alienation and distress they experienced was
   a. socioeconomic class.
   b. marital status.
   c. race.
   d. physical appearance.

B
p. 423

7. In terms of the empty nest syndrome, Dolores Borland hypothesizes that
   a. the syndrome affects all women who have children.
   b. it may occur to a greater degree in a particular cohort of white, middle-class women.
   c. the syndrome is most likely to affect black women.
   d. the empty nest no longer exists because children tend to remain in the parental home.

D
p. 424

8. Which statement has been found to be true concerning employment patterns and economic well-being
   a. launching the last child improved both.
   b. marital dissolution decreased both.
   c. no changes were detected in employment or well-being by either launching the last child or marital dissolution.
   d. both (a) and (b) above are true.

C
p. 424

9. Modern grandparenthood in the United States has been significantly shaped by
   a. a younger age at marriage and an increase in family size.
   b. an increased spacing of children and a later age at retirement.
   c. an increased life expectancy and women having their last child at a younger age.
   d. all of the above three have significantly shaped grandparenthood.

A
p. 425

10. The text suggests that the middle class grandparent role in the United States in one which can be described as
   a. a "roleless role" with few normative restrictions.
   b. the ultimate parenting situation.
   c. dysfunctional in kinship interaction patterns.
   d. filled with sorrow and grief due to frequent divorce situations and high mobility patterns.

D
p. 427

11. The term "roleless role" has been used in the test to describe
   a. grandparenthood.
   b. stepgrandparenthood.
   c. great-grandparenthood.
   d. all of the first three.

B
p. 428

12. In the United States, life expectancy at birth is longest for
   a. white males.
   b. white females.
   c. black males.
   d. black females.

A
p. 428

13. The biological age limit beyond which on one can expect to live is the
   a. life span.
   b. live expectancy.
   c. life course or life cycle.
   d. age/sex dependency ratio.

D
p. 431

14. Social gerontology is the study of
   a. female illness in old age.
   b. medical and health need throughout the life span.
   c. communications patterns among widows.
   d. older persons and the aging process.

A
p. 432

15. As of 1997, the percent of men and women over age 75 who were married was closest to
   a. 64 percent of the men and 27 percent of the women.
   b. 64 percent of the men and 50 percent of the women.
   c. 50 percent of the men and 60 percent of the women.
   d. 40 percent of the men and 27 percent of the women.

C
p. 435

16. Research suggests that people over age 65
   a. are alienated from their children.
   b. experience high levels of conflict when two or more generations live together.
   c. get more support from daughters rather than sons.
   d. experience all of the above three.

B
p. 435

17. Support for older parents by daughters seems to be motivated primarily by
   a. principles of obligation.
   b. intergenerational affection and altruism.
   c. expectations of inheritance.
   d. receiving child-care and financial assistance.

C
p. 436

18. After age 65, the majority of men and women are living
    a. with friends.
    b. in institutions or home for the elderly.
    c. in households or families of their own.
    d. with children or other relatives.

D
p. 438

19. Residents of nursing homes are predominately
    a. white.
    b. widowed.
    c. over age 75.
    d. all of the above three.

B
p. 438

20. The number of older people living in long-term care institutions is about
    _____ percent of those over age 65 and _____ percent of those over age 85.
    a. four; ten
    b. four; twenty
    c. ten; twenty
    d. twenty; thirty

D
p. 441

21. In the United States the poverty rate for the elderly, compared to that of
    children under age eighteen, is about
    a. three times as high.
    b. twice as high.
    c. the same.
    d. half as high.

A
p. 445

22. The statement about retirement found to be true is that
    a. retired elderly turn to family members rather than formal sources.
    b. it is a less stressful event for women than for men.
    c. males have significantly more contact with siblings and children than
       do females.
    d. all of the above three are true about retirement.

B
p. 445

23. Which statement about retirement is not true.
    a. Retired elderly people are not neglected nor abandoned by their families.
    b. Retirement threatens marital quality.
    c. Retirement is not materially different for women than for men.
    d. Retirement requires major role readjustments for both men and women.

D
p. 447

24. Elderly bedridden people first turn for help to
    a. bureaucratic organizations.
    b. friends.
    c. neighbors.
    d. families.

A
p. 447
25. Health care plans which emphasize a therapeutic environment designed from the patients' point of view and stress space for interaction with other people are called
   a. hospice.
   b. nursing care.
   c. hospital based.
   d. Health maintenance organizations.

B
p. 447
26. A study of 44,000 deaths in Sweden found the highest mortality risk to exist among
   a. widowed women.
   b. divorced women.
   c. separated men.
   d. cohabiting women.

D
p. 450
27. The chances for remarriage are higher for
   a. the widowed than the divorced.
   b. women than for men.
   c. older people than for younger people.
   d. widowers than widows.

C
p. 450
28. In 1997, the sex ratio of married males age 65 and over to unmarried females of the same age was about
   a. 71
   b. 51
   c. 31
   d. 11

Fill-in Questions

1. Mitchell and Gee refer to children who leave home and return as _____ kids.

2. To the extent that a "mid-life crisis" occurs at all, it appears to be more prevalent among white middle class women and _____ class men.

3. Grandparenthood, stepgrandparenthood, and great grandparenthood have all been described as _____ roles.

4. By race and sex, life expectancy in the United States is <u>highest</u> for _____ .

5. The biological age limit beyond which no one can expect to live is the _____ .

6. The study of older persons and the aging process is known as social _____ .

7. Parents in the middle years squeezed between the need of their children and those of their aging parents have been referred to as the _____ .

8. The myth of _____ suggests that families are less willing today than those of the past to care for their elderly family members.

9. _____, which may be active or passive, refers to the deliberate ending of a persons life to spare her or him from the suffering of an agonizing disease or illness.

10. _____ is a program that emphasized a therapeutic environment for dying patients that involves extensive interaction with family and friends.

Fill-in answers	Page Reference
1. boomerang	421
2. lower	423
3. roleless	427
4. white females	428
5. life span	428
6. gerontology	431
7. sandwich generation	434
8. abandonment	439
9. Euthanasia	446
10. Hospice	447

Short Answer/Essay Questions

1. What changes in family composition and in the timing of family transitions may account for the change in length of the post-parental period?

2. What does research suggest about a mid-life crisis? Examine differences by sex and by social class.

3. Contrast the different circumstances facing grandparents, stepgrandparents, and great grandparents. What is meant by each being a "roleless role". Illustrate.

4. What is the difference between life span and life expectancy? How does life expectancy differ by race and sex? What factors account for these differences?

5. Contrast the marital status differences of men and women over age 65. List three major consequences of these differences.

6. What/who is the "sandwich generation"? Describe the support patterns of this generation and the motivational differences for this support by sons and daughters.

7. Madonna Mayer shows how social security, private pensions, and personal pensions such as Individual Retirement Accounts are all structured around gender. How? Explain.

8. Describe marriages and families in the later years in terms of (a) marital status, (b) living arrangements, (c) poverty, and (d) relationships with children.

9. Of what importance is socialization to the elderly? Socialization to what? By whom?

10. Contrast widows and widowers in terms of (a) numbers, (b) adjustment to the death of a spouse, and (c) remarriage.

CHAPTER 15

True/False Questions

T p. 457	1. Pauline Boss views stress as an outcome, as a disturbance resulting from change in the family.
T p. 458	2. Some external stressors (such as war, flood, or depression) may unify the family into a more cohesive unit rather than cause it to break down.
F p. 458	3. Joyous events such as a pay raise, a child's graduation, or the birth of a child seldom results in or produces stress.
F p. 459	4. According to the ABCX model, death, divorce, and unemployment in families can always be expected to be major stressor and crisis events.
T p. 460	5. It was documented that home-to-work stress occurs more strongly among men than women.
F p. 461	6. Children are more likely to be kidnapped by in-laws and extended kin than by anyone else.
F p. 462	7. Levinson, in examining violence cross-culturally, notes that violence is an inevitable consequence of family life.
T p. 462	8. Family violence is more common in societies in which men control women's lives and mothers bear the major responsibility for childrearing.
F p. 463	9. Abusers (about 40 percent or more) tend to be mentally disturbed, psychologically unbalanced, or even psychotic.
F p. 464	10. A structural cultural theory of violence suggests that most violence can be attributed to psychopathologies and the misuse of alcohol and drugs that are available in our culture.
T p. 465	11. Straus found that over 90 percent of parents of children ages three and four in the United States used physical punishment to correct behavior.
T p. 466	12. A law passes in 1979 made it illegal for Swedish parents to spank their children or treat them in a humiliating way.
T p. 466	13. Straus argues that empirical findings lend support to the hypothesis that physical punishment produces conformity in the immediate situation but in the long run increases the probability of divorce.

T
p. 466

14. A longitudinal study in New Zealand reported that exposure to abusive treatment during childhood resulted in elevated roles of juvenile offending, alcohol abuse, and mental health problems.

F
p. 467

15. Straus and Gelles, in comparing the rate of physical abuse of children in 1975 and 1985, found that the child abuse rate had increased slightly over the 10 year period.

F
p. 469

16. The consequence of child sexual abuse, while very traumatic at the time, appears to have little severe or long lasting effects.

T
p. 470

17. Research on over 500 young women in Washington State found that two-thirds of those who became pregnant as adolescents had been sexually abused.

T
p. 470

18. Research has consistently shown that physical aggression is at least twice as common among cohabiting couples as it is among married couples.

F
p. 472

19. Due to norms of egalitarianism, the incidence of wife abuse in China is very low.

F
p. 473

20. Wife beating, according to national studies by Straus and Gelles in 1975 and again in 1985, increased by 27 percent in the 10 year interval.

T
p. 475

21. In the Colonial period, a woman who was raped could not expect to marry into a respectable family since virginity before marriage reigned supreme.

F
p. 476

22. Due to tremendous legal changes in the 1980s, as of 1990 only two states prevented a husband from being persecuted for raping his wife.

T
p. 476

23. Diana Russelll, in her study of marital rape, reported that one out of every seven ever-married women reported one or more experiences of rape by her husband.

T
p. 477

24. Research by Straus and Gelles found that assaults by women on their male partners occur at about the same rate as assaults by men on their female partners.

F
p. 477

25. Males who viewed parental violence were more likely to experience depression than females who viewed parental violence.

T
p. 478

26. Both spouse and child abuse are more likely in stepfamilies and families in which one or both spouses have beeen divorced than in never-divorced families.

F   27. The greatest amount of sibling violence occurs between brother-brother pairs.
p. 479

F   28. A national sample of never-married persons ages 18-30 found that women
p. 480   are much less likely than men to be physically aggressive.

T   29. Calling the police is the last response when women react to violence.
p. 482

F   30. A review of studies over the past 40 years revealed a very low correlation
p. 482   (not statistically significant) between television violence and aggressive
             behavior.

Multiple-Choice Questions

B   1. Stressor or crisis-producing events have been seen by Reuben Hill as
p. 457   a. the result of stress.
             b. situations for which families have little or no preparation.
             c. events that drain available family resources.
             d. all of the above three.

A   2. Certain events outside of a group, such as war or depression, tend to
p. 458   a. unify the family into a more cohesive unit.
             b. turn the group against the government or system that created or
                permitted them to happen.
             c. lead to interpersonal conflict, a high degree of stress, and eventual
                marital breakdown.
             d. illustrate the accuracy of the ABCX model.

C   3. The ABCX model of stress would suggest that death or unemployment
p. 458   a. are inevitably stressful events.
             b. are only stressful events if we loved the person and didn't have another job.
             c. are only stressful if we define them as such and don't have adequate
                resources to deal with them.
             d. are never stressful events unless we make them such.

D   4. The double ABCX model illustrates
p. 459   a. positive events such as winning the lottery and negative events such
                as death.
             b. the responses of women and the responses of men.
             c. the meaning given to an event and the actual reality of an event.
             d. the pre-crisis and post-crisis variables.

A
p. 461

5. Compared to any other place or person, people are more likely to be beaten, raped, or killed
   a. in their own home by loved ones.
   b. in their own home by strangers.
   c. within walking distance of their homes by strangers.
   d. in poor areas of large cities by gangs or criminals.

B
p. 461

6. Results from several countries, including the United States, suggest that one out of every _____ murder victims are killed by a member of his or her own family.
   a. two
   b. four
   c. six
   d. eight

C
p. 462

7. Levinson suggests that in societies without family violence
   a. the respondents don't tell the truth since family violence is universal.
   b. marriages tend to be polygamous.
   c. family life is characterized by sharing and equality.
   d. men control women's lives with the support of clearly defined patriarchal norms.

A
p. 463

8. Which one of the following is <u>not</u> a myth of family violence according to Gelles and Straus?
   a. violence and love are compatible.
   b. abusers tend to be psychologically unbalanced while victims tend to be defenseless victims.
   c. alcohol and drugs are the real causes of violence in the home.
   d. abuse is confined to poor minority families.

D
p. 464

9. A social factor that contributes to high rates of family violence includes
   a. male dominance in the family and in society.
   b. pervasiveness of violence in society.
   c. neither a nor b above.
   d. both a and b above.

A
p. 465

10. In Sweden, corporal punishment and striking a child is
    a. illegal and can mean imprisonment for a parent.
    b. a necessary and legitimate form of discipline for parents.
    c. is granted approval for school teachers and administrators under conditions of severe student misbehavior.
    d. true under conditions cited in both b and c above.

C
p. 466

11. That violence in one sphere of life tends to engender violence in other spheres is what Straus terms
   a. the multiplying theory.
   b. social diffusion theory.
   c. cultural spillover theory.
   d. cultural dissemination theory.

C
p. 467

12. Results by Gelles indicate that very severe violence toward children is
   a. 25 percent higher among the upper classes.
   b. 50 percent higher among the middle classes.
   c. 100 percent higher among households below the poverty level.
   d. found at all class levels with relatively insignificant differences between them.

B
p. 468

13. A Gallup poll revealed that
   a. abuse is greater in two-parent than in one-parent households.
   b. mothers are more than twice as likely to have physically abused their children than are fathers.
   c. more than 90 percent of children were subject to severe verbal aggression.
   d. all of the above three are true.

D
p. 468

14. Murray Straus and Richard Gelles compared the rate of physical abuse of children from a 1975 study with the rates from a 1985 replication. They found that the rate from the 1985 study was
   a. 47 percent higher than in 1975.
   b. 17 percent higher than in 1975.
   c. 17 percent lower than in 1975.
   d. 47 percent lower than in 1975.

D
p. 469

15. Declines in levels of child abuse have been found to be related to
   a. a lower age at marriage.
   b. an increase in the number of children per family.
   c. higher rates of unemployment with inflation.
   d. a perceived high probability of getting caught.

B
p. 469

16. Which statement is not true about childhood sexual abuse?
   a. biological related caretakers are overrepresented and nonbiological caretakers are underrepresented in sexual abuse.
   b. boys are more likely to be abused by strangers whereas girls are more likely to be abused by family members.
   c. consequences of child sexual abuse are severe and long-lasting in terms of adolescent sexual dysfunctions, homosexual experiences and depression.
   d. more girls than boys report sexual victimization.

B
p. 469

17. Adolescents who assault parents are <u>less</u> likely to
    a. have friends who assaulted parents.
    b. be black or Hispanic than white.
    c. approve of delinquency.
    d. be any of the above three.

A
p. 471

18. Michael Johnson agures that there are two distinct forms of violence against women: common couple violence and
    a. patriarchal terrorism.
    b. retaliatory sexism.
    c. masculine supremecy.
    d. male brutality.

B
p. 472

19. Nursing research on battering during pregnancy reveals that
    a. approximately 25 percent of women are physically abused.
    b. approximately 8 percent of women are physically abused.
    c. pregnant women are only abused if they were abused when not pregnant.
    d. pregnant women experience considerably lower rates of abuse than nonpregnant women.

D
p. 473

20. Murray Straus and Richard Gelles compared the rate of wife or spouse abuse from a 1975 study with the rates from a 1985 replication. They found that the rate from the 1985 study was
    a. 47 percent higher than in 1975.
    b. 27 percent higher than in 1975.
    c. 17 percent lower than in 1975.
    d. 27 percent lower than in 1975.

D
p. 475

21. Research efforts to answer the question, "Why do physically abuse wives stay with their husbands? " reveal that
    a. the less severe but frequent the violence, the more a woman will remain with her spouse and not seek outside aid.
    b. the more a wife was struck by her parents, the less inclined she is to stay with her abusive husband.
    c. wives who stay do so because of the inability to make a choice among the many alternatives available to them.
    d. women employ cognitive strategies that help them perceive their relationship in a positive light.

D
p. 475

22. Legal definitions of rape include
    a. actual vaginal, anal, or oral penetration.
    b. force or theat of force.
    c. nonconsent of the victim.
    e. all of the above.

C
p. 476

23. As of 1990, the number of states that allow the prosecution of husbands for raping their wives without exception was
   a. all but one, that is, 49 states.
   b. all but twelve, that is, 38 states.
   c. 16 states.
   d. only North and South Carolina, that is, two states.

C
p. 477

24. In explaining the high rates of violence by women, Murray Straus suggests that
   a. non-retaliatory violence increases the probability of initiating family violence.
   b. implicit cultural norms disallow the marriage license to become a hitting license.
   c. childhood training allows violence within the family to be appropriate for females.
   d. the home is the one place where women are as powerful and dominant as men.

A
p. 478

25. According to the text, sibling abuse and violence
   a. is the most frequent and acceptable form of violence within families.
   b. occurs most frequently among boy-boy pairs.
   c. is usually explained in terms of parental jealousy.
   d. revolves around parental aggression.

B
p. 479

26. Elder abuse
   a. is not a substantial problem since most abuse occurs among young people.
   b. includes passive neglect such as being ignored.
   c. is done almost exclusively by ones own children.
   d. includes none of the above three as true.

D
p. 480

27. Physical violence among intimates
   a. seldom involves females as aggressors.
   b. is less likely to occur among fraternity members than nonmembers.
   c. has little, if any, relationship to verbal aggression.
   d. seems to occur nearly equally among males and females.

B
p. 482

28. In the prevention of family violence, Gelles and Straus argue that policies and programs must be directed primarily toward
   a. counseling and therapy for the abusive family member.
   b. cultural norms and values that support violence.
   c. educating parents about the need for strict discipline, including corporal punishment, in rearing their children.
   d. any and all of the above.

Fill-in Questions

1. The ABCX model suggests that the extent to which an event (A) leads to a crisis (X) is dependent on _____ (B) and the definition of the event (C).

2. Children are more likely to be kidnapped by _____ than by strangers.

3. A _____ theory of violence suggests that incompatabilies of income,education, and occupational prestige between men and women give men greater power and control.

4. In _____, a parent can be imprisoned for striking a child.

5. Straus suggests that violence in one sphere of life tends to engender violence in other spheres. This was termed_____ theory.

6. Michael Johnson argues that there are two distinct forms of violence against women. The one he call common couple violence. The other he calls _____, which is based on traditional notions of men's right to control "their" partners.

7. A theory of _____ suggests that there is nothing that can be done to stop violence, so the people involved quit trying.

8. In the colonial period, a woman who was raped could not marry into a respectable family because female _____ was held in high esteem.

9. More than one-half of the women who experiences violence said their first response was to cry. The response in last place was to _____.

10. The primary goal of Gelles and Straus in preventing violence is to eliminate _____ that support violence.

Fill-in answers	Page Reference
1. resources	458
2. parents	461
3. feminist	464
4. Sweden	465
5. cultural spillover	466
6. patriarchal terrorism	471
7. learned helplessness	474
8. virginity / sexual purity	475
9. call the police	482
10. cultural norms / values	482

Short Answer/Essay Questions

1. What is meant by the ABCX model of stress? Give examples.

2. Select three of the following statements and respond to their accuracy or inaccuracy.
    a. the family is nonviolent.
    b. most abusers are psychologically unbalanced and most victims are innocent.
    c. abuse is confined to poor and minority families.
    d. the real causes of violence are alcohol and drugs.
    e. children who are abused grow up to be abusers.
    f. battered women like being hit.
    g. violence and love are incompatible.

3. Straus and Smith suggest five social factors that converge to cause the high rates of intrafamily violence. Select three of them. Explain each.

4. What does Straus mean by a cultural spillover theory in regard to violence?

5. In regard to child abuse, what differences exist by (a) social class, (b) males and females, and (c) biological and nonbiological relationships?

6. Michael Johnson argues that there are two distinct forms of violence against women. What are they? How do they differ?

7. What is known about child sexual abuse in terms of (1) the perpetrators, (2) male-female differences, and (3) consequences?

8. What does research suggest about why many abused wives stay with their husbands? Explain.

9. List any three findings about marital rape in regard to factors such as it's frequency, it's consequences for the wife, the law regarding marital rape, and so forth.

10. In both an insert (p. 474) and in the text itself (p. 478) reference is made to a theory of learned helplessness. What does this mean? How is it relevant to understanding either abuse itself or remaining in an abusive relationship?

11. What is known about violence and sexual coercion among intimates? How frequent is courtship violence? What male-female differences exist? What is the effect of factors such as fraternity membership or drinking behavior on violence?

12. Straus and Gelles argue that violence prevention policies and programs must be directed at two factors. What are they? How can they be accomplished?

CHAPTER 16

True/False Questions

T
p. 489

1. The official law of Islam and of Judaism grants free power of the husband to terminate his marriage by repudiation of the wife.

F
p. 490

2. Informal separation is simply another term for desertion.

T
p. 491

3. Divorce is a factor in nearly all of the world's nations, including most tribal societies.

F
p. 492

4. Data that is available tends to support the idea that no other country in history had higher divorce rates than did the United States in the 1980s.

T
p. 493

5. Divorce by agreement, where both husband and wife desire divorce, is a simple procedure and without cost to the applicants in China.

F
p. 495

6. The divorce data reported by the National Vital Statistics Division are highly accurate since they are based on a 100 percent count of all divorces recorded in the United States each year.

F
p. 496

7. U.S. divorce rates were higher in the 1990s than at any time since records were kept.

T
p. 498

8. Generally, divorce rates decline in times of economic depression and rise during time of prosperity.

F
p. 498

9. Divorce rates, by region of the United States, are lowest in the south.

T
p. 499

10. A Gallup poll revealed that Americans are happy with their marriages with about 80 percent giving it an A grade.

F
p. 500

11. More than half of all divorces occur among persons under age 25 with the largest number of these being marriages among teenagers.

T
p. 500

12. The second, third, and fourth years of marriage appear to be the modal years for divorce.

F
p. 501

13. Evidence suggests an increase in mid-life divorce as couples experience a mid-life crisis.

T 14. In spite of their disapproval of divorce, Protestant fundamentalists have high
p. 503   dissolution rates.

T 15. With some exceptions, such as among professional women, the divorce rate
p. 504   tends to go up as socioeconomic level goes down.

F 16. Studies suggest that divorcing mothers are faring much better economically
p. 507   under the no-fault system in comparison to the former adversary system.

T 17. An increase in marital alternatives appears to be more important than
p. 508   attitudinal factors in hastening the transition to divorce.

T 18. Emile Durkheim theorized that societies with lower degrees of social
p. 509   integration typically share higher rates of suicide.

F 19. Divorced men report more frequent depression than divorced women.
p. 509

T 20. National data suggest that more than one-fourth of divorced women fall into
p. 510   poverty for at least some time during the first five years after divorce while men
              who divorce are immediately better off financially.

T 21. Close to half of all children living in the United States today will reach age
p. 511   eighteen without having lived continuously with both biological parents.

F 22. The presence of children not only deters divorce, it prevents it as well.
p. 511

F 23. Based on research findings, it appears that adolescent children are better off
p. 513   in intact homes with parental conflict than in homes with divorced parents.

F 24. Joint custody is generally defined as an arrangement where the child
p. 515   spends nearly equal time with each of the two parents.

T 25. Custodial fathers represent about one case in seven or 14 percent
p. 515   while custodial mothers represent about six cases in seven or 86 percent.

T 26. Child support has been found to be a negative factor in the remarriage of
p. 517   divorced mothers.

T 27. Over 40 percent of marriages in the United States are remarriages for one
p. 518   or both partners.

T 28. Remarriage rates are higher for men than for women, but women are
p. 518   just as prone to cohabit as men.

T
less
p. 519

29. The mean age at remarriage after widowhood for women is ten　　　years that the mean age at widowhood.

F
p. 519

30. By race, remarriage is both more likely and more quickly experienced for black women than for white women.

F
p. 519

31. Divorced Japanese women are much more likely to remarry than their American female counterparts.

F
p. 522

32. Most children of divorce have two homes with the majority living most of the time with their mothers but spending week-ends and vacation times with their nonresident fathers.

T
p. 523

33. Parents who cohabited before remarriage had less negative parent-child relationships after marriage.

F
p. 523

34. The stepparenting experience is more difficult for the stepfather than the stepmother and made more difficult with live-in stepchildren.

F
p. 524

35. There was no difference found in the scores of complex versus simple stepfamilies in areas of financial management, communications, personality, or adjustment.

Multiple-Choice Questions

A
p. 489

1. According to the text, in regard to desertion and marital separation,
   a. desertion is not institutionalized.
   b. the majority of separations are legalized.
   c. limited divorce and partial dissolution are both used interchangeably with informal separation.
   d. desertion is usually associated with legal separation.

B
p. 491

2. To say that a marriage is annulled is to indicate that
   a. the couple in the marriage was incompatible.
   b. a court found causes existed prior to the marriage that made the marriage contract void.
   c. the Catholic church disapproved of it and failed to recognize it as legitimate.
   d. the marriage never existed except if the birth of child is involved which legitimizes the union.

D
p. 491

3. Which of the following would be the least likely basis for an annulment?
   a. being underage for marriage.
   b. having another spouse.
   c. impotence not known to the spouse before marriage.
   d. adultery.

C
p. 492

4. In Sweden, marital and couple breakup
   a. is very low compared to most industrialized countries.
   b. is easy to determine since most people cohabit rather than marry.
   c. may be the highest in the industrialized world.
   d. is highest for those with two or more children.

D
p. 492

5. A study of 66 countries found that a societal-level correlate to an increased likelihood of divorce was
   a. increased female labor force participation in the countries early stages of industrialization.
   b. the level of socioeconomic development in the countries early stages of industrialization.
   c. a late average age at marriage for women.
   d. a low sex ratio.

A
p. 493

6. Divorce in China
   a. is simple and without cost if both parties agree to it.
   b. requires that both parties agree to it.
   c. has rates very similar to industrialized countries.
   d. is illegal and no accurate data is available on informal separation.

D
p. 494

7. In 1997, the divorce rate in the United States was approximately
   a. 4.3 per 1,000 persons in the total population.
   b. 19.5 per 1.000 married women, age 15 and over.
   c. 49 per 100 marriages begun in that year.
   d. all of the above three.

C
p. 498

8. According to the text, in the United States divorce rates
   a. are very low among young marriages.
   b. are highest eight to ten years after the marriage.
   c. tend to increase as one moves from east to west.
   d. are very low among conservative Protestant denominations.

B
p. 500

9. The most common years for divorce is during
   a. the first year of marriage.
   b. the second, third or fourth year of marriage.
   c. the middle years as couples face a mid-life crisis.

d. old age.

B
p. 501

10. The statement that is true about divorce in the United States as of the early 1990s is that
   a. the modal years for divorce were the tenth and eleventh years of marriage.
   b. the average interval between the first marriage and divorce was about eleven years.
   c. the median length of all marriages is about eleven years.
   d. all of the above three are true.

A
p. 503

11. Divorce differentials on the basis of major religious affiliation reveal that
   a. considered as a whole, Protestants have a rate of marital dissolution that is moderately higher than for Catholics.
   b. Catholics have the lowest divorce rate of all major groups.
   c. the highest rates of divorce exist among those with high religious involvement.
   d. the lowest rates of divorce exist among the most conservative Protestant denominations.

D
p. 504

12. The statement that is true about divorce rates is
   a. they tend to increase during times of prosperity and decrease in times of depression.
   b. they tend to increase as socioeconomic level goes down.
   c. professional women, compared to women in general, are more likely to get divorced.
   d. all of the above three statements are true.

B
p. 507

13. Under no-fault divorce
   a. consent of both parties is required.
   b. women and mothers are faring more poorly than under the fault system.
   c. the person not at fault gets a disproportionate amount of the settlement.
   d. all of the above three are true.

C
p. 509

14. Divorce mediation is a conflict resolution process that occurs
   a. in the early years of a marriage to prevent future marital dissolution.
   b. during legal separation to prevent a subsequent divorce.
   c. during the divorce process to help negotiate mutually agreeable decisions regarding property distribution, support, and child custody.
   d. following divorce to facilitate adjustment to singlehood.

A
p. 510

15. The consequences of divorce for adults include
   a. women reporting more frequent depression than men.
   b. no direct relationship with suicide.
   c. an increase in standard of living for both men and women.
   d. an opening up of and greater availability of close, confiding relationships.

C
p. 510

16. By gender, the economic consequences of divorce
    a. improve for both men and women.
    b. improve for women and decline for men.
    c. improve for men and decline for women.
    d. decline for both men and women.

B
p. 511

17. Are children a deterrent to the divorce of their parents?
    a. Yes. Children of all ages deter divorce.
    b. Yes and no. Young preschool children deter divorce but older children
       increase the chances.
    c. No and yes. Young children increase the chances of divorce but older
       children deter the chances.
    d. No. Children of all ages increase divorce.

D
p. 513

18. Compared to adolescent children in intact parental homes, adolescent
    children of divorced parents
    a. show few differences in behavior from other adolescents.
    b. are more likely to get married themselves.
    c. delay marriage, that is, marry at a later age.
    d. none of the above three are true.

D
p. 515

19. Joint custody (as opposed to single custody) arrangements appear to result in
    a. fewer emotional and behavior problems in the children.
    b. greater father compliance in financial child support obligations.
    c. higher satisfaction among both parents and children with the arrangements
    d. all of the above happening.

A
p. 515

20. Although mothers are far more likely to get custody of their children, the
    odds of father custody improves when
    a. the oldest child is male.
    b. the father is the defendant rather than the plaintiff.
    c. the mother has a higher educational level and is employed.
    d. all of the above occur.

C
p. 516

21. Census and other reports document the fact that child support awards are
    received in full by close to
    a. 100 percent of the children.
    b. 75 percent of the children with the other 25 percent receiving less than
       the full amount.
    c. 50 percent of the children, with 25 percent receiving less than the full
       amount and 25 percent getting nothing.
    d. 25 percent of the children, with 50 percent receiving less than the full
       amount and 25 percent getting nothing.

A

p. 517

22. When compared to heterosexual parents, the literature concludes that granting custody and visitation rights to homosexual parents
    a. results in no differences in parenting styles, child adjustment, or sexual orientation.
    b. is not in the best interest of the child.
    c. results in a tendency for the children to become confused over their own sexual orientation.
    d. causes children to fail to develop an appropriate role model of the opposite sex.

C

p. 518

23. Which statement is true about remarriage.
    a. over two-thirds of all marriages are remarriages for one or both partners.
    b. men are less likely to remarry than women.
    c. the rate of remarriage has declined over the past few decades.
    d. none of the above three statements about remarriage are true.

D

p. 519

24. In the United States, remarriage is more likely for
    a. black than for white women.
    b. women than for men.
    c. women with higher incomes.
    d. women not in the paid labor force.

D

p. 520

25. When compared to first marriages, it appears that remarriages
    a. are more stable as a result of prior marital experience.
    b. are less likely to end in divorce.
    c. have fewer financial difficulties as a result of being older and more secure.
    d. are or have none of the above. All are false.

A

p. 521

26. Remarriages
    a. have higher rates of divorce if adolescent stepchildren are present.
    b. are more likely among Japanese women than American women.
    c. tend to be more stable than first marriages.
    d. both a and b of the above three are true.

B

p. 522

27. Which statement has research shown to be true about stepfamilies and children in stepfamilies?
    a. complex stepfamilies experience greater satisfaction and less stress than do those in simple stepfamilies.
    b. nearly half of all children in stepfamilies had not seen their nonresident fathers in the past year.
    c. the role of the stepfather is more difficult than that of the stepmother.
    d. the longer the time period between a divorce and remarriage, the better the adjustment of the children to the remarriage.

28. Which statement is true about stepfamilies?
   a. stepfamilies have less pathological behaviors than first families.
   b. stepmothers are more satisfied with their relationships with stepchildren than are stepfathers.
   c. complex stepfamilies experience greater dissatisfaction and stress than simple stepfamilies.
   d. none of the above statements are true.

Fill-in Questions

1. In cases of _____, the husband and wife are married but authorized to live apart with formal agreements specifying visiting patterns, support and so forth.

2. Based on causes that existed prior to the marriage, _____ renders a marriage contract void.

3. In the country of _____ a divorce by agreement is simple and of no cost to the applicants when both husband and wife agree to it.

4. _____ is the state in the United States with the highest rate of divorce.

5. A major exception to the inverse relationship between socioeconomic status and the divorce rate is among _____ .

6. The adversary divorce system in which one person is guilty and the other innocent has been replaced in all states with _____ divorce.

7. Divorce _____ is a conflict resolution process to help negotiate mutually agreeable decisions regarding property and so forth.

8. Two key determinants of economic well-being for divorced custodial mothers are (1) child support, and (2) _____ .

9. A key explanation for the decline in the rate of remarriage over the past several decades is the rising rate of _____ .

10. Remarriage is more likely for men with _____ incomes and for women with _____ incomes.

11. Remarriage was said to create _____ where uncertainty exists as to who is part of the family and is responsible for certain roles and responsibilities.

12. Stepfamilies with children from just one parent are termed _____ stepfamilies in contrast to _____ stepfamilies that have children from both parents.

Fill-in answers

	Fill-in answers	Page Reference
1.	legal separation	490
2.	annulment	491
3.	China	493
4.	Nevada	498
5.	professional women	504
6.	no-fault	506
7.	mediation	507
8.	remarriage	517
9.	cohabitation	518
10.	higher / lower	519
11.	boundary ambiguity	523
12.	simple / complex	524

Short Answer/Essay Questions

1. Define desertion, marital separation, annulment, and divorce. How does desertion differ from marital separation? How does annulment differ from divorce? Provide examples.

2. Divorce rates tend to be calculated in three ways. What are they? What are some advantages and limitations of each method?

3. Describe variations in divorce in the United States by (a) geography, (b) age of husband and wife, (c) duration of marriage, (d) race, (e) religion, and (f) socioeconomic status.

4. How is it possible that divorce rates decrease during depressions when time are hard and increase among the lower strata where times are also difficult? Explain.

5. Why are marriages more unstable and divorce rates higher at lower socioeconomic levels? In light of this, how does one explain the exception that exists for professional women?

6. What have been the consequences of no-fault divorce laws (a) in divorce rates and (b) for mothers and women.

7. What does research suggest are some of the consequences of divorce for (a) adults and (b) the children of divorced parents.

8. Compare custodial fathers, custodial mothers and joint custody. What differences exist in terms of (a)frequency, (b) income, and (c) parent-child relationships?

9. Who is most likely to remarry (a) by race, (b) by age, (c) by children, (d) by education, (e) by employment, and (f) by income? Why?

10. Is there a difference in marital satisfaction between first marriages and remarriages? If so, how do you explain the difference? What is the effect of having stepchildren on the husband-wife relationship?

11. How do stepfamilies differ from first families? How are stepmothers and stepfathers differently affected by children? What do we know about child/parent/stepparent relationships?

12. It was said that many structural variations of remarriage have the potential to create boundary ambiguity. Explain.

CHAPTER 17

True/False Questions

T
p. 530

1. The United States has no explicit national policy for families and no agency devoting its attention directly to families.

T
p. 531

2. Implicit family policy is not directed specifically at families but has significant consequences for them.

F
p. 532

3. Zimmerman says the goal of family policy should be directed toward two-parent families, births within wedlock, and the elimination of divorce.

F
p. 532

4. In establishing family policy, the text suggests that families should be defined as any two or more persons related by birth, marriage, or adoption.

F
p. 533

5. The text takes the position that the family policy researcher should not attempt to be value free but rather should lend support to the causes that improve family life.

T
p. 534

6. Bogenschneider argues that family policy advocacy is an appropriate professional role when done within the context of family policy alternative education.

F
p. 535

7. The Heritage Foundation defines it's policy role as nonpolitical and to objectively sharpen thinking and increase public awareness of important issues.

F
p. 535

8. An investigation of low-income female-headed households in New Jersey concluded that welfare dependency can be reduced by expanding the number of low level jobs available.

T
p. 536

9. Evaluation research is conducted at a programmatic level to determine the degree to which social programs have achieved or are achieving the stated goals of a public policy program.

T
p. 536

10. A study of two thousand firms with ten or more employees indicated that where job guaranteed parental leave existed, leave taking was not a problem and firms dealth with it without increasing substantial direct costs.

F
p. 537

11. Zimmerman, in conducting research that assessed the impact of welfare, concluded that states that spent more on welfare had higher divorce rates.

T
p. 538

12. Conventionals believe that the normal family is conjugal.

F p. 538	13. Groups representing the conventional perspective believe that involved adults should strive to become equal partners.
T p. 539	14. Progressives take a pluralistic view of families.
F p. 539	15. Scanzoni points out that there is a relationship between progressives and the functionalist perspective.
F p. 541	16. The one-child policy introduced in China in 1979 was basically a failure in that the desire for children, particularly sons, led to most families having two or three children.
T p. 541	17. A philosophy stressing hard work, thrift, and minimum government intervention in the lives of citizens has been found to hurt the poor more than those in a better position economically.
T p. 542	18. A privacy position argues that the family or an intimate relationship is a matter of personal concern and the state or community should stay out of their affairs.
T p. 543	19. Welfare, AFDC, and Social Security all support families in need but stigma is less for Social Security recipients because they are defined as deserving of support while the others are undeserving.
T p. 544	20. Sweden's parental leave policy encourages fathers to participate in prenatal care, take time off to care for sick children, or to reduce their workday to six hours for child-care purposes.
F p. 545	21. A social relationship focus assumes that the woman who gave birth to a child should have priority above all other issues in keeping and caring for the child.
F p. 546	22. Macro-level policy focuses on patterns of personal interactions that characterize everyday life.
F p. 549	23. The text concludes that most changes in the family such as divorce, unwed parenthood, or same-sex marriages are destructive of the social order.
F p. 551	24. DaVanzo and others predict that the conservative religious and political movements in the United States in the 1980s and 1990s will lead to more people marrying, having children, and staying married (fewer divorces).
T p. 551	25. The author of the text states unequivocally that as long as society exists the family will survive.

Multiple-Choice Questions

B
p. 532

1. A continuing difficulty in family policy is determining
   a. the priorities.
   b. who and what is family.
   c. family needs.
   d. family wants.

D
p. 532

2. Moen and Schorr, for purposes of establishing family policy, say that families should be defined
   a. as husband, wife, and children.
   b. as intimate primary relationships including cohabiting adults.
   c. as whoever occupies a household.
   d. in numerous ways according to the issues involved.

A
p. 532

3. What function of the family is served by programs such as child care, health care, and services to the elderly?
   a. nurturance
   b. economic
   c. political
   d. advocacy

C
p. 533

4. Someone who endorses and works for a course of action to improve family life is a
   a. family policy liberal.
   b. family policy researcher.
   c. family policy advocate.
   d. family policy patriot.

D
p. 535

5. The Urban Institute has been stated in the text to be an organization that
   a. fights urban crime.
   b. is the research unit of the American Civil Liberties Union.
   c. is aimed at providing conservative policymakers with arguments to bolster their view.
   d. attempts to improve government decisions and increase citizens awareness of important public issues.

B
p. 535

6. The text suggests that the research done in most of the "think tanks" such as the Brookings Institute or the Urban Institute would fall into the category of
   a. political action committees.
   b. research to establish family policy.
   c. family evaluation research.
   d. family impact analysis.

C
p. 535

7. An investigation of low-income female-headed households concluded that welfare dependency can be reduced by
   a. having women work at any type of job they can get.
   b. expanding the number of low level jobs that require few skills.
   c. producing fewer but better paying jobs.
   d. emphasizing or doing all of the above three about equally.

C
p. 536

8. Shirley Zimmerman looked at state per capita expenditures for public welfare in all fifty states and found that lower state expenditures for public welfare was
   a. not related to state divorce rates.
   b. directly related to state poverty rates.
   c. inversely related to suicide rates.
   d. related to all of the above three as stated.

A
p. 536

9. The purpose of family evaluation research is to
   a. determine the degree to which social programs have achieved or are achieving the stated goals of a public policy or resultant program.
   b. assess the intended and unintended consequences of public policy and social programs.
   c. examine certain categories of persons who have a particular life style and to discover the outcomes of that life style for the individuals involved and for society.
   d. determine causal relationships among societal level variables with little concern for potential application of findings.

D
p. 537

10. The type of family policy research designed to assess the intended and unintended consequences of public policy and social programs is
    a. family evaluation research.
    b. research for family policy.
    c. family policy advocacy.
    d. family impact analysis.

A
p. 538

11. Conventionals support the position that
    a. the normal family is conjugal.
    b. adults in families should strive to become equal partners.
    c. corporal punishment (spanking) is abusive and should be discouraged.
    d. all of the above three about equally.

A
p. 539

12. Scanzoni most closely links the category he calls progressives with the
    a. conflict approach.
    b. functionalist approach.
    c. social exchange approach.
    d. developmental approach.

D
p. 540

13. According to Scanzoni, in spite of the unified efforts of the conventionals, the major weakness of their model is it
   a. lacks a broad base of support.
   b. allows the individual too much freedom.
   c. is liberal in its definitions of family.
   d. is out of sync with the times.

B
p. 540

14. The Reagan and Bush administrations took the position that the level of government responsible for the formulation and enforcement of family policy should be
   a. the federal government.
   b. state governments.
   c. county governments.
   d. municipal governments.

D
p. 541

15. The one-child policy in China
   a. can be considered a failed family planning policy.
   b. offered certificates to those couples who agreed to have no children at all.
   c. made no exceptions to having more than one child.
   d. allows two children in many rural provinces if the first child is a girl.

C
p. 541

16. The impact of supply-side economics of the Reagan administration on family support services, food-related programs and housing was that it
   a. helped most the poorer states at the expense of the wealthier ones.
   b. proved highly beneficial to all states.
   c. affected the poor more negatively than the economically better off.
   d. affected everyone negatively.

B
p. 543

17. A policy directed at families with problems tends to support the idea that
   a. select groups of families have problems but the help resides with groups such as kin, church or local community.
   b. some families with problems such as the elderly are deserving whereas others such as welfare recipients are undeserving.
   c. a policy should be directed at all families so as to prevent problems in specific families.
   d. all of the above three are true of policies directed at families with problems.

C
p. 543

18. To label specific types of structures or relationships as problems or as pathological will
   a. almost guarantee the government will take action to resolve it.
   b. almost guarantee that public sentiment will be supportive of policies to correct it.
   c. in itself affect the type of policy directed at it.
   d. in itself have little impact on anything.

D
p. 544

19. Sweden's parental leave policy
    a. doesn't exist. That is, there is no such policy in Sweden.
    b. is very beneficial to mothers but not fathers.
    c. requires employers to offer and pay full salaries and benefits whenever parents take a leave from work.
    d. allows fathers and mothers time off with pay and benefits at births, to care for sick children, or to visit day-care centers or schools.

A
p. 544

20. Parental leave in Sweden
    a. is paid from social insurance offices rather than from employers.
    b. is offered primarily for employed mothers.
    c. is offered without any time limitation and with pay equal to about 90 percent of the employment pay.
    d. includes all of the above three characteristics.

C
p. 544

21. A biological focus on parent-child relationships suggests
    a. the best interests of the child are of prime importance.
    b. gay couples can keep their child only if one parent is the biological father or mother.
    c. assumes that "blood is thicker than water."
    d. all of the above three.

A
p. 546

22. According to the text, policy at a micro-level
    a. focuses on patterns of personal interactions that characterize everyday life.
    b. is related to such areas as taxation, medical care, employment, housing, education, and leisure.
    c. focuses on the social patterns and forms of social organization that shape an entire society.
    d. is identical to that of a meso-level policy.

C
p. 547

23. In her investigation of the consequences of unemployment on families in the 1980s, Phyllis Moen noted that
    a. most families of the unemployed who suffered financial hardship received adequate income support from the government.
    b. the duration of unemployment should not be limited if families are to be assisted satisfactorily by government.
    c. families with more than a single wage earner are much more able to avoid economic deprivation.
    d. unemployment benefits have no value with regard to coping with long-term unemployment.

D
pp. 541-
547

24. There is widespread agreement that family policy should
    a. be non-existent since the family is a private institution.
    b. be aimed at families with problems rather than at all families.
    c. operate at a micro level.
    d. none of the first three have widespread agreement.

A
p. 548

25. John Scanzoni argues that the most effective level at which to target social policy pertaining to families is on the "meso" level. This focuses on
    a. community groups and organizations that can mediate, provide training, and offer direct support to families.
    b. social patterns and forms of social organization that shape an entire society.
    c. patterns of personal behaviors and interactions that characterize everyday life.
    d. students who get frustrated taking exams in family courses.

B
p. 549

26. According to the test's discussion of the future of the family system
    a. most changes in the American family structure have been regrettable from a social standpoint.
    b. the family is changing and likely to continue to change in the future.
    c. the family can only be fully understood by isolating it from other influences and institutions.
    d. only a and b above are true.

B
p. 551

27. DaVanzo and others predict that over the next few decades
    a. the labor force participation of women will level off or even decrease.
    b. the incentive to marry will be reduced and childbearing will be delayed.
    c. conservative religious and political trends will lead to a decrease in the trend toward cohabitation.
    d. all of the above three will likely happen.

D
p. 551

28. With regard to the future of the family system, the text points out that
    a. the family will, in time, probably cease to exist.
    b. any type of projection into the future is pure speculation and quite useless.
    c. families will no longer be the primary source of socialization.
    d. the passing of the conventional family will leave many traumas and many loose ends.

Fill-in Questions

1. The text makes a distinction between policies and _____ , the practical application used to fulfill policy goals.

2. The text distinguishes between family policy research and family policy _____ , which takes one side or position on an issue and works actively to process or achieve that position.

3. Bogenschneider argues for a new professional role in family policy, that of _____, which clarifies the potential consequences of a range of policy choices.

4. Policy research aimes at determining the degree to which programs fulfill or achieve their stated goals is _____ research.

5. _____ is the type of family policy research that attempts to assess the intended and unintended consequences of public policy and social programs.

6. Scanzoni differentiates conventionals, those traditionally oriented families who want to maintain the status quo, from the _____ who want change and believe a normal family can take many forms.

7. Scanzoni links the perspective of conventionals with the _____ approach or frame of reference.

8. A _____ policy emphasizes heterosexual marriages and genetic ties of parent and child as best suited to childrearing.

9. _____ level policy focuses on the social patterns and forms of social organization, system, or society that extend beyond any person or group.

10. Scanzoni argues for policy at a _____ level, an alternative model that supplies a fit between the macro- and micro-levels.

Fill-in answers	Page Reference	Fill-in answers	Page Reference
1. programs	531	6. progressives	539
2. advocacy	533	7. functionalist	539
3. alternative education	534	8. biological or birth	544
4. evaluation	536	9. Macro	546
5. Family impact analysis	537	10. meso	548

Short Answer/Essay Questions

1. Differentiate between (1) implicit and explicit family policy, (2) family policies and family programs, and (3) family policy research and family policy advocacy.

2. Define family policy. What definition(s) of "family" can be used to improve the well-being of persons and relationships?

3. Differentiate the role of the family policy researcher from the policy advocate and the alternative education professional.

4. What are the three directions of or types of policy research cited in the text? Show how they differ and give an example of each.

5. Differentiate between what Scanzoni labels conventionals and progressives. How does either or both impact policy decisions?

6. What are arguments for and against policy at a federal or national level and policy at a state or local level? Provide an example to illustrate different likely consequences resulting from each.

7. Should policies be established for all families or simply those with problems? Give arguments for both. Why are certain families who receive government support, such as those on welfare, stigmatized differently from social security recipients who also receive government support?

8. What are the major arguments for or against a biological versus a relationship policy as applied to (1) birth-parent versus social-parent custody, and (2) heterosexual versus homosexual marriage and children.

9. Scanzoni argues for family policy at a mesolevel. what does he mean?

10. What does the text suggest about the future of the family system?

NOTES

NOTES

NOTES

NOTES

NOTES

NOTES

NOTES

NOTES

NOTES

NOTES